# THE KANJI ABC

# ANDREW DYKSTRA

PROVOST

KANSAI GAIDAI HAWAII COLLEGE

KANJI PRESS

2440 KUHIO AV. SUITE 1512
HONOLULU, HAWAII 96815
USA

OTHER BOOKS BY ANDREW DYKSTRA:

KANJI 1-2-3
KANJI ICHI NI
SEXY LAUGHING STORIES OF OLD JAPAN

ISBN 0-917880-00-5

Library of Congress Catalog Card Number: 76-58964

ISBN 0-913232-37-8

# CONTENTS

### THE KANJI ABC

---

## KANJINN KOBOLD IST GEKOMMEN

秦 CH'IN

商 SHANG

陰 YIN

陽 YANG

The shadowed Yin and crimsoned Yang,
Vermilion Ch'in and yellowed Shang
Cry out, cry out with fearful shout!
"Who's here?  Who's here to hear?  Thou lout!

Dost keen the warf my skein doth make?
The mien of whose forgotten line
To thee doth mean and signify
That hath the single piercing eye;

In lines together gather take,
In scene to thee alone is seen
Where warp, where weft, where east, where west
Doth intersecting meeting lie."

"If I shall rake and slash thy mesh,
Thy mask no more shall faces hold;
Thy spaces without lines are won
And I am free, a spirit bold!"          DYKSTRA

# THE KANJI ABC

The KANJI or characters of Japan and China, invented by the Yellow Emperor in the legendary dawn of China's history, are found in primitive form on the oracle "dragon bones" of the Shang Dynasty.  They are on the bright-colored signs of San Francisco's Chinatown and in the flashing neon lights of the Tokyo Ginza District.

THE KANJI ABC explains the origin of these three-thousand-year-old pictographs to make them easy for you to learn and understand.  At the same time you will discover how the users of the KANJI thought and lived.

The KANJI are an international language of symbols.  Korea, Okinawa, Vietnam, and Japan, although speaking languages very different from Chinese, all accepted the KANJI with the culture of China.  Thus the different peoples of the "World of Chopsticks" could communicate by writing KANJI.

Japan's Ministry of Education has helped all students of the KANJI by numbering in order of importance the KANJI which are necessary in reading Japanese.  THE KANJI ABC gives you the Japanese Ministry of Education (JME) number, the radical (RAD) number for finding KANJI in the dictionary, and the number of strokes in the KANJI, also for dictionary use. The little numbers with each KANJI tell you the direction and order of the strokes.  The Japanese words in large capital letters are of Chinese origin;  those in small capital letters are of native origin.

The "ABC" in the title of these volumes stands for the order, simplicity, and explanation in learning to read, write, and understand.  It also emphasizes the international quality of the KANJI which can also be used to write English or Swahili.

The purpose of THE KANJI ABC is to help you learn.  To be scholarly is not the purpose.  Some of the explanations of the KANJI can be found in other books.  Many are original with us, but seem obviously correct.  We have studied the KANJI or characters for many years with famous authorities like Professor Ch'en Shou-yi of the Claremont University Center, and in books like the Shuo Wen.  You will notice that explanations are usually easy and consistent.

We hope that by learning the KANJI in this way, you will come to enjoy and love the KANJI.  The ancient style of the KANJI or pictographic writing is often far superior to the alphabet writing of the Western world.  Nowadays, for impact and retention as in international road signs and in many advertisements, the Western world turns to the earlier picture writing, the symbolism that unites and belongs to all of us as human beings.

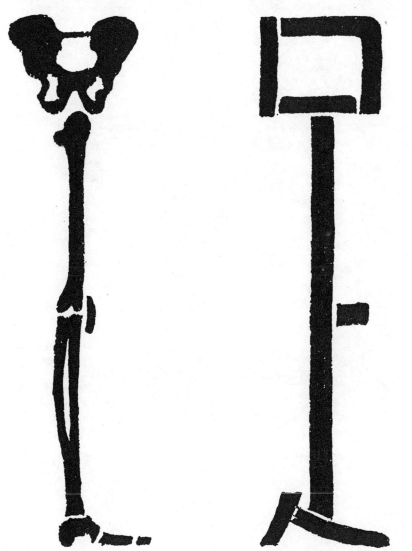

means
FOOT, LEG
in Japanese _kanji_
+ Chinese characters

ICHI; HITOTSU, HITO, ONE, THE FIRST.

THE KANJI ONE 一, THE KANJI TWO 二, AND THE KANJI THREE 三 ARE WRITTEN HORIZONTALLY AS STRAIGHT LINES.

THE KANJI ONE 一 TURNED NINETY DEGREES FORMS THE ARABIC 1.

THE LINE FOR ONE 一 REPRESENTS THE UNITY, THE ONENESS OF THE EARTH AND SKY OR THE OCEAN AND SKY MEETING AT THE HORIZON.

| RAD | STROKE | JME |
|-----|--------|-----|
| 1   | 1      | 1   |

NI, JI; FUTATSU, FUTA, FU, TWO, THE SECOND.

THE TWO HORIZONTAL STROKES OF THE KANJI TWO 二 BECOME THE ARABIC 2 WHEN A CURVED LINE IS DRAWN TO JOIN THE SEGMENTS.

COMMON AMONG MANY ANCIENT PEOPLES IS THE BELIEF IN THE SKY-FATHER ABOVE WHO IMPREGNATES WITH SEED AND FERTILIZES WITH RAIN THE EARTH-MOTHER BELOW. AN EARLY MALE CHAUVINISM, PERHAPS.

SKY-FATHER

EARTH-MOTHER

| RAD | STROKE | JME |
|-----|--------|-----|
| 7   | 2      | 2   |

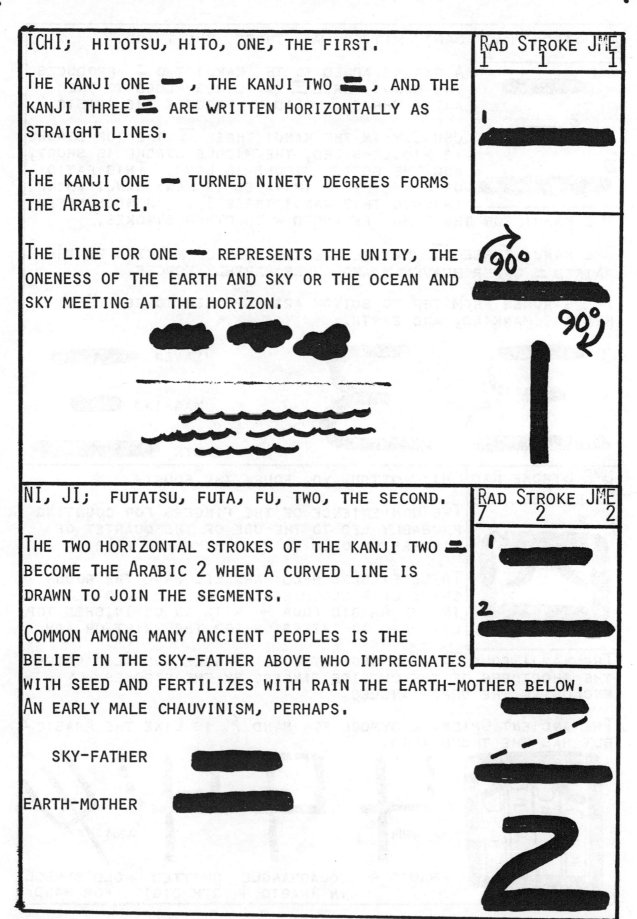

| JME | STROKE | RAD |
|-----|--------|-----|
| 3 | 3 | 1 |

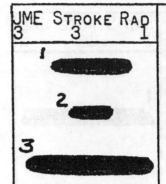

SAN; MITTSU, MI, THREE, THE THIRD.

A STROKE ADDED TO THE KANJI TWO 二 PRODUCES THE KANJI THREE 三. LINES ADDED TO THE KANJI THREE 三 READILY PRODUCE THE ARABIC 3.

USUALLY IN THE KANJI THREE 三 THE TOP STROKE IS MIDDLE-SIZED, THE MIDDLE STROKE IS SHORT, AND THE BOTTOM STROKE IS LONG. THIS RATIO OR SYMMETRY IS IMITATED IN MANY KANJI WHICH INCLUDE THIS KANJI THREE 三. IN SUCH CASES THE KANJI FOR THREE MAY BE FUSED WITH OTHER STROKES.

THE KANJI THREE 三 MAY BE THE CREATION OF MANKIND BY THE PAIRED 二 UPPER HEAVENLY AND LOWER EARTHLY FORCES.

THE STROKES FROM TOP TO BOTTOM ARE SUPPOSED TO REPRESENT HEAVEN, MANKIND, AND EARTH.

HEAVEN

MANKIND

EARTH

| JME | STROKE | RAD |
|-----|--------|-----|
| 4 | 5 | 31 |

SHI; YOTTSU, YO, FOUR, THE FOURTH.

THE CONVENIENCE OF THE FINGERS FOR COUNTING PROBABLY LED TO THE USE OF THE QUARTET OF FINGERS OPPOSED TO THE THUMB FOR FOUR.

THESE FINGERS HELD PARALLEL HAVE THE ROUGH SHAPE OF A QUADRANGLE WHICH CAN ALSO BE SEEN IN THE ARABIC FOUR 4 WITH AN UNFINISHED TOP LINE AND AN EXTENSION FOR THE WRIST OR ARM.

THE KANJI FOUR 四 ALSO SHOWS THE QUADRANGLE AND ALSO NOTES THE SHORTNESS OF THE OUTSIDE FINGERS BY THE STROKES ハ ENCLOSING THE UPPER ANGLES.

THE ANCIENT ORIENTAL SYMBOL FOR HAND 푸 IS LIKE THE ARABIC 4 BUT HAS THE THUMB ALSO.

ARM

ARM

ARABIC 4　　QUADRANGLE OMITTED　　OLD SYMBOL
　　　　　IN ARABIC 4  5TH DIGIT  FOR HAND

GO;   ITSUTSU, ITSU, FIVE, THE FIFTH.

| Rad | Stroke | JME |
|-----|--------|-----|
| 7   | 4      | 5   |

THE KANJI FIVE 五 CONTAINS ALL PARTS OF THE ARABIC 5 BUT INCLUDES A COMPLETE VERTICAL STROKE AND OTHER SLIGHT DIFFERENCES.

THE KANJI FIVE 五 MAY BE REGARDED AS A KANJI ONE 一 ABOVE ATTACHED TO A QUADRANGLE ▢ BELOW REPRESENTING THE KANJI FOUR 四 .

WHAT IS BELOW CAN ALSO BE REGARDED AS AN INVERTED AND CLOSED ARABIC 4.

KANJI ONE OVER THE QUADRANGLE

KANJI ONE OVER INVERTED ARABIC 4

KANJI ONE ATTACHED TO ARABIC 4 INVERTED & FINISHED TO SUGGEST THE KANJI FIVE

SUPERIMPOSITION

KANJI FIVE     ARAB. 5

---

ROKU;   MUTTSU, SIX, THE SIXTH.

| Rad | Stroke | JME |
|-----|--------|-----|
| 12  | 4      | 6   |

THE KANJI SIX 六 MAY BE REGARDED AS A HUMAN FIGURE WITH FOUR LIMBS, BODY, AND HEAD.  THE TOTAL IS SIX.

SINCE THE STANDARD HUMAN FIGURE IS A MALE, WE HAVE A FIGURE ANALOGOUS TO THE WESTERN PHALLIC SYMBOL SIX 6 .  THE SYMBOL IS ALSO WRITTEN ♂ .  MALENESS IN BOTH CASES.

NOTE HOW THIS HUMAN FIGURE IS ALSO FOUND IN THE KANJI TO STAND JME149 WHERE IT STANDS ON A BASELINE.

TWO ARMS & BODY     HEAD

TWO LEGS

OLD KANJI FOR SIX, (MAN)

TWO ARMS AND BODY     HEAD

TWO LEGS

BASELINE

KANJI SIX (SIX PARTS OF A MAN)

KANJI TO STAND (SHOWS THE MAN STANDING)

| JME | Stroke | Rad |
|---|---|---|
| 7 | 2 | 1 |

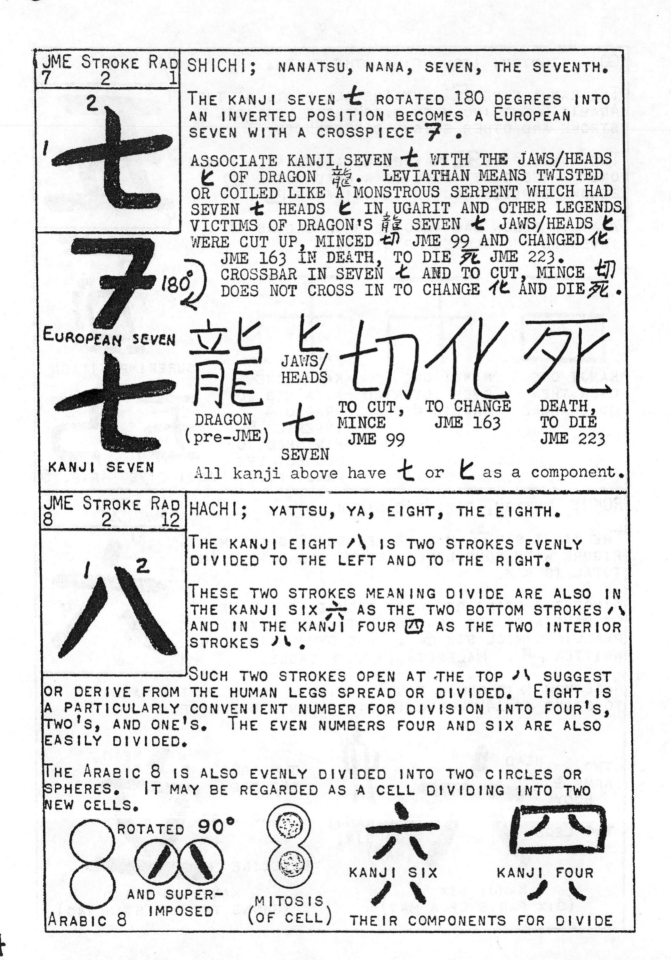

SHICHI; NANATSU, NANA, SEVEN, THE SEVENTH.

THE KANJI SEVEN 七 ROTATED 180 DEGREES INTO AN INVERTED POSITION BECOMES A EUROPEAN SEVEN WITH A CROSSPIECE 7.

ASSOCIATE KANJI SEVEN 七 WITH THE JAWS/HEADS ヒ OF DRAGON 龍. LEVIATHAN MEANS TWISTED OR COILED LIKE A MONSTROUS SERPENT WHICH HAD SEVEN 七 HEADS ヒ IN UGARIT AND OTHER LEGENDS. VICTIMS OF DRAGON'S 龍 SEVEN 七 JAWS/HEADS ヒ WERE CUT UP, MINCED 切 JME 99 AND CHANGED 化 JME 163 IN DEATH, TO DIE 死 JME 223. CROSSBAR IN SEVEN 七 AND TO CUT, MINCE 切 DOES NOT CROSS IN TO CHANGE 化 AND DIE 死.

EUROPEAN SEVEN

龍  ヒ JAWS/HEADS   切 化   死

DRAGON (pre-JME)   七 SEVEN

TO CUT, MINCE JME 99    TO CHANGE JME 163    DEATH, TO DIE JME 223

KANJI SEVEN

All kanji above have 七 or ヒ as a component.

| JME | Stroke | Rad |
|---|---|---|
| 8 | 2 | 12 |

HACHI; YATTSU, YA, EIGHT, THE EIGHTH.

THE KANJI EIGHT 八 IS TWO STROKES EVENLY DIVIDED TO THE LEFT AND TO THE RIGHT.

THESE TWO STROKES MEANING DIVIDE ARE ALSO IN THE KANJI SIX 六 AS THE TWO BOTTOM STROKES 八 AND IN THE KANJI FOUR 四 AS THE TWO INTERIOR STROKES 八.

SUCH TWO STROKES OPEN AT THE TOP 八 SUGGEST OR DERIVE FROM THE HUMAN LEGS SPREAD OR DIVIDED. EIGHT IS A PARTICULARLY CONVENIENT NUMBER FOR DIVISION INTO FOUR'S, TWO'S, AND ONE'S. THE EVEN NUMBERS FOUR AND SIX ARE ALSO EASILY DIVIDED.

THE ARABIC 8 IS ALSO EVENLY DIVIDED INTO TWO CIRCLES OR SPHERES. IT MAY BE REGARDED AS A CELL DIVIDING INTO TWO NEW CELLS.

ARABIC 8   ROTATED 90° AND SUPER-IMPOSED   MITOSIS (OF CELL)   KANJI SIX   KANJI FOUR

THEIR COMPONENTS FOR DIVIDE

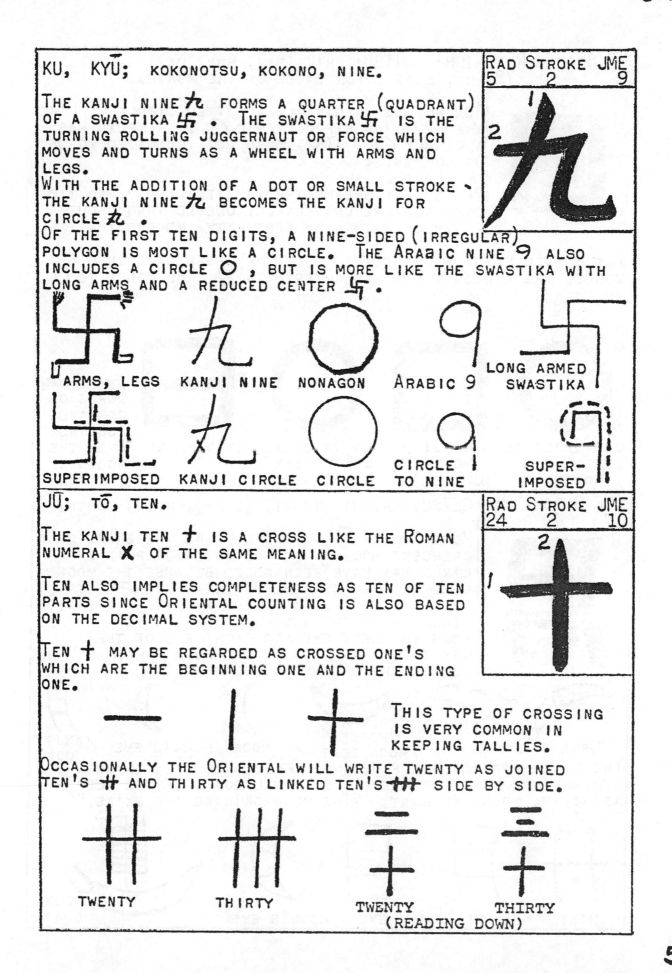

KU, KYŪ; KOKONOTSU, KOKONO, NINE.

| Rad | Stroke | JME |
|-----|--------|-----|
| 5   | 2      | 9   |

THE KANJI NINE 九 FORMS A QUARTER (QUADRANT) OF A SWASTIKA 卐. THE SWASTIKA 卐 IS THE TURNING ROLLING JUGGERNAUT OR FORCE WHICH MOVES AND TURNS AS A WHEEL WITH ARMS AND LEGS.

WITH THE ADDITION OF A DOT OR SMALL STROKE ˎ THE KANJI NINE 九 BECOMES THE KANJI FOR CIRCLE 丸.

OF THE FIRST TEN DIGITS, A NINE-SIDED (IRREGULAR) POLYGON IS MOST LIKE A CIRCLE. THE ARABIC NINE 9 ALSO INCLUDES A CIRCLE O, BUT IS MORE LIKE THE SWASTIKA WITH LONG ARMS AND A REDUCED CENTER 卐.

ARMS, LEGS     KANJI NINE     NONAGON     ARABIC 9     LONG ARMED SWASTIKA

SUPERIMPOSED     KANJI CIRCLE     CIRCLE     CIRCLE TO NINE     SUPER-IMPOSED

JŪ; TŌ, TEN.

| Rad | Stroke | JME |
|-----|--------|-----|
| 24  | 2      | 10  |

THE KANJI TEN 十 IS A CROSS LIKE THE ROMAN NUMERAL X OF THE SAME MEANING.

TEN ALSO IMPLIES COMPLETENESS AS TEN OF TEN PARTS SINCE ORIENTAL COUNTING IS ALSO BASED ON THE DECIMAL SYSTEM.

TEN 十 MAY BE REGARDED AS CROSSED ONE'S WHICH ARE THE BEGINNING ONE AND THE ENDING ONE.

一     |     十     THIS TYPE OF CROSSING IS VERY COMMON IN KEEPING TALLIES.

OCCASIONALLY THE ORIENTAL WILL WRITE TWENTY AS JOINED TEN'S 廿 AND THIRTY AS LINKED TEN'S 卅 SIDE BY SIDE.

TWENTY          THIRTY          TWENTY          THIRTY
                                (READING DOWN)

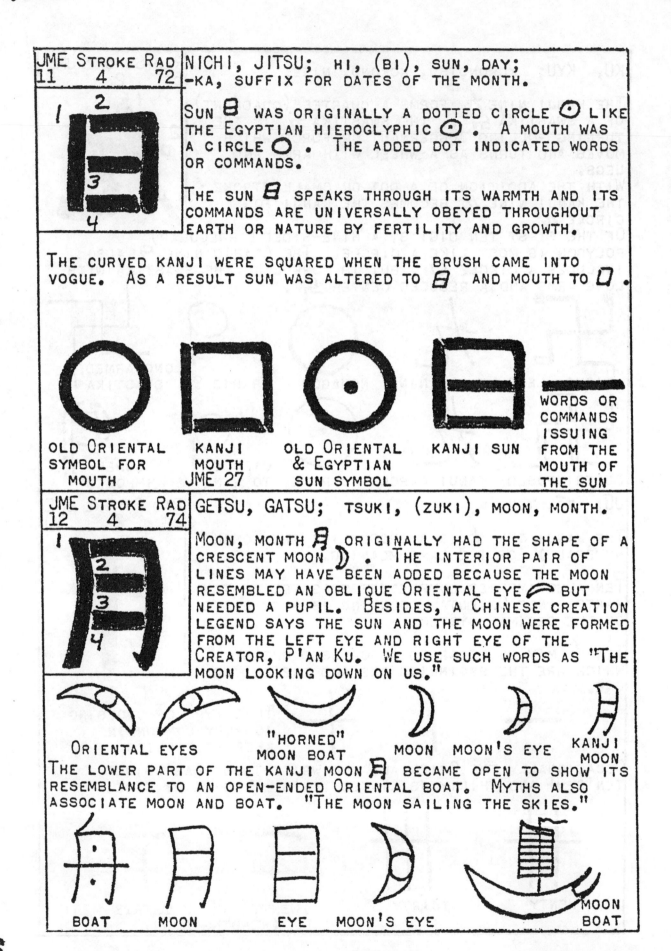

| JME | Stroke | Rad |
|---|---|---|
| 11 | 4 | 72 |

NICHI, JITSU; HI, (BI), SUN, DAY; -KA, SUFFIX FOR DATES OF THE MONTH.

SUN 日 WAS ORIGINALLY A DOTTED CIRCLE ⊙ LIKE THE EGYPTIAN HIEROGLYPHIC ⊙ . A MOUTH WAS A CIRCLE ◯ . THE ADDED DOT INDICATED WORDS OR COMMANDS.

THE SUN 日 SPEAKS THROUGH ITS WARMTH AND ITS COMMANDS ARE UNIVERSALLY OBEYED THROUGHOUT EARTH OR NATURE BY FERTILITY AND GROWTH.

THE CURVED KANJI WERE SQUARED WHEN THE BRUSH CAME INTO VOGUE. AS A RESULT SUN WAS ALTERED TO 日 AND MOUTH TO 口 .

OLD ORIENTAL SYMBOL FOR MOUTH    KANJI MOUTH JME 27    OLD ORIENTAL & EGYPTIAN SUN SYMBOL    KANJI SUN    WORDS OR COMMANDS ISSUING FROM THE MOUTH OF THE SUN

| JME | Stroke | Rad |
|---|---|---|
| 12 | 4 | 74 |

GETSU, GATSU; TSUKI, (ZUKI), MOON, MONTH.

MOON, MONTH 月 ORIGINALLY HAD THE SHAPE OF A CRESCENT MOON ) . THE INTERIOR PAIR OF LINES MAY HAVE BEEN ADDED BECAUSE THE MOON RESEMBLED AN OBLIQUE ORIENTAL EYE ⌒ BUT NEEDED A PUPIL. BESIDES, A CHINESE CREATION LEGEND SAYS THE SUN AND THE MOON WERE FORMED FROM THE LEFT EYE AND RIGHT EYE OF THE CREATOR, P'AN KU. WE USE SUCH WORDS AS "THE MOON LOOKING DOWN ON US."

ORIENTAL EYES    "HORNED" MOON BOAT    MOON    MOON'S EYE    KANJI MOON

THE LOWER PART OF THE KANJI MOON 月 BECAME OPEN TO SHOW ITS RESEMBLANCE TO AN OPEN-ENDED ORIENTAL BOAT. MYTHS ALSO ASSOCIATE MOON AND BOAT. "THE MOON SAILING THE SKIES."

BOAT    MOON    EYE    MOON'S EYE    MOON BOAT

KA;  HI, (BI), FIRE.

| RAD | STROKE | JME |
|-----|--------|-----|
| 86  | 4      | 13  |

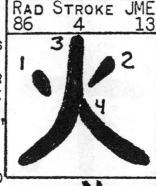

THE NEXT FIVE KANJI RELATE TO THE SUBSTANCES FIRE 火, WATER 水, WOOD 木, METAL 金, AND EARTH 土. THE ANCIENT ORIENTAL PHILOSOPHER LIKE HIS GREEK COUNTERPART SPECULATED ON THE COMPOSITION OF OUR WORLD AND HAD SOME SIMILAR ANSWERS.  THUS THESE FIVE "ELEMENTS."

IN THE KANJI FIRE 火 YOU SEE THE PILE OF COMBUSTIBLES WITH SMOKE OR FLAMES RISING AND A SMALL STROKE TO EACH SIDE FOR THE FLAMES FLICKERING OR THE CONVECTION CURRENTS.

AS A KANJI COMPONENT FIRE MAY ALSO BE WRITTEN 灬.  THIS COMPONENT REPRESENTS FOUR FLAMES AND MAY BE CONFUSED WITH A SIMILAR COMPONENT DEPICTING THE FOUR LEGS OF AN ANIMAL, ETC.

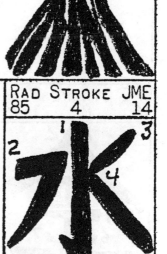

COMPONENT FOR FIRE AS USED IN A KANJI

COMPONENT FOR FIRE

SUI;  MIZU, WATER.

| RAD | STROKE | JME |
|-----|--------|-----|
| 85  | 4      | 14  |

IN THE KANJI WATER 水 THE MIDDLE VERTICAL | STROKE IS THE MAIN CURRENT AS YOU LOOK DOWN ON THE STREAM OR RIVER.  THE SIDE STROKES TO THE LEFT フ AND TO THE RIGHT く ARE THE EDDIES STRIKING THE BANKS AND SWIRLING ABOUT.

THERE IS A COMPONENT FORM FOR WATER WRITTEN AS THREE FALLING SPLASHING DROPS.

COMPONENT FOR WATER (THREE FALLING AND SPLASHING DROPS) AS USED IN A KANJI

COMPONENT FOR WATER

THE KANJI FOR WATER SUPERIMPOSED ON A STREAM AND SHOWING THE SWIRLING CURRENTS

| JME | Stroke | Rad |
|-----|--------|-----|
| 15  | 4      | 75  |

MOKU, BOKU;  KI, (GI), TREE, WOOD.

TREE IS AN EXCELLENT PICTOGRAPH.  THE CENTRAL VERTICAL STROKE IS THE TRUNK AND TAP ROOT. THE HORIZONTAL LINE REPRESENTS BRANCHES. THE LOWER OBLIQUE LINES ARE THE SPREADING ROOTS.

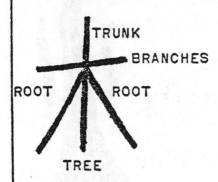

TREE

WOODS, GROVE
JME 150

FOREST
JME 41

| JME | Stroke | Rad |
|-----|--------|-----|
| 16  | 8      | 167 |

KIN, GOLD; KON, (GOLD); KANE, MONEY

GOLD 金 IS A COMPOSITE KANJI CONSISTING OF A MINE TUNNEL ROOF 𠆢 ABOVE, A SHIELD 干 AS A SUPPORT FOR THE ROOF, TWO SMALL OBLIQUE STROKES FOR GRAINS OR NUGGETS ′′ OF GOLD, AND EARTH 土 JME 17 BELOW TO SHOW THE BASE AND SOURCE OF THE GOLD.  THE KANJI FOR THE SHIELD 干 AND THE EARTH 土 ARE FUSED 壬.

THE KANJI GOLD 金 ALSO MEANS MONEY 金 .  AS A LEFT COMPONENT THE KANJI GOLD USUALLY INDICATE A METAL OR SOMETHING METALIC.

MINE TUNNEL ROOF SUPPORTED BY A SHIELD OVER THE EARTH WITH NUGGETS OR GRAINS OF GOLD SHINING FROM THE EARTH'S SURFACE.

MINE TUNNEL ROOF

SHIELD

SHIELD AND EARTH FUSED

EARTH

GRAINS OR NUGGETS OF GOLD

DO, TO; TSUCHI, EARTH, SOIL.

| Rad | Stroke | JME |
|---|---|---|
| 32 | 3 | 17 |

EARTH 土 HAS A BASELINE ― AND A PLANT OR A
STEM OF GRASS 十 GROWING VERTICALLY / ,
ORIGINALLY ψ , MUCH LIKE THE ANCIENT
PICTOGRAPH FOR HAND ψ .

LIKE THE KANJI TREE 木 WHICH HAS A HORIZON-
TAL LINE ― FOR BRANCHES, THE ENDS OF THE
HORIZONTAL LINE ― OF GRASS 十 WERE ONCE
CURVED UPWARDS ψ TO INDICATE SPROUTS FROM
THE MAIN STEM ψ . THUS THERE IS A CLOSE RELATIONSHIP IN
THE PAST REPRESENTATION OF GRASS ψ AND HAND ψ .

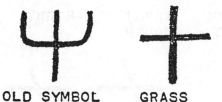

OLD SYMBOL    GRASS        BASELINE OF      EARTH
FOR GRASS                       EARTH        PILED UP AS
                                                A MOUND
                                                OR ALTAR

(SUPERIMPOSITION)

SA; HIDARI, LEFT.

| Rad | Stroke | JME |
|---|---|---|
| 48 | 5 | 18 |

IN LEFT 左 THE COMPONENT 工 REPRESENTS A
PLUMB LINE HANGING AS FROM CEILING TO FLOOR.
SUCH A PLUMB LINE IS USED BY A WORKER SUCH
AS A CARPENTER OR OTHER ARTISAN AND IMPLIES
SKILL OR CRAFTSMANSHIP.

THE LEFT COMPONENT 𠂇 OF THE KANJI LEFT
IS A HAND 𠂇 ORIGINALLY ψ . THE COMMON
UNSKILLED LABORER IS RIGHTHANDED AND USES
PRIMARILY THE RIGHT HAND. THE SKILLED WORKMAN IS AMBI-
DEXTROUS AND USES HIS LEFT HAND ALSO AS HE PRACTICES HIS
CRAFT. THEREFORE 左 MEANS LEFT.

THINK OF THE CARPENTER WITH THE HAMMER IN HIS RIGHT HAND,
THE NAIL IN HIS LEFT; OR THE MASON WITH THE TROWEL IN HIS
RIGHT HAND, THE BRICK IN HIS LEFT. THE KANJI 工 JME 71
IMPLIES WORKER OR CONSTRUCTION.

COMPONENT   OLD SYMBOL   WORKER   HAND & SQUARE   SUPERIMPOSED
FOR HAND     LEFT HAND    CONST.    OR PLUMB LINE

| JME 19 | Stroke 5 | Rad 30 |
|---|---|---|

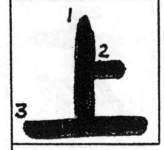

YŪ, U;  MIGI, RIGHT.

RIGHT 右 ALSO HAS THE COMPONENT FOR HAND ナ, ORIGINALLY ⼿ .  IN THE KANJI RIGHT 右 , HAND ナ FORMS A COMPOSITE WITH THE KANJI MOUTH 口 JME 27 ORIGINALLY O .  THE RIGHT HAND ナ IS THE ONE GENERALLY USED TO FEED THE MOUTH.  THUS THE KANJI 右 MEANS RIGHT.

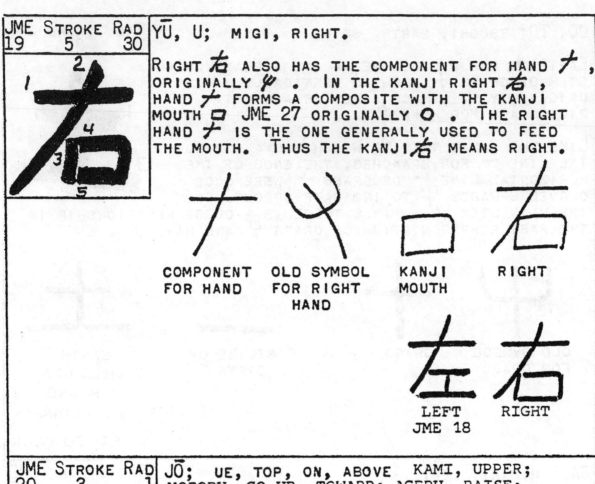

| COMPONENT FOR HAND | OLD SYMBOL FOR RIGHT HAND | KANJI MOUTH | RIGHT |

LEFT
JME 18　　RIGHT

| JME 20 | Stroke 3 | Rad 1 |
|---|---|---|

JŌ;  UE, TOP, ON, ABOVE  KAMI, UPPER; NOBORU, GO UP, TOWARD; AGERU, RAISE; AGARU, RISE.

ABOVE, ON TOP, TO RISE, UPPER 上 SHOWS A FIGURE STANDING ON A BASELINE GESTURING ABOVE.  (WITH THE PASSING OF TIME, THE GESTURING ARM HAS BECOME MORE AND MORE TIRED AND NOW IS OFTEN HORIZONTAL OR NEARLY SO).

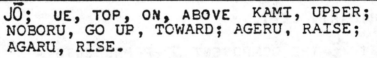

UP....ON HIS
FLYING CARPET

KA, GE;  SHITA, UNDER, LOWER, BOTTOM;
MOTO, UNDER;  SHIMO, LOWER PART, BOTTOM;
KUDARU, COME DOWN, GO DOWN;
SAGERU, KUDASU, OROSU, TO LOWER;
SAGARU, TO HANG, TO FALL

IF THE KANJI UP 上 JME 20 IS LEFT ON ITS
BASELINE AND TURNED TO FALL ON ITS FACE, IT
WILL MAKE THE KANJI 下 BELOW, UNDER, BOTTOM,
DOWN, ETC.

| Rad | Stroke | JME |
|-----|--------|-----|
| 1 | 3 | 21 |

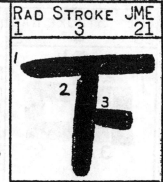

上        下

TOP,ON      UNDER,
ABOVE       LOWER,
JME 19      BOTTOM

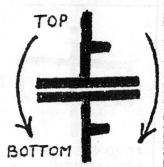

TOP

BOTTOM

KANJI TOP
FLIPPED TO
KANJI BOTTOM

---

DAI, TAI;  ŌKII, LARGE, BIG, GREAT.

THE KANJI GREAT, BIG, LARGE 大 IS A MAN
STANDING WITH HIS LEGS SPREAD 人 AND
EXTENDING HIS ARMS HORIZONTALLY TO SHOW
GREATNESS OR BIGNESS (AS OF THE FISH HE DID
NOT CATCH).

| Rad | Stroke | JME |
|-----|--------|-----|
| 37 | 3 | 22 |

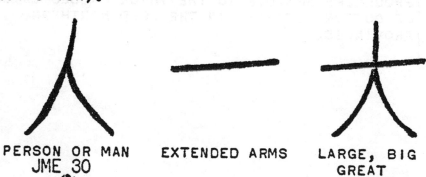

人            一            大

PERSON OR MAN    EXTENDED ARMS    LARGE, BIG
   JME 30                          GREAT

| JME 23 | Stroke 4 | Rad 2 |
|---|---|---|

CHŪ, JŪ; NAKA, MIDDLE, INSIDE, WITHIN, AMONG.

MIDDLE, INSIDE, WITHIN 中 SHOWS A TARGET OR MOUTH 口, ORIGINALLY A CIRCLE OR DISC O, WITH A VERTICAL LINE REPRESENTING THE ARROW | STRIKING OR PASSING THROUGH IT.

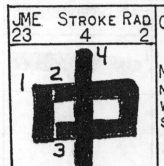

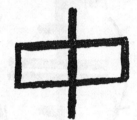

ARROW STRIKES OR PASSES THROUGH TARGET (MOUTH OR APERTURE)

VERTICAL LINE REPRESENTING THE ARROW

TARGET (MOUTH OR APERTURE) ORIGINALLY A CIRCLE OR DISC

A DRAWING FOR IMPROVED VISUALIZATION (NOT AN ALTERNATE STYLE OF WRITING THE KANJI)

| JME 24 | Stroke 3 | Rad 42 |
|---|---|---|

SHŌ; CHIISAI, KO, O, LITTLE, SMALL.

LITTLE, SMALL, MINOR 小 HAS A VERTICAL LINE FOR THE CHILD |, LITTLE 小 CONTRASTED TO AN ADULT, WITH ITS ARMS HANGING OBLIQUELY ハ DUE TO THE NARROWNESS OF ITS LITTLE SHOULDERS AND DUE TO THE THICK PADDED LAYERS OF COTTON CLOTHING IN THE COLD NORTHERN PROVINCES.

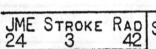

SUPERIMPOSED

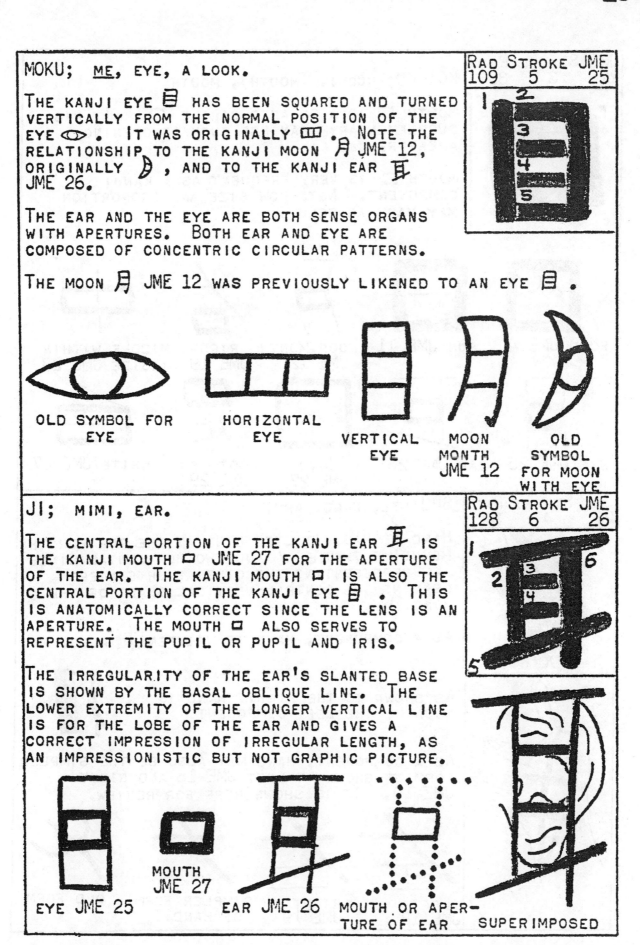

MOKU; ME, EYE, A LOOK.

| RAD | STROKE | JME |
|-----|--------|-----|
| 109 | 5 | 25 |

THE KANJI EYE 目 HAS BEEN SQUARED AND TURNED VERTICALLY FROM THE NORMAL POSITION OF THE EYE ⬮. IT WAS ORIGINALLY ▭. NOTE THE RELATIONSHIP TO THE KANJI MOON 月 JME 12, ORIGINALLY ☽, AND TO THE KANJI EAR 耳 JME 26.

THE EAR AND THE EYE ARE BOTH SENSE ORGANS WITH APERTURES. BOTH EAR AND EYE ARE COMPOSED OF CONCENTRIC CIRCULAR PATTERNS.

THE MOON 月 JME 12 WAS PREVIOUSLY LIKENED TO AN EYE 目 .

OLD SYMBOL FOR EYE     HORIZONTAL EYE     VERTICAL EYE     MOON MONTH JME 12     OLD SYMBOL FOR MOON WITH EYE

JI; MIMI, EAR.

| RAD | STROKE | JME |
|-----|--------|-----|
| 128 | 6 | 26 |

THE CENTRAL PORTION OF THE KANJI EAR 耳 IS THE KANJI MOUTH 口 JME 27 FOR THE APERTURE OF THE EAR. THE KANJI MOUTH 口 IS ALSO THE CENTRAL PORTION OF THE KANJI EYE 目 . THIS IS ANATOMICALLY CORRECT SINCE THE LENS IS AN APERTURE. THE MOUTH 口 ALSO SERVES TO REPRESENT THE PUPIL OR PUPIL AND IRIS.

THE IRREGULARITY OF THE EAR'S SLANTED BASE IS SHOWN BY THE BASAL OBLIQUE LINE. THE LOWER EXTREMITY OF THE LONGER VERTICAL LINE IS FOR THE LOBE OF THE EAR AND GIVES A CORRECT IMPRESSION OF IRREGULAR LENGTH, AS AN IMPRESSIONISTIC BUT NOT GRAPHIC PICTURE.

EYE JME 25     MOUTH JME 27     EAR JME 26     MOUTH OR APERTURE OF EAR     SUPERIMPOSED

| JME 27 | Stroke 3 | Rad 30 |
|---|---|---|

KŌ, KU; KUCHI, (MOUTH), MOUTH.

MOUTH 口 IS A SQUARED CIRCLE ○. IT HAS SUPPLEMENTARY MEANINGS SUCH AS OPENING, APERTURE.

MOUTH 口 IS VERY FREQUENT AS A KANJI COMPONENT. NOTE HOW SIZE AND PROPORTION MAY VARY AS BELOW.

| FOUR JME 4 | SUN JME 11 | MOON, MONTH JME 12 | RIGHT JME 19 | MIDDLE, WITHIN INSIDE JME 23 |
|---|---|---|---|---|

| EYE JME 25 | EAR JME 26 | MOUTH JME 27 | FOOT, LEG JME 29 | WHITE JME 37 |
|---|---|---|---|---|

| JME 28 | Stroke 4 | Rad 30 |
|---|---|---|

SHU; TE, HAND, ARM.

HAND 手 HAS A TILTED LINE AT THE TOP FOR THE HORNLIKE THUMB ノ AND TWO HORIZONTAL LINES 二 REPRESENTING THE OTHER FOUR FINGERS LEAVING THE CENTRAL VERTICAL SHAFT OF THE HAND ｜.

AS A COMPONENT, HAND IS WRITTEN 扌 ALSO.

AS SHOWN TO THE RIGHT, HAND IS USUALLY THE LEFT COMPONENT.

AS A COMPONENT, HAND MAY ALSO BE THE SIMPLER FORM 手 SHOWN IN LEFT JME 18 AND RIGHT JME 19. IT IS SHOWN HERE FOR REVIEW.

| LEFT JME 18 | RIGHT JME 19 | SIMPLER FORM OF HAND | OLD FORM |
|---|---|---|---|

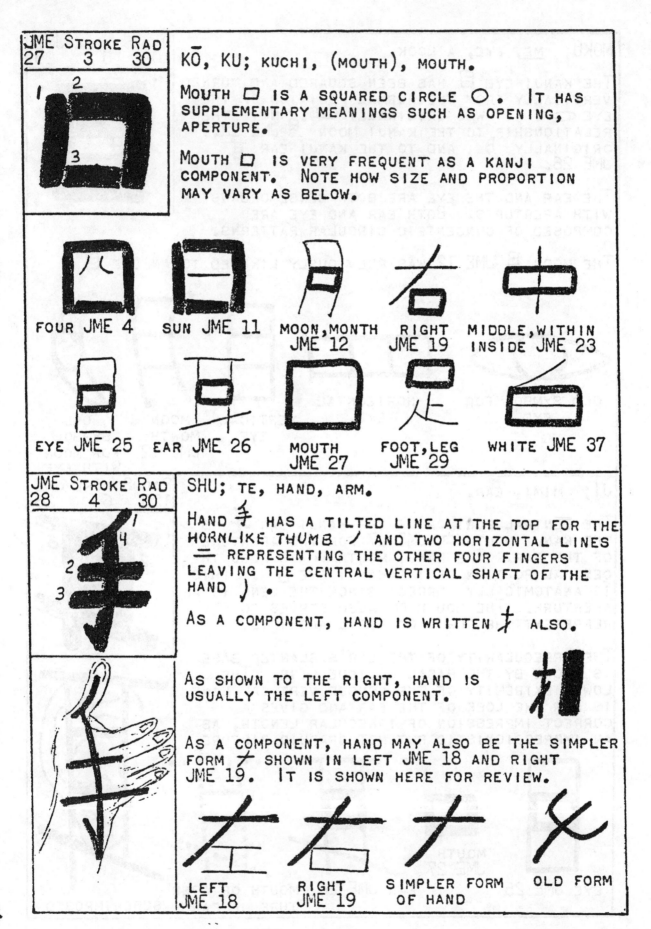

14

SOKU, (ZOKU) MAY MEAN PAIR AS A SUFFIX; ASHI, FOOT, LEG, PAW; TARU, BE ENOUGH, BE SUFFICIENT.

| RAD | STROKE | JME |
|-----|--------|-----|
| 157 | 7 | 29 |

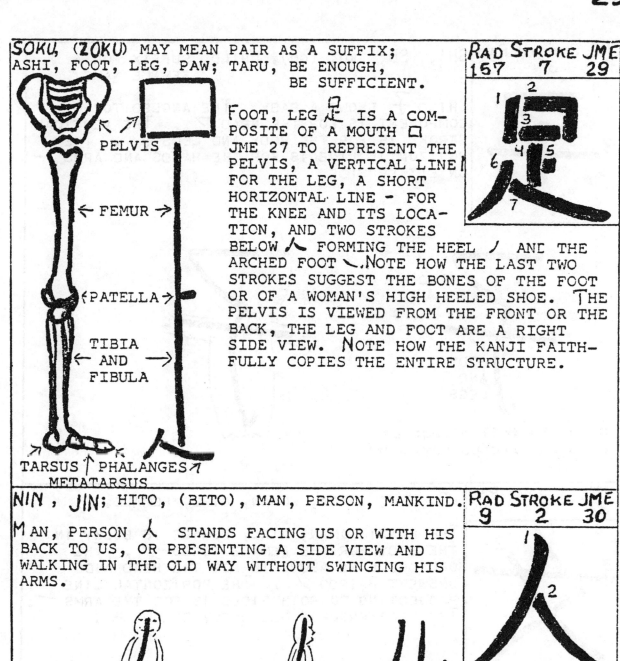

FOOT, LEG 足 IS A COMPOSITE OF A MOUTH ロ JME 27 TO REPRESENT THE PELVIS, A VERTICAL LINE FOR THE LEG, A SHORT HORIZONTAL LINE - FOR THE KNEE AND ITS LOCATION, AND TWO STROKES BELOW 人 FORMING THE HEEL ノ AND THE ARCHED FOOT ＼. NOTE HOW THE LAST TWO STROKES SUGGEST THE BONES OF THE FOOT OR OF A WOMAN'S HIGH HEELED SHOE. THE PELVIS IS VIEWED FROM THE FRONT OR THE BACK, THE LEG AND FOOT ARE A RIGHT SIDE VIEW. NOTE HOW THE KANJI FAITHFULLY COPIES THE ENTIRE STRUCTURE.

PELVIS

← FEMUR →

← PATELLA →

TIBIA ← AND → FIBULA

TARSUS ↑ PHALANGES ↗
METATARSUS

---

NIN, JIN; HITO, (BITO), MAN, PERSON, MANKIND.

| RAD | STROKE | JME |
|-----|--------|-----|
| 9 | 2 | 30 |

MAN, PERSON 人 STANDS FACING US OR WITH HIS BACK TO US, OR PRESENTING A SIDE VIEW AND WALKING IN THE OLD WAY WITHOUT SWINGING HIS ARMS.

MAN AS TWO LEGS (COMPONENT)

THE TOP COMPONENT MAN

THESE TWO STROKES FOR MAN, PERSON DRAWN SLIGHTLY DIFFERENTLY MAY BECOME A TOP ノ OR A LEFT イ COMPONENT IN KANJI. (THE MAN HOLDS UP ONE LEG).

MAN AS LEFT COMPONENT

人
MAN

イ ノ
LIFTS ONE LEG, LIFTS OTHER LEG

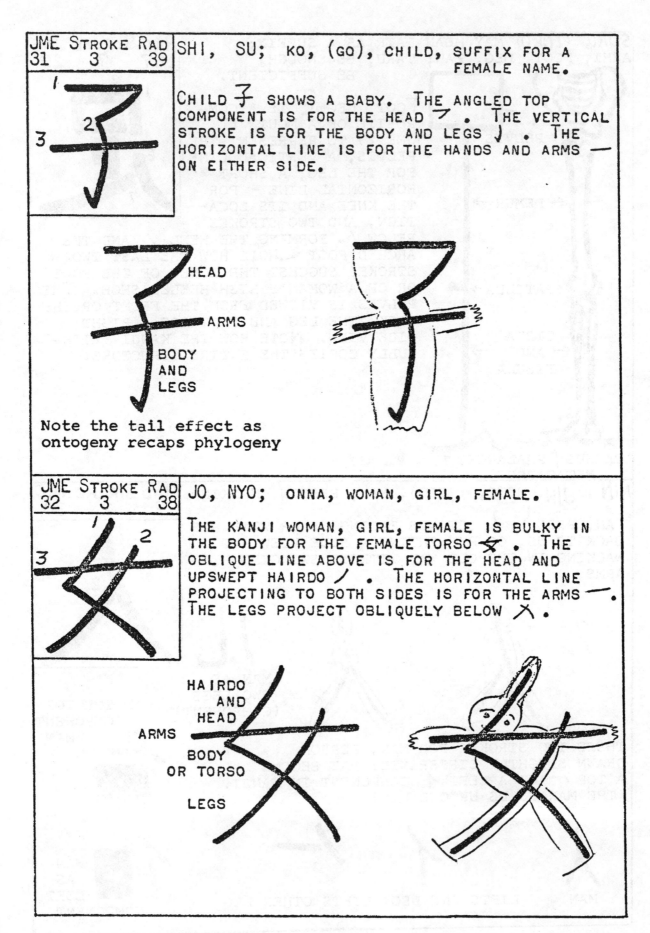

| JME 31 | Stroke 3 | Rad 39 |
|---|---|---|

SHI, SU; KO, (GO), CHILD, SUFFIX FOR A FEMALE NAME.

CHILD 子 SHOWS A BABY. THE ANGLED TOP COMPONENT IS FOR THE HEAD ㇇. THE VERTICAL STROKE IS FOR THE BODY AND LEGS 亅. THE HORIZONTAL LINE IS FOR THE HANDS AND ARMS ― ON EITHER SIDE.

HEAD

ARMS

BODY
AND
LEGS

Note the tail effect as ontogeny recaps phylogeny

| JME 32 | Stroke 3 | Rad 38 |
|---|---|---|

JO, NYO; ONNA, WOMAN, GIRL, FEMALE.

THE KANJI WOMAN, GIRL, FEMALE IS BULKY IN THE BODY FOR THE FEMALE TORSO 女. THE OBLIQUE LINE ABOVE IS FOR THE HEAD AND UPSWEPT HAIRDO ノ. THE HORIZONTAL LINE PROJECTING TO BOTH SIDES IS FOR THE ARMS ―. THE LEGS PROJECT OBLIQUELY BELOW 乂.

HAIRDO
AND
HEAD

ARMS

BODY
OR TORSO

LEGS

SEN; SAKI, PREVIOUS, IN ADVANCE, AHEAD.

| RAD | STROKE | JME |
|-----|--------|-----|
| 10  | 6      | 33  |

PREVIOUS, AHEAD 先 IS A COMPOSITE OF TWO LEGS 儿 BELOW REPRESENTING A MAN WALKING, AND THE KANJI FOR COW 牛 ABOVE, ABBREVIATED TO 土 TO CONVENIENCE THE MAN'S LEGS 儿. OX, COW 牛 IS DRAWN AS A TOP VIEW, PERHAPS A STRETCHED HIDE. THE OBLIQUE LINE ノ ON THE UPPER LEFT IS THE HORN(S). THE TWO ニ HORIZONTAL LINES ARE THE FOUR LEGS PROJECTING FROM THE VERTICAL LINE | OF THE BODY. THE VERTICAL LINE CONTINUES BELOW AS THE TAIL.

IN WRITING THE KANJI PREVIOUS, AHEAD 先 THE TAIL IS REPLACED BY THE TWO LEGS 儿 OF THE MAN AHEAD 先 LEADING THE COW. TWO LEGS 儿 IS LEADING FOUR LEGS 牛.

THE ORIENTAL METHOD OF CONTROLING THE COW, OX 牛 WAS TO PLACE A RING THROUGH THE SEPTUM OF ITS SENSITIVE NOSE FOR LEADING PURPOSES. THE LEADING PERSON 儿 WAS AHEAD OF, PREVIOUS, OR IN ADVANCE 先. THE SAME TECHNIQUE WAS USED IN EUROPE. RECALL "THE OWL AND THE PUSSY CAT" GETTING THE PIG'S NOSE RING FOR THEIR WEDDING?

先

牛 COW

先 PREVIOUS, IN ADVANCE, AHEAD

儿 LEGS

TAIL REPLACED BY TWO LEGS, MAN

---

SEI, SHŌ, EXISTENCE, LIFE; UMARERU, TO BE BORN; UMU, TO GIVE BIRTH; IKIRU, TO LIVE; NAMA, RAW; KI, GENUINE, PURE.

| RAD | STROKE | JME |
|-----|--------|-----|
| 100 | 5      | 34  |

EXISTENCE, LIFE, TO BE BORN, TO LIVE 生 IS A GROWING STEM | COMING UP WITH LATERAL SHOOTS 十 FROM THE EARTH 土. THE OBLIQUE STROKE ノ IS FOR THE HEAD OF THE GRAIN, ETC. TO SHOW THE YIELD. THUS EARTH 土 AND THE PLANT ARE COMBINED AND HEADED 生. ALWAYS CONSIDER THE POSSIBILITY THAT LATERAL LINES MAY ONCE HAVE CURVED UPWARDS, ESPECIALLY IN KANJI OF MEANINGS SUCH AS THE ABOVE. THE ORIGINAL FORM OF 十 WAS ψ.

NOTICE THE RATIO OF THE THREE HORIZONTAL STROKES 三. IT IS THE SAME AS IN THE KANJI THREE 三 JME 3.

EXISTENCE, LIFE, TO BE BORN, TO LIVE 生 IS CLOSELY LINKED TO THE YIELD OF THE EARTH, ESPECIALLY FOR THE NOMADIC HERDSMAN. 生 MAY REPRESENT THE SPIKELETS, EARS, HEADS ノ OF GRAIN, ETC. OVER PLANT LAYERS, FOLIAGE 主.

ノ HEAD OR YIELD OF THE PLANT

十 PLANT   ψ PLANT (OLD SYMBOL)

生   土 EARTH JME 17

| JME | STROKE | RAD |
|-----|--------|-----|
| 35 | 7 | 155 |

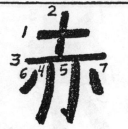

SEKI, SHAKU; AKAI, AKA, RED, CRIMSON, SCARLET.

RED 赤 IS A COMPOSITE OF EARTH 土 JME 17 AND FIRE 火 JME 13 WRITTEN IN A SLIGHTLY DIFFERENT FORM 小 BELOW.

IT REFERS TO THE COLOR OF LAVA OR THE VOLCANIC FIRES 小 CRATERS IN OR UNDER THE EARTH 土 .

EARTH (GRAVE-MOUND, ALTAR, ETC.) JME 17

RED CRIMSON SCARLET

EARTH, SOIL OVER FIRE COMPONENT

FIRE JME 13

FIRE COMPONENT

| JME | STROKE | RAD |
|-----|--------|-----|
| 36 | 8 | 174 |

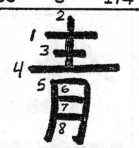

LAYERS OF PLANT LIFE

MOONLIGHT CASTING BLUISH OR GREENISH SHADOWS

SEI, SHŌ; AOI, AO, BLUE, GREEN, UNRIPE, INEXPERIENCED.

BLUE, GREEN UNRIPE, INEXPERIENCED 青 IS A COMPOSITE OF LAYERS 圭 OF PLANT LIFE ABOVE THROUGH WHICH THE MOON 月 LIGHT BELOW HAS DIFFUSED GIVING A BLUISH OR GREENISH TINGE.

JUST AS IN THE ENGLISH WORD "GREENHORN" FOR A NOVICE OR THE BLUE GRASS OF KENTUCKY, BLUE, GREEN, OR BLUISH-GREEN IS THE COLOR FOR INEXPERIENCE 青 OR UNRIPENESS SINCE NEW SHOOTS OR PLANTS ARE OF THAT COLOR BEFORE MATURATION.

NOTE HOW THE UPPER COMPONENT 圭 RESEMBLES JME 34 生 BUT DOES NOT HAVE THE HEAD / INDICATING RIPENESS OR YIELD. MOON WAS JME 12 月 .

"Old thujas thickly grew Casting their shades of blue.
                    Su Tung-p'o (Trans. by Dykstra)

"And smitten trees in groups and rows Beneath the tempest's tune, Stand in the mists of midnight drooping,
By moss-grown rocks fantastic stooping, In the blue shadows of the yellow moon.   J. Sheridan Le Fanu (1815-73)

HAKU, BYAKU; SHIROI, SHIRO, SHIRA, WHITE.

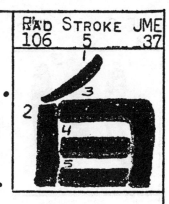

| Rad | Stroke | JME |
|-----|--------|-----|
| 106 | 5 | 37 |

WHITE 白 IS THE COLOR OF LIGHT WHICH COMES FROM THE SUN 日 JME 11 AS RAYS OR SHAFTS /. THE RAYS / BRING THE SUN 日 DOWN TO US.

"WAKE! For the Sun....

....strikes The Sultan's Turret with a Shaft of Light.
(Rubáiyát)

WHITE

SUN JME 11

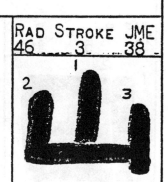

RAYS WHICH BRING SUN (LIGHT) DOWN TO US.

SAN, (ZAN); YAMA, MOUNTAIN.

| Rad | Stroke | JME |
|-----|--------|-----|
| 46 | 3 | 38 |

MOUNTAIN 山 IS COMPOSED OF THREE VERTICAL LINES FOR PEAKS OF IRREGULAR HEIGHT RELATED TO A HORIZONTAL BASELINE.

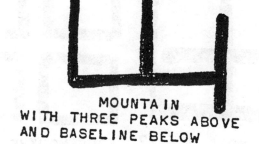

OLD SYMBOL HAD THREE PEAKS STILL PRESENT

MOUNTAIN WITH THREE PEAKS ABOVE AND BASELINE BELOW

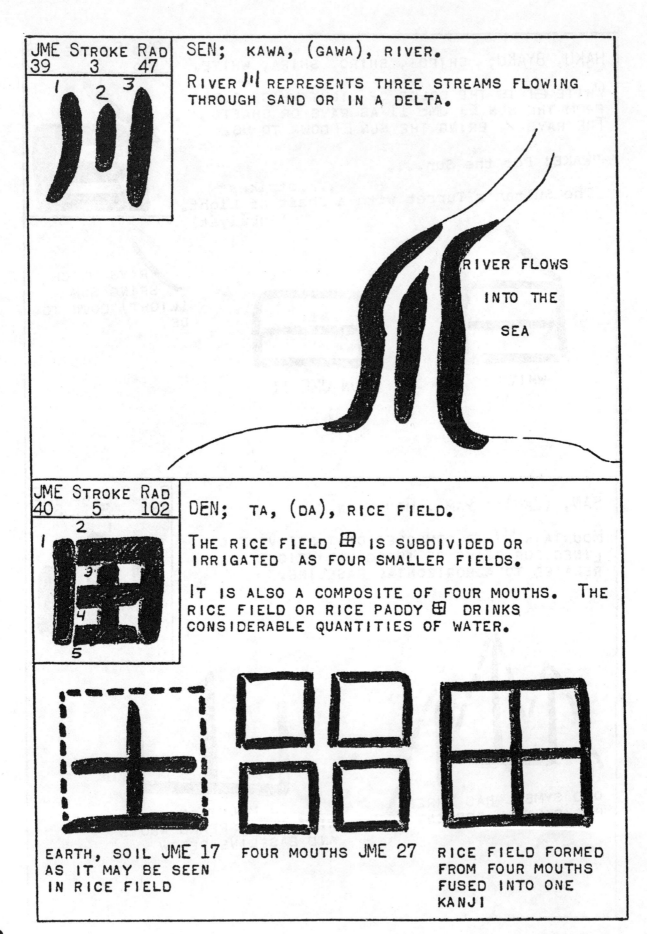

| JME 39 | Stroke 3 | Rad 47 |
|--------|----------|--------|

SEN; KAWA, (GAWA), RIVER.

RIVER 川 REPRESENTS THREE STREAMS FLOWING THROUGH SAND OR IN A DELTA.

RIVER FLOWS

INTO THE

SEA

| JME 40 | Stroke 5 | Rad 102 |
|--------|----------|---------|

DEN; TA, (DA), RICE FIELD.

THE RICE FIELD 田 IS SUBDIVIDED OR IRRIGATED AS FOUR SMALLER FIELDS.

IT IS ALSO A COMPOSITE OF FOUR MOUTHS. THE RICE FIELD OR RICE PADDY 田 DRINKS CONSIDERABLE QUANTITIES OF WATER.

EARTH, SOIL JME 17 AS IT MAY BE SEEN IN RICE FIELD

FOUR MOUTHS JME 27

RICE FIELD FORMED FROM FOUR MOUTHS FUSED INTO ONE KANJI

SHIN; MORI, FOREST.

Forest 森 IS REPRESENTED BY THREE TREES
JME 15. THREE OF A KIND MAY BE USED TO
SHOW AN INCREASE IN QUANTITY, QUALITY, OR
NUMBERS. THREE OF A KIND IS COMMONLY DONE
AS IN THIS CASE BY PLACING ONE OF THE ITEM
ABOVE AND TWO BELOW.

| Rad | Stroke | JME |
|---|---|---|
| 75 | 12 | 41 |

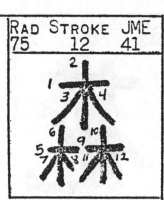

TREE, WOOD JME 15

WOODS, GROVE JME 150

FOREST
JME 41

---

U; AME, RAIN.

Rain 雨 IS DROPS ∴ OF WATER FALLING ｜
IN THE ENCLOSURE OR SPACE ⊓ UNDER HEAVEN
—

THE RAIN KANJI 雨 IS A TOP COMPONENT IN THE
KANJI FOR SNOW, FROST, HAIL, THUNDER, CLOUD,
ETC.

| Rad | Stroke | JME |
|---|---|---|
| 173 | 8 | 42 |

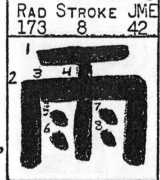

CLOUD JME 47

SNOW JME 100

RAIN

FROM HEAVEN

FALLS

INTO THE
ENCLOSURE
OR SPACE

THE RAIN,
RAINDROPS

"The hooded clouds, like friars,
  Tell their beads in drops of rain.
                    Longfellow
"The mist and cloud will turn to rain,
  The rain to mist and cloud again,
                    Longfellow

| JME | Stroke | Rad |
|-----|--------|-----|
| 43  | 7      | 140 |

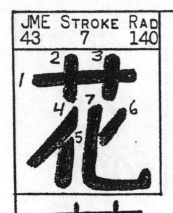

FUSED GRASSES
(DOUBLED)

亻 UPRIGHT MAN

匕 MAN IN INVERTED FETAL, SITTING, OR MUMMY POSITION

KA; HANA, FLOWER.

FLOWER 花 IS A COMPOSITE. THE TOP ⺾ COMPONENT MEANING GRASS OR PLANT 十 IS A SINGLE GRASS OR PLANT DOUBLED AND FUSED ⺾. IT IS ANOTHER INSTANCE OF CURVED UPWARDS LINES ψ BECOMING HORIZONTAL FOR WRITING SPEED AND CONVENIENCE.

THE LOWER PORTION 化 OF FLOWER 花 SHOWS A MAN STANDING 亻 TO THE LEFT AND A MAN SITTING 匕 WITH ARMS EXTENDED ON THE RIGHT.

THE COMBINATION 化 MEANS CHANGE OR TO CHANGE 化 BECAUSE OF THE CHANGE IN POSITION DESCRIBED. WHEN GRASS OR A PLANT CHANGES, IT BECOMES A FLOWER.

SOMETIMES 匕 IS REGARDED AS THE DEATH FORM, NOTE THE MUMMY OR FETAL POSITION 匕, OR AS THE INVERTED FORM WITH LEGS UP OF 人 WHICH IS THE LIFE FORM OR NATURAL POSITION. IN ANY CASE THE TRANSITION FROM 亻 TO 匕 IS CHANGE. ("All flesh is grass, and all the goodliness thereof is as the flower of the field... Grass withereth, flower fadeth:" Is.)

| JME | Stroke | Rad |
|-----|--------|-----|
| 44  | 5      | 112 |

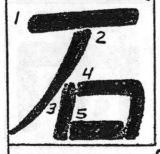

CLIFFS WITH MORE OR LESS OVERHANG

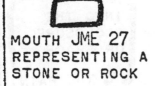

MOUTH JME 27 REPRESENTING A STONE OR ROCK

SEKI, SHAKU, KOKU; ISHI, STONE.

STONE, ROCK 石 IS ANOTHER COMPOSITE. 丁 IS A CLIFF IN PROFILE WITH MORE OR LESS OVERHANG 丁厂 AND A STONE 口 AT ITS BASE. THE COMPOSITE 石 IS NECESSARY TO INDICATE STONE OR ROCK SINCE MOUTH IS WRITTEN WITH 口 JME 27 ALONE. IN STONE, ROCK 石 WE HAVE AN INSTANCE OF HOW 口 AS A KANJI MEANS MOUTH BUT IS USED IN A COMPONENT TO CREATE A COMPOSITE WITH A DIFFERENT MEANING.

STONES AT THE BASE OF
MESA-LIKE CLIFFS

HON, (BON), (PON), SUFFIX IN COUNTING LONG
SLENDER ARTICLES, BOOK;  MOTO, ROOT, SOURCE.

| RAD | STROKE | JME |
|-----|--------|-----|
| 75  | 5      | 45  |

BOOK, ROOT, SOURCE 本 CONSISTS OF TREE 木
JME 15 WITH A SHORT HORIZONTAL STROKE —
ADDED TO ALTER THE MEANING TO BOOK, ROOT,
SOURCE 本.

A BOOK 本 IS THE ROOT OR SOURCE 本 OF
KNOWLEDGE AND WOODEN (TREE) BLOCKS WERE USED
FOR EARLY PRINTING.  THE SCOPE AND POWER OF
THE TREE USED AS A SOURCE OF WRITING MATERIALS AND FOR
PRINTING BLOCKS WERE ENORMOUSLY INCREASED.  THE SHORT
STROKE OR DOT SIGNIFIES THIS, ANALOGOUS TO SUN 日 JME 11.

TREE, WOOD JME 15

SHORT STROKE
HAS THE EFFECT
OF A DOT AS IN
JADE JME 64 AND
DOG JME 66

BOOK, ROOT, SOURCE

---

SEI, SHŌ; TADASHII, CORRECT, RIGHT.

| RAD | STROKE | JME |
|-----|--------|-----|
|     | 5      | 46  |

CORRECT, RIGHT 正 IS REPRESENTED BY A HALTED
UP- 上 (RIGHT) POSITION UNDER THE HORIZONTAL
LINE FOR HEAVEN 一 .  UPRIGHT UNDER HEAVEN
AS THE BIBLE PHRASES IT.  TO STOP, TO BRING
TO A STOP 止 IS FOOT, LEG 足 JME 29 WITH THE
PELVIS REMOVED 止 AND THE FOOT FLATTENED 止
AS THOUGH SCREECHING TO A HALT.  THUS RIGHT,
CORRECT 正 IS A FUSION OF UP 上 , TO STOP 止 ,
AND HEAVEN . 

FOOT, LEG
JME 29
(WITH AN
ARCHED
FOOT)

CORRECT,
RIGHT
JME 46
(WITH THE
FOOT FLAT)

HEAVEN
(AS PART
OF WORKER
AND CON-
STRUCTION)

TO STOP, TO
BRING TO A
STOP
JME 220

UPPER, ABOVE,
TOP, ON, UP,
TO GO UP
JME 20

| JME 47 | Stroke 12 | Rad 173 | UN; KUMO, (GUMO), CLOUD. |
|---|---|---|---|

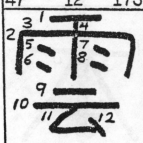

CLOUD 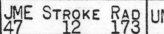 IS A COMPOSITE WITH RAIN  JME 42 AS THE TOP COMPONENT AND A COILED CLOUD ム AT THE BOTTOM UNDER LAYERS OF CLOUD = ABOVE. THE SYMBOL FOR THE COILED CLOUD ム IS GENERIC FOR CERTAIN THINGS WHICH ARE COILED, LAYERED, OR HOLDING. EXAMPLES ARE A MOUTH SPEAKING, A BASKET, A (PINE) CONE, OR AN ARM WITH THE MUSCLE CONTRACTED. THE COILED CLOUD WITH LAYERS ABOVE 云 MAY ALSO MEAN A MOUTH ム SPEAKING IN SOUND WAVES OR VIBRATIONS = AS IN WEATHER CAUSING FROSTY PUFFS OF BREATH LIKE CLOUDS. THIS MOUTH IS CONCEPTUALLY DIFFERENT THAN ロ JME 27 SINCE ム SENDS FORTH AS A GENESIS OF EXPANSION LIKE THE PINE CONE WHICH IS THE SOURCE OF SEEDLINGS, THE CLOUD WHICH CAN EXPAND AND COVER THE SKY, THE BASKET WHOSE CONTENTS CAN BE SPREAD, OR THE CONTRACTED ARM MUSCLE WHICH CAN OPEN THE ARM.

RAIN JME 42

CLOUD LAYERS

COILED CLOUD

CLOUD JME 47

| JME 48 | Stroke 4 | Rad 31 | EN; CIRCLE, YEN, JAPANESE UNIT OF CURRENCY. |
|---|---|---|---|

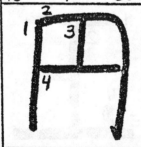

CIRCLE, YEN 円 IS TWO DOORS 門 JOINED 円 WITH THEIR PANELS RAISED AS WITH A PAIR OF SWINGING DOORS. THE MOST PICTURESQUE DOORS ARE THOSE OF A "MOON-GATE" WHICH IS CIRCULAR LIKE A FULL MOON. SOME OLD ORIENTAL COINS WERE CIRCULAR AND HAD HOLES FOR STRINGING. THE KANJI HAS BEEN SQUARED FROM ITS ORIGINAL CURVED FORM.

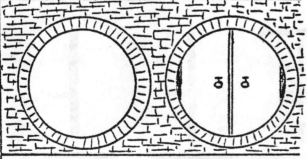

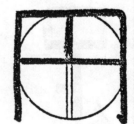

CIRCULAR AND OPEN "MOON-GATE" AS IN A BRICK WALL

DOORS SET IN "MOON-GATE"

OLD COIN WITH SQUARE HOLE FOR STRINGING

SUPER-IMPOSITION

Ō; KING.

KING 王 IS A COMPOSITE INCLUDING THREE HORIZONTAL LINES 三. THE TOP HORIZONTAL LINE IS FOR HEAVEN, THE MIDDLE HORIZONTAL LINE IS FOR THE PEOPLE, THE BOTTOM HORIZONTAL LINE IS FOR THE EARTH. THE VERTICAL LINE REPRESENTS THE KING WHO OFFERS PRAYERS ON THE ALTARS OF EARTH FOR THE PEOPLE TO HEAVEN. THUS THE KING MEDIATES BETWEEN EARTH AND HEAVEN FOR HIS PEOPLE.

| RAD | STROKE | JME |
|-----|--------|-----|
| 96 | 4 | 49 |

HEAVEN

MANKIND, MAN

EARTH          KING MEDIATES   KING JME 49

(TRIAD IN THREE JME 3)

ON, IN; NE, OTO, SOUND.

SOUND 音 IS A COMPOSITE. SOUND 音 ISSUES FROM THE MOUTH 日 OF A PERSON OR MAN 立 STANDING 立. NOTE JME 6. A STANDING 立 POSITION IS THE BEST FOR MAKING SOUND BY SINGING, SHOUTING, ETC. TO STAND 立 IS APPROPRIATELY ABOVE SINCE SOUND WILL CARRY BETTER FROM AN ELEVATION.

| RAD | STROKE | JME |
|-----|--------|-----|
| 180 | 9 | 50 |

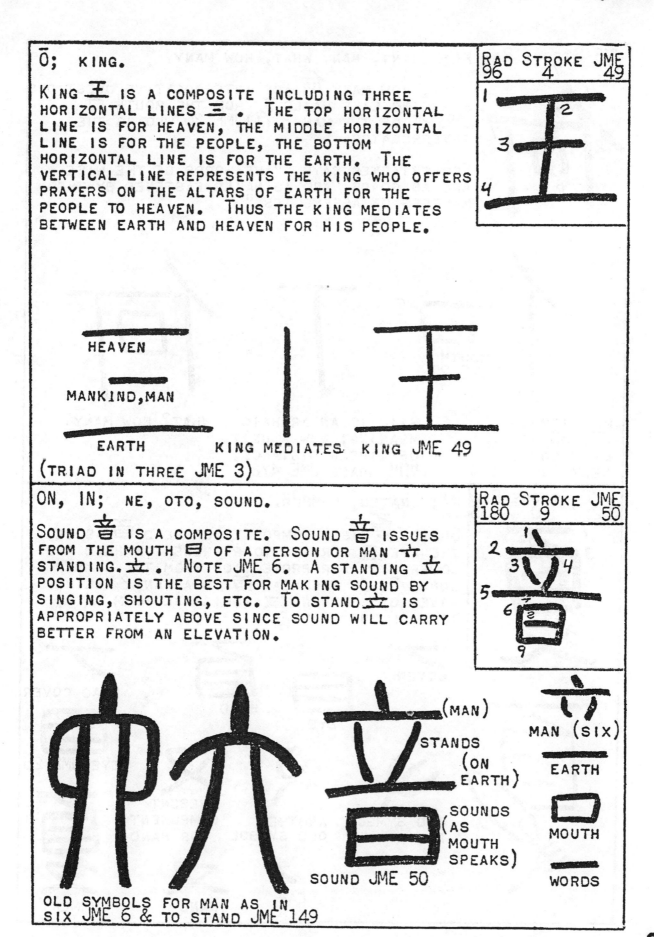

(MAN)

STANDS (ON EARTH)

SOUNDS (AS MOUTH SPEAKS)

SOUND JME 50

MAN (SIX)

EARTH

MOUTH

WORDS

OLD SYMBOLS FOR MAN AS IN SIX JME 6 & TO STAND JME 149

| JME 51 | Stroke 7 | Rad 9 |
|---|---|---|

KA; NANI, NAN, WHAT, HOW MANY.

WHAT, HOW MANY 何 ARE INTERROGATIVE QUESTIONS STRIKING LIKE NAILS 丁 FROM THE MOUTH 口 JME 27 OF THE MAN 亻(人) JME 30 WHO IS THE INTERROGATOR.

ECCLESIASTES SAYS, "THE WORDS OF THE WISE ARE AS GOADS, AND AS NAILS FASTENED BY THE MASTERS OF ASSEMBLIES."

MOUTH JME 27

MAN, PERSON JME 30 AS LEFT COMPONENT

NAIL IS AN ARCHAIC MEANING; NOW A UNIT OF LINEAR DISTANCE, "D" GRADE JME 473

WHAT? HOW MANY?

| JME 52 | Stroke 10 | Rad 35 |
|---|---|---|

KA; NATSU, SUMMER.

SUMMER 夏 IS A COMPOSITE OF HEAD 百 ABOVE, THE EYE 目 SERVING TO REPRESENT A HEAD AND COVERED 冖 FOR PROTECTION FROM THE SUMMER SUN. BELOW THE HEAD 百 IS A FAN ノ BEING WAVED BY THE HAND 又 (ORIGINAL FORM ) TO COOL THE HEAD 百.

COVER

EYE

HEAD

HEAD COVER

EYE JME 25

OLD SYMBOL FOR HAND

ANOTHER OLD SYMBOL

PRESENT COMPONENT FOR HAND

FAN

HAND

SUMMER

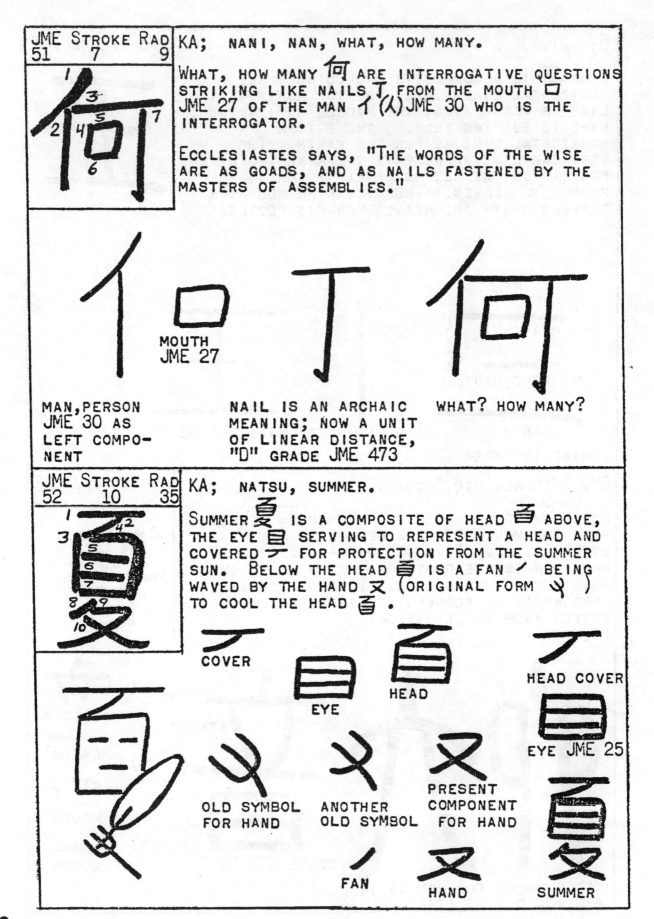

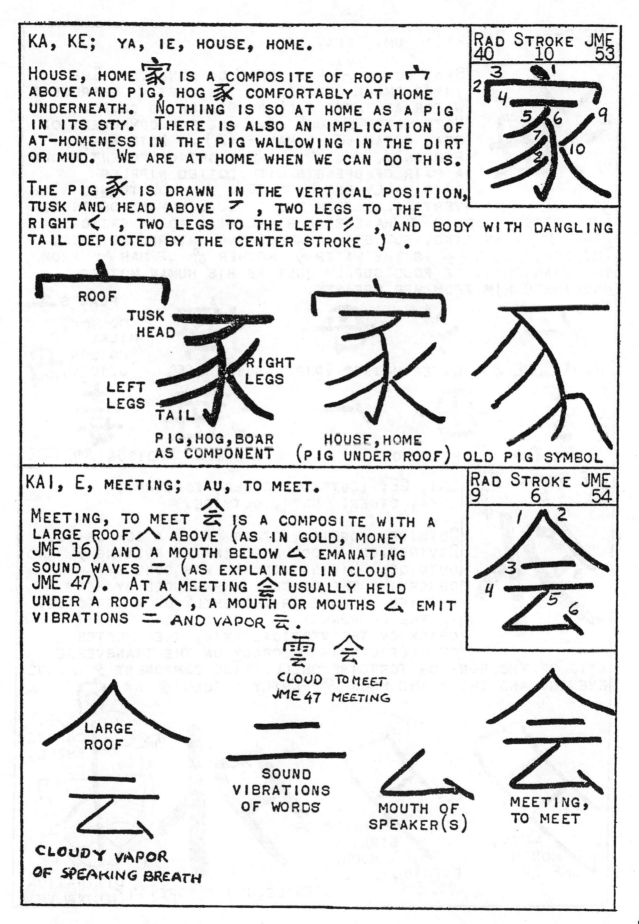

KA, KE; YA, IE, HOUSE, HOME.

| Rad | Stroke | JME |
|-----|--------|-----|
| 40 | 10 | 53 |

HOUSE, HOME 家 IS A COMPOSITE OF ROOF 宀 ABOVE AND PIG, HOG 豕 COMFORTABLY AT HOME UNDERNEATH. NOTHING IS SO AT HOME AS A PIG IN ITS STY. THERE IS ALSO AN IMPLICATION OF AT-HOMENESS IN THE PIG WALLOWING IN THE DIRT OR MUD. WE ARE AT HOME WHEN WE CAN DO THIS.

THE PIG 豕 IS DRAWN IN THE VERTICAL POSITION, TUSK AND HEAD ABOVE ⼸ , TWO LEGS TO THE RIGHT ⼃ , TWO LEGS TO THE LEFT ⼆ , AND BODY WITH DANGLING TAIL DEPICTED BY THE CENTER STROKE ⼁ .

ROOF

TUSK
HEAD

LEFT LEGS    RIGHT LEGS

TAIL

PIG, HOG, BOAR AS COMPONENT

HOUSE, HOME (PIG UNDER ROOF)

OLD PIG SYMBOL

KAI, E, MEETING; AU, TO MEET.

| Rad | Stroke | JME |
|-----|--------|-----|
| 9 | 6 | 54 |

MEETING, TO MEET 会 IS A COMPOSITE WITH A LARGE ROOF 𠆢 ABOVE (AS IN GOLD, MONEY JME 16) AND A MOUTH BELOW ム EMANATING SOUND WAVES = (AS EXPLAINED IN CLOUD JME 47). AT A MEETING 会 USUALLY HELD UNDER A ROOF 𠆢 , A MOUTH OR MOUTHS ム EMIT VIBRATIONS = AND VAPOR 云.

雲 会
CLOUD   TO MEET
JME 47   MEETING

LARGE ROOF

SOUND VIBRATIONS OF WORDS

MOUTH OF SPEAKER(S)

MEETING, TO MEET

CLOUDY VAPOR OF SPEAKING BREATH

| JME | Stroke | Rad |
|-----|--------|-----|
| 55  | 9      | 85  |

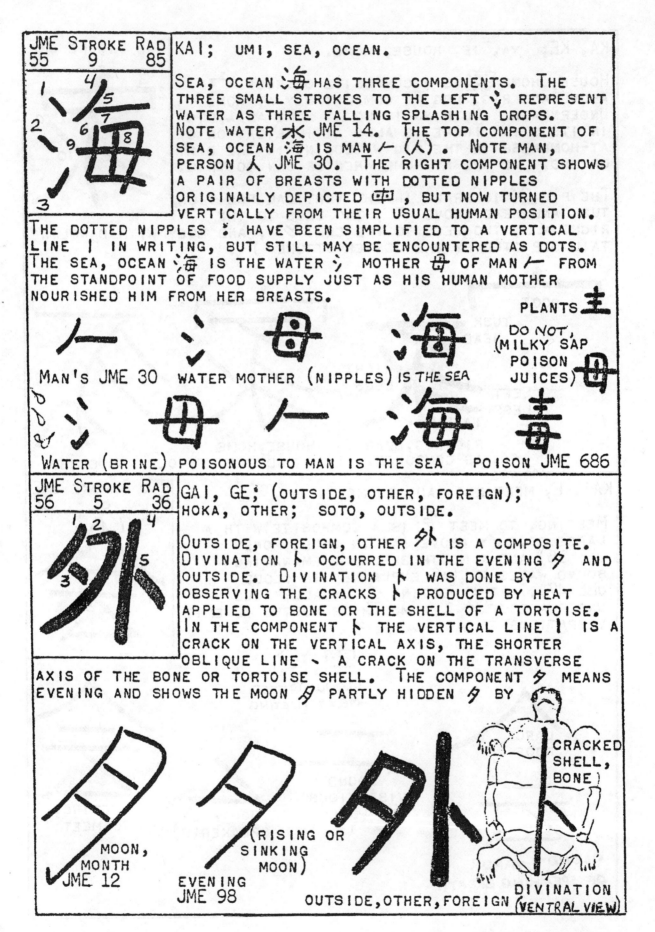

KAI; UMI, SEA, OCEAN.

SEA, OCEAN 海 HAS THREE COMPONENTS. THE THREE SMALL STROKES TO THE LEFT 氵 REPRESENT WATER AS THREE FALLING SPLASHING DROPS. NOTE WATER 水 JME 14. THE TOP COMPONENT OF SEA, OCEAN 海 IS MAN 𠂉 (人). NOTE MAN, PERSON 人 JME 30. THE RIGHT COMPONENT SHOWS A PAIR OF BREASTS WITH DOTTED NIPPLES ORIGINALLY DEPICTED 申, BUT NOW TURNED VERTICALLY FROM THEIR USUAL HUMAN POSITION.

THE DOTTED NIPPLES ⁝ HAVE BEEN SIMPLIFIED TO A VERTICAL LINE | IN WRITING, BUT STILL MAY BE ENCOUNTERED AS DOTS. THE SEA, OCEAN 海 IS THE WATER 氵 MOTHER 母 OF MAN 𠂉 FROM THE STANDPOINT OF FOOD SUPPLY JUST AS HIS HUMAN MOTHER NOURISHED HIM FROM HER BREASTS.

PLANTS 主

𠂉  氵  母  海      DO NOT, (MILKY SAP POISON JUICES) 母

MAN'S JME 30   WATER MOTHER (NIPPLES) IS THE SEA

氵  母  𠂉  海  毒

WATER (BRINE) POISONOUS TO MAN IS THE SEA     POISON JME 686

| JME | Stroke | Rad |
|-----|--------|-----|
| 56  | 5      | 36  |

GAI, GE; (OUTSIDE, OTHER, FOREIGN); HOKA, OTHER; SOTO, OUTSIDE.

OUTSIDE, FOREIGN, OTHER 外 IS A COMPOSITE. DIVINATION 卜 OCCURRED IN THE EVENING 夕 AND OUTSIDE. DIVINATION 卜 WAS DONE BY OBSERVING THE CRACKS 卜 PRODUCED BY HEAT APPLIED TO BONE OR THE SHELL OF A TORTOISE. IN THE COMPONENT 卜 THE VERTICAL LINE | IS A CRACK ON THE VERTICAL AXIS, THE SHORTER OBLIQUE LINE ヽ A CRACK ON THE TRANSVERSE AXIS OF THE BONE OR TORTOISE SHELL. THE COMPONENT 夕 MEANS EVENING AND SHOWS THE MOON 月 PARTLY HIDDEN 夕 BY

月  夕  外      CRACKED SHELL, BONE

MOON, MONTH JME 12

(RISING OR SINKING MOON)

EVENING JME 98

OUTSIDE, OTHER, FOREIGN      DIVINATION (VENTRAL VIEW)

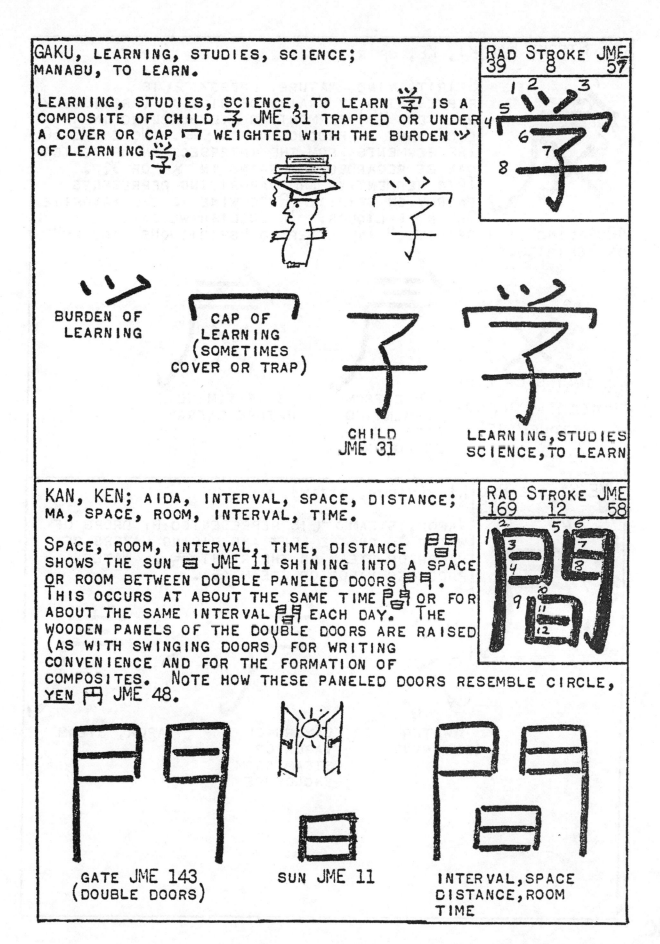

GAKU, LEARNING, STUDIES, SCIENCE;
MANABU, TO LEARN.

LEARNING, STUDIES, SCIENCE, TO LEARN 学 IS A
COMPOSITE OF CHILD 子 JME 31 TRAPPED OR UNDER
A COVER OR CAP ⌐ WEIGHTED WITH THE BURDEN ⋎
OF LEARNING 学.

| Rad | Stroke | JME |
|-----|--------|-----|
| 39  | 8      | 57  |

BURDEN OF
LEARNING

CAP OF
LEARNING
(SOMETIMES
COVER OR TRAP)

CHILD
JME 31

LEARNING, STUDIES
SCIENCE, TO LEARN

KAN, KEN; AIDA, INTERVAL, SPACE, DISTANCE;
MA, SPACE, ROOM, INTERVAL, TIME.

SPACE, ROOM, INTERVAL, TIME, DISTANCE 間
SHOWS THE SUN 日 JME 11 SHINING INTO A SPACE
OR ROOM BETWEEN DOUBLE PANELED DOORS 門.
THIS OCCURS AT ABOUT THE SAME TIME 間 OR FOR
ABOUT THE SAME INTERVAL 間 EACH DAY. THE
WOODEN PANELS OF THE DOUBLE DOORS ARE RAISED
(AS WITH SWINGING DOORS) FOR WRITING
CONVENIENCE AND FOR THE FORMATION OF
COMPOSITES. NOTE HOW THESE PANELED DOORS RESEMBLE CIRCLE,
YEN 円 JME 48.

| Rad | Stroke | JME |
|-----|--------|-----|
| 169 | 12     | 58  |

GATE JME 143
(DOUBLE DOORS)

SUN JME 11

INTERVAL, SPACE
DISTANCE, ROOM
TIME

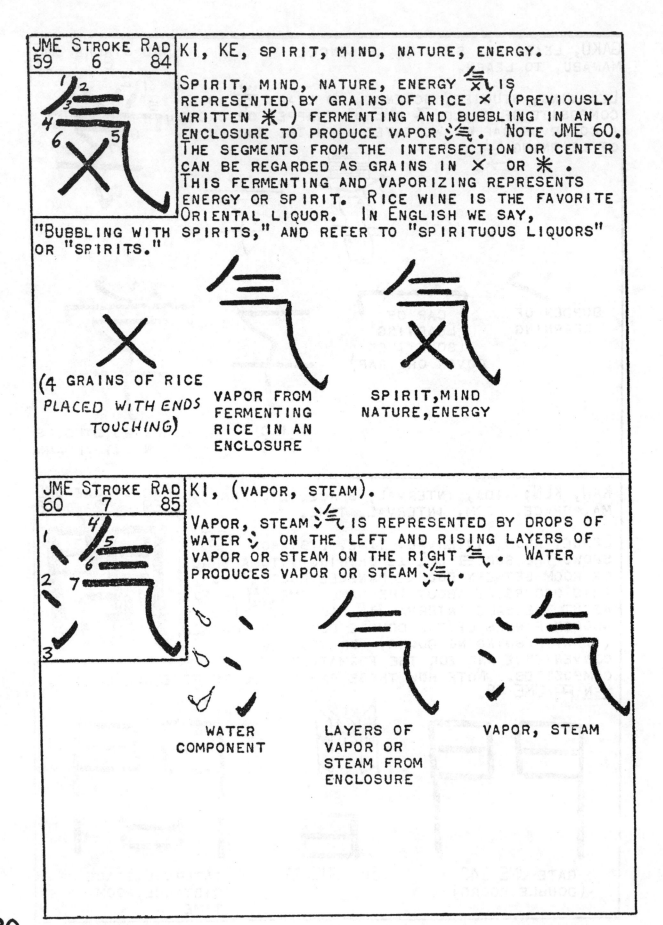

| JME 59 | Stroke 6 | Rad 84 |
|---|---|---|

KI, KE, SPIRIT, MIND, NATURE, ENERGY.

SPIRIT, MIND, NATURE, ENERGY 気 IS REPRESENTED BY GRAINS OF RICE ╳ (PREVIOUSLY WRITTEN 米) FERMENTING AND BUBBLING IN AN ENCLOSURE TO PRODUCE VAPOR 气. NOTE JME 60. THE SEGMENTS FROM THE INTERSECTION OR CENTER CAN BE REGARDED AS GRAINS IN ╳ OR 米. THIS FERMENTING AND VAPORIZING REPRESENTS ENERGY OR SPIRIT. RICE WINE IS THE FAVORITE ORIENTAL LIQUOR. IN ENGLISH WE SAY, "BUBBLING WITH SPIRITS," AND REFER TO "SPIRITUOUS LIQUORS" OR "SPIRITS."

(4 GRAINS OF RICE PLACED WITH ENDS TOUCHING)

VAPOR FROM FERMENTING RICE IN AN ENCLOSURE

SPIRIT, MIND NATURE, ENERGY

| JME 60 | Stroke 7 | Rad 85 |
|---|---|---|

KI, (VAPOR, STEAM).

VAPOR, STEAM 汽 IS REPRESENTED BY DROPS OF WATER ⺡ ON THE LEFT AND RISING LAYERS OF VAPOR OR STEAM ON THE RIGHT 气. WATER PRODUCES VAPOR OR STEAM 汽.

WATER COMPONENT

LAYERS OF VAPOR OR STEAM FROM ENCLOSURE

VAPOR, STEAM

| RAD | STROKE | JME |
|-----|--------|-----|
| 9   | 6      | 61  |

KYU; YASUMI, REST, VACATION;
YASUMU, TO REST.

REST, VACATION 休 IS A COMPOSITE OF A MAN イ
JME 30 TO THE LEFT OF A TREE 木 JME 15 BY
OR UNDER WHICH HE CAN REST OR VACATION.

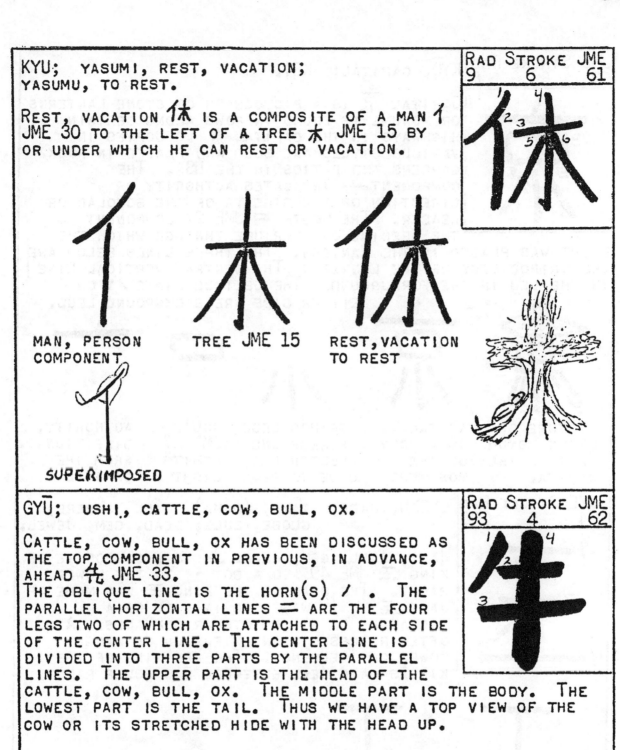

MAN, PERSON
COMPONENT

TREE JME 15

REST, VACATION
TO REST

SUPERIMPOSED

| RAD | STROKE | JME |
|-----|--------|-----|
| 93  | 4      | 62  |

GYŪ; USHI, CATTLE, COW, BULL, OX.

CATTLE, COW, BULL, OX HAS BEEN DISCUSSED AS
THE TOP COMPONENT IN PREVIOUS, IN ADVANCE,
AHEAD 先 JME 33.
THE OBLIQUE LINE IS THE HORN(S) ノ . THE
PARALLEL HORIZONTAL LINES ニ ARE THE FOUR
LEGS TWO OF WHICH ARE ATTACHED TO EACH SIDE
OF THE CENTER LINE. THE CENTER LINE IS
DIVIDED INTO THREE PARTS BY THE PARALLEL
LINES. THE UPPER PART IS THE HEAD OF THE
CATTLE, COW, BULL, OX. THE MIDDLE PART IS THE BODY. THE
LOWEST PART IS THE TAIL. THUS WE HAVE A TOP VIEW OF THE
COW OR ITS STRETCHED HIDE WITH THE HEAD UP.

HORN(S)

HEAD

BODY

TAIL

FOUR LEGS

HEAD, BODY, TAIL

MINUS HORN(S)

COW, BULL
CATTLE, OX

| JME | Stroke | Rad |
|-----|--------|-----|
| 63 | 8 | 8 |

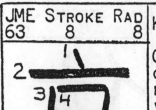

KYŌ, CAPITAL; KEI.

CAPITAL 京 IS A PICTOGRAPH OF STONE LANTERNS OR MONUMENTS FOUND IN ROWS ALONG CERTAIN HIGHWAYS IN THE CAPITAL 京 . COPIES IN VARIOUS STYLES ARE SOLD AND PLACED IN ROCK GARDENS AND PATIOS IN THE USA. THE COMPONENT ⊥ INDICATES AUTHORITY OR DIRECTION OR THE BIRETTA OF THE SCHOLAR OR LEADER. THE MOUTH ロ JME 27 COMPONENT IS THE OPENING OR APERTURE THROUGH WHICH THE LIGHT WAS PLACED IN THE LANTERN. THE THREE LINES BELOW ARE THE TRIPOD LEGS OF THE LANTERN. THE CENTRAL VERTICAL LINE⌡ IS THE LEG IN THE FOREGROUND. THE OBLIQUE LINES ハ ON EITHER SIDE ARE BACKGROUND LEGS.

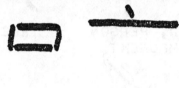

| PICTURE OF STONE MONU- MENT IN THE CAPITAL | CAPITAL... IS A COPY OF THE MONUMENT | TRIPOD LEGS FOREGROUND CENTER LEG SIDE TO REAR | MOUTH JME 27 ADMITS LIGHT | AUTHORITY, DIRECTION... FROM THE CAPITAL |
|---|---|---|---|---|

| JME | Stroke | Rad |
|-----|--------|-----|
| 64 | 5 | 96 |

GYOKU, JADE; TAMA, (DAMA), BALL, SPHERE, GLOBE, BULB, BEAD, GEM, JEWEL.

JADE, BALL, GEM, JEWEL 玉 IS A COMPOSITE OF KING 王 JME 49 AND A DOT ﹅ TO THE LOWER RIGHT. THE SEAL OF THE KING 王 WAS MADE OF JADE 玉. IT WAS USED IN LIEU OF A SIGNATURE ON HIS EDICTS OR COMMANDS. A DOT﹅ OFTEN REPRESENTS AN EXTENSION OF RANGE, POWER OR INFLUENCE. THE AFFIXING OF THE KING'S JADE SEAL EXTENDED HIS POWER RANGE.

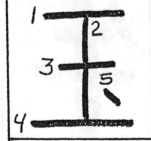

| KING JME 49 MEDIATES FROM EARTH TO HEAVEN FOR HIS PEOPLE | JADE, BALL, SPHERE, GEM JME 64 KING'S AUTHORITY | DOT EXTENDS POWER, RANGE INFLUENCE |
|---|---|---|

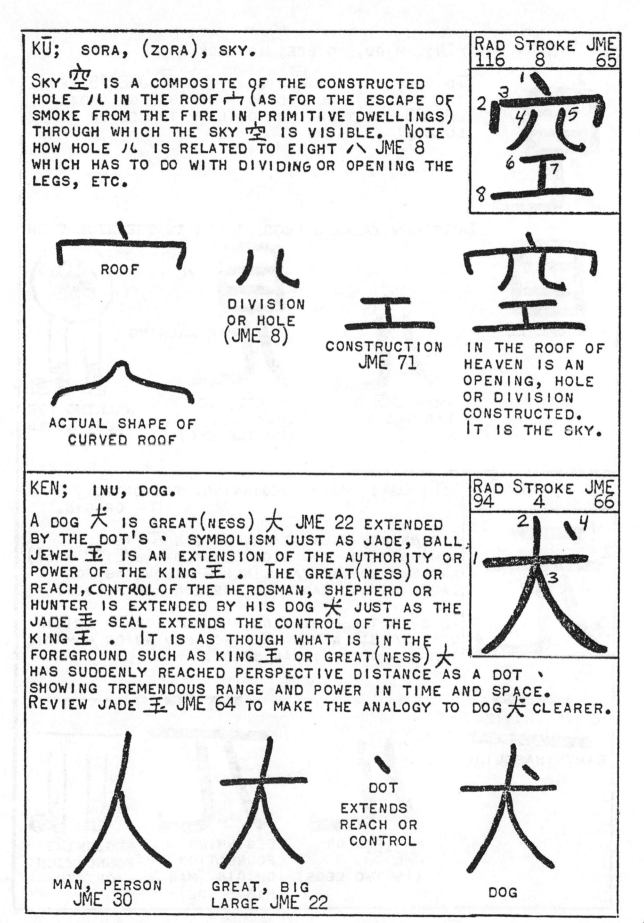

KŪ;　SORA, (ZORA), SKY.

| RAD | STROKE | JME |
|-----|--------|-----|
| 116 | 8 | 65 |

SKY 空 IS A COMPOSITE OF THE CONSTRUCTED HOLE ハ IN THE ROOF 宀 (AS FOR THE ESCAPE OF SMOKE FROM THE FIRE IN PRIMITIVE DWELLINGS) THROUGH WHICH THE SKY 空 IS VISIBLE. NOTE HOW HOLE ハ IS RELATED TO EIGHT 八 JME 8 WHICH HAS TO DO WITH DIVIDING OR OPENING THE LEGS, ETC.

ROOF

DIVISION OR HOLE (JME 8)

ACTUAL SHAPE OF CURVED ROOF

CONSTRUCTION JME 71

IN THE ROOF OF HEAVEN IS AN OPENING, HOLE OR DIVISION CONSTRUCTED. IT IS THE SKY.

KEN;　INU, DOG.

| RAD | STROKE | JME |
|-----|--------|-----|
| 94 | 4 | 66 |

A DOG 犬 IS GREAT(NESS) 大 JME 22 EXTENDED BY THE DOT'S ` SYMBOLISM JUST AS JADE, BALL, JEWEL 玉 IS AN EXTENSION OF THE AUTHORITY OR POWER OF THE KING 王. THE GREAT(NESS) OR REACH, CONTROL OF THE HERDSMAN, SHEPHERD OR HUNTER IS EXTENDED BY HIS DOG 犬 JUST AS THE JADE 玉 SEAL EXTENDS THE CONTROL OF THE KING 王. IT IS AS THOUGH WHAT IS IN THE FOREGROUND SUCH AS KING 王 OR GREAT(NESS) 大 HAS SUDDENLY REACHED PERSPECTIVE DISTANCE AS A DOT ` SHOWING TREMENDOUS RANGE AND POWER IN TIME AND SPACE. REVIEW JADE 玉 JME 64 TO MAKE THE ANALOGY TO DOG 犬 CLEARER.

MAN, PERSON JME 30

GREAT, BIG LARGE JME 22

DOT EXTENDS REACH OR CONTROL

DOG

| JME 67 | Stroke 7 | Rad 147 |
|--------|----------|---------|

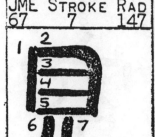

KEN; MIRU, TO SEE, TO LOOK.

TO SEE, TO LOOK 見 IS AN EYE 目 JME 25 (FOR THE VIEWER) MOUNTED ON A MAN'S LEGS (NOTE JME 33) SO THERE IS MOBILITY TO SEE OR TO LOOK 見.

NOTE HOW WALKING LEGS DIFFER IN THE SIDE VIEW.

EYE JME 25

MAN JME 30
(AS TWO LEGS)

TO SEE, TO
LOOK
(MOBILE EYE)

EYE

MAN WALKING

WALKING EYE
SEES, LOOKS

| JME 68 | Stroke 4 | Rad 8 |
|--------|----------|-------|

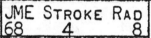

GEN; GAN; MOTO, BEGINNING, FOUNDATION, ORIGIN.

BEGINNING, FOUNDATION, ORIGIN 元 IS A COMPOSITE OF TWO LEGS 儿 BELOW (JME 33 & 67) AND TWO HORIZONTAL LINES 二 ABOVE AS FOR BASELINE AND EARTH OR HORIZON AND HEAVEN.

THIS IS THE BEGINNING, FOUNDATION OR ORIGIN OF THINGS: A MAN WALKING, MOVING OR NOMADIC AND HIS OPERATIONAL SPACE.

HEAVEN, HORIZON

EARTH, BASELINE

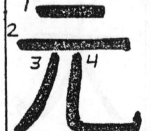

MAN, PERSON
JME 30
(AS TWO LEGS)

BEGINNING
FOUNDATION
ORIGIN (MAN &
HIS SPACE)

BEGINNING
FOUNDATION
ORIGIN

KO; TO, (DO), DOOR, SUFFIX IN COUNTING HOUSES. (ENGLISH CONCEPT: "THREE DOORS DOWN THE STREET.")

| RAD | STROKE | JME |
|-----|--------|-----|
| 63 | 4 | 69 |

THE DOOR 戸 IS A SINGLE DOOR IN CONTRAST TO THE CIRCLE 円 (OF THE MOON-GATE PAIRED DOORS) JME 48 AND THE GATE 門 (DOUBLE DOORS) JME 143 USUALLY USED FOR GATEWAYS TO ENCLOSURES AND FOR MAIN ENTRANCES. ORIENTAL DOORS WERE NOT HINGED, BUT TURNED ON PINS EXTENDING FROM THE DOOR AND SET IN SOCKETS ABOVE AND BELOW. THE TOP LINE WHICH MAY BE OBLIQUE OR HORIZONTAL REPRESENTS ONE OF THESE PINS.

CIRCLE, YEN JME 48 (MOON-GATE)

GATE JME 143 (DOUBLE DOORS)

PICTURE OF SOCKETED PINS OF THE SINGLE DOOR

DOOR JME 69 (UPPER PIN MAY BE OBLIQUELY DRAWN)

PIN
DOOR
PIN

KO; FURUI, OLD, ANCIENT.

| RAD | STROKE | JME |
|-----|--------|-----|
| 24 | 5 | 70 |

OLD, ANCIENT 古 IS A COMPOSITE OF TEN 十 JME 10 AND MOUTH 口 JME 27. IT INDICATES SOMETHING ENDURING OR PASSED ON BY TEN 十 GENERATIONS OF MOUTHS 口 IS OLD, ANCIENT 古.

ORIENTALS RECKON A GENERATION AS THIRTY YEARS. TEN GENERATIONS IS THREE HUNDRED YEARS, A GREAT CYCLE OF THE ORIENTAL SIXTY YEAR CALENDAR CYCLE, OR FIVE LESSER CYCLES.

TEN JME 10

MOUTH JME 27

OLD, ANCIENT JME 70

TEN (GENERATIONS OF) MOUTHS

| JME 71 | STROKE 3 | RAD 48 |
|---|---|---|

KŌ, KU; WORKER, ENGINEERING, CONSTRUCTION.

WORKER, ENGINEERING, CONSTRUCTION 工 IS A SMALL CARPENTER'S SQUARE OR A PLUMB LINE FROM THE CEILING OR HEAVEN TO THE FLOOR OR EARTH. WORKER, ENGINEERING, CONSTRUCTION 工 WAS A COMPONENT IN LEFT 左 JME 18 AND A COMPONENT IN SKY 空 JME 65.

THE SQUARE OR PLUMB LINE IS ESSENTIAL TO A WORKER IN CONSTRUCTION OR ENGINEERING 工.

HEAVEN

PLUMB LINE

EARTH

 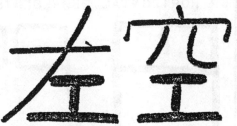

| THE CONCEPT OF THE SQUARE OR PLUMB LINE AS APPLIED TO HEAVEN AND EARTH AS A DIVINE CONSTRUCTION JME 71 | WORKER, ENGINEERING, CONSTRUCTION AS SUPERIMPOSED PLUMB LINE OR SQUARE | LEFT JME 18 WORKER, OR ENGINEERING CONSTRUCTION IS THE LOW COMPONENT | SKY JME 65. WORKER, OR ENGINEERING, CONSTRUCTION IS THE LOW COMPONENT |
|---|---|---|---|

| JME 72 | STROKE 6 | RAD 42 |
|---|---|---|

KŌ; HIKARI, LIGHT, BRILLIANCE; HIKARU, TO SHINE.

LIGHT, BRILLIANCE, TO SHINE 光 IS A COMPOSITE OF A WALKING MAN (ON TWO LEGS 儿) CARRYING A FIRE 火 (TORCH). THE BOTTOM PORTION OF THE KANJI FOR FIRE 火 HAS BEEN FLATTENED: 丷. 丷 CAN ALSO BE INTERPRETED AS RAYS OF LIGHT 丷.

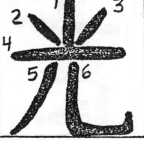

| MAN IS PORTRAYED BY TWO LEGS WALKING (WHICH WILL CARRY THE FIRE, TORCH) | LIGHT, BRILLIANCE, TO SHINE (FIRE ABOVE, MAN CARRYING THE FIRE OR TORCH) | THE LOWER PART OF FIRE HAS BEEN FLATTENED AND RAISED FROM DOTS | DOTTED LINE SHOWS THE FUTURE POSITION OF THE LOWER PART OF FIRE | FIRE JME 13 BECOMES TOP COMPONENT IN LIGHT, BRILLIANCE, TO SHINE JME 72 |
|---|---|---|---|---|

KŌ, GYŌ, AN;  IKU, YUKU, TO GO;
OKONAU, TO DO, TO ACT;  OKONAI, ACT, DEED.

| RAD | STROKE | JME |
|-----|--------|-----|
| 144 | 6 | 73 |

TO GO, TO DO, TO ACT, ACT, DEED 行 HAD ITS
ORIGIN AS A CROSSROADS 什 .

AT PRESENT, TO GO, TO DO, TO ACT, ACT,
DEED 行 ALSO SUGGESTS TWO FEET OR LEGS
IN THE ACT OR DEED 行 OF GOING OR DOING 行 .

ADDITIONAL MEANINGS SUCH AS TO CONDUCT,
TO PRACTICE 行 DERIVE FROM THE CONCEPT OF TRAVELING THE
CORRECT (RIGHTEOUS) ROAD OR PATH.

| CROSSROADS & NECESSARY TO GO, TO DO, TO ACT | LINES OF CROSSROADS SHIFT AND STRAIGHTEN | TO GO, TO DO, TO ACT | TO GO, TO DO, TO ACT SUGGESTS LEGS, FEET JME 29 | CORRECT CONDUCT, FOLLOW LEADER |

KŌ;  KANGAERU, TO THINK;
KANGAE, IDEA, THOUGHT, OPINION

| RAD | STROKE | JME |
|-----|--------|-----|
| 125 | 6 | 74 |

TO THINK, IDEA, THOUGHT, OPINION 考 IS FOR
THE FILIAL CONFUCIAN TO THINK OR TO REFLECT
ON HIS (DEAD) FATHER.
EARTH 土 CARRIED ON A SLANTED STICK OR
BACK / CONNOTES BURDEN.  THE SAME SLANTED
LINE IS SEEN IN AGED, OLD 老 JME 541 AND IN
FEW, LITTLE, SCARCE 少 .  THE OLD AND THE
LITTLE ARE THE BURDEN.
THE COMPONENT 丂 MAY BE THE ASTHMATIC GROAN OF FATHER OR
THE RASP 丂 OF THE BOWSTRING.  LINKED HERE IS THE THOUGHT OF
HOW HE CARRIED YOU DURING YOUR FIRST THREE YEARS.  THAT IS
WHY THE OFFICIAL MOURNING PERIOD FOR A PARENT WAS THREE
YEARS.

| EARTH (BURDEN) | BENT SLANTED BACK OR STICK CARRYING | RASP OF BOWSTRING OR GROAN | THOUGHT, OPINION, IDEA | ASIAN COMPOUND BOW | FEW, LITTLE, SCARCE JME 93 (ALSO IS A BURDEN) |

MOVEMENT OF BOWSTRING

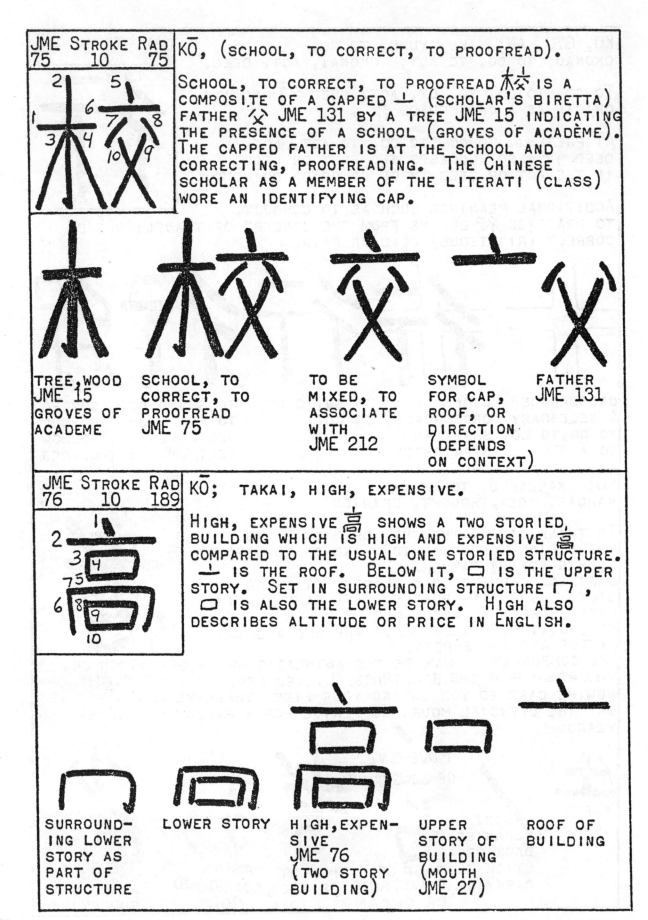

| JME 75 | STROKE 10 | RAD 75 |
|---|---|---|

**KŌ, (SCHOOL, TO CORRECT, TO PROOFREAD).**

SCHOOL, TO CORRECT, TO PROOFREAD 校 IS A COMPOSITE OF A CAPPED 亠 (SCHOLAR'S BIRETTA) FATHER 父 JME 131 BY A TREE JME 15 INDICATING THE PRESENCE OF A SCHOOL (GROVES OF ACADÈME). THE CAPPED FATHER IS AT THE SCHOOL AND CORRECTING, PROOFREADING. THE CHINESE SCHOLAR AS A MEMBER OF THE LITERATI (CLASS) WORE AN IDENTIFYING CAP.

TREE, WOOD JME 15 GROVES OF ACADEME

SCHOOL, TO CORRECT, TO PROOFREAD JME 75

TO BE MIXED, TO ASSOCIATE WITH JME 212

SYMBOL FOR CAP, ROOF, OR DIRECTION (DEPENDS ON CONTEXT)

FATHER JME 131

| JME 76 | STROKE 10 | RAD 189 |
|---|---|---|

**KŌ; TAKAI, HIGH, EXPENSIVE.**

HIGH, EXPENSIVE 高 SHOWS A TWO STORIED, BUILDING WHICH IS HIGH AND EXPENSIVE 高 COMPARED TO THE USUAL ONE STORIED STRUCTURE. 亠 IS THE ROOF. BELOW IT, 口 IS THE UPPER STORY. SET IN SURROUNDING STRUCTURE 冂, 口 IS ALSO THE LOWER STORY. HIGH ALSO DESCRIBES ALTITUDE OR PRICE IN ENGLISH.

SURROUNDING LOWER STORY AS PART OF STRUCTURE

LOWER STORY

HIGH, EXPENSIVE JME 76 (TWO STORY BUILDING)

UPPER STORY OF BUILDING (MOUTH JME 27)

ROOF OF BUILDING

GŌ; AU, TO FIT, TO SUIT, TO AGREE, TO BE TOGETHER.

TO FIT, TO SUIT, TO AGREE, TO BE TOGETHER 合 IS A COMPOSITE OF A LARGE ROOF 𠆢 ABOVE WITH THE COMBINATION OF ONE ― AND MOUTH 口 BELOW.

ONE MOUTH 合 INDICATES UNIFORMITY OF OPINION AND/OR ECONOMIC AGREEMENT SINCE THE COMMON MOUTH MUST BE NOURISHED AND THIS IS ACCOMPLISHED BY AGREEING, BEING TOGETHER.

THE IDEALIZED CHINESE PATRIARCHAL FAMILY HAD FIVE 五 GENERATIONS UNDER "ONE ROOF."

| RAD 30 | STROKE 6 | JME 77 |
|---|---|---|

|  | | | | |
|---|---|---|---|---|
| LARGE ROOF (OR MT. PEAK DEPENDING ON THE CONTEXT | TO FIT, TO SUIT, TO AGREE, TO BE TOGETHER (ROOF, UNITY) | ONE JME 1 OVER MOUTH (UNITY) | FIVE JME 5 (GENERATIONS) | MEETING, TO MEET JME 54 SOUND VIBRATIONS FROM MOUTH |

KOKU; TANI, VALLEY.

VALLEY 谷 IS A COMPOSITE OF TWO SEPARATED OBLIQUE LINES 八 AT THE TOP WHICH MEAN DIVIDE, DIVIDED 八 (REFER TO EIGHT 八 JME 8) SINCE VALLEYS DIVIDE OR SEPARATE MOUNTAINS, THE MOUNTAIN PEAK ABOVE 𠆢 THE VALLEY 口 REPRESENTED BY A MOUTH 口 SINCE THE VALLEY MAY BE USED FOR INGRESS AND SINCE THE VALLEY BY ITS SHAPE AND FERTILITY HOLDS THE PEOPLE, JUST AS A MOUTH HOLDS FOOD, ETC.

| RAD 150 | STROKE 7 | JME 78 |
|---|---|---|

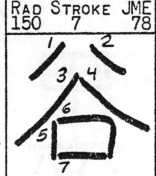

| DIVIDED, SEPARATED (REVIEW JME 8) | VALLEY JME 78 (DIVIDED MOUNTAIN VALLEYS) | MOUTH OR APERTURE UNDER MOUNTAIN | MOUTH OR APERTURE (MAY HAVE HOLDING FUNCTION |
|---|---|---|---|

| JME 79 | Stroke 8 | Rad 31 |
|---|---|---|

KOKU, (GOKU); KUNI, (GUNI), COUNTRY.

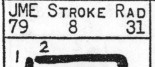
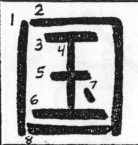

COUNTRY 国 HAS TWO COMPONENTS, JEWEL OR JADE 玉 REPRESENTING THE AUTHORITY OF THE RULER THROUGH HIS JADE SEAL 王, AND AN ENCLOSURE 口 AS THE NATIONAL BORDER OR BOUNDARY. THE ENCLOSURE 口 IS THE SAME SHAPE AS MOUTH 口 JME 27, BUT IS LARGER AND IS ONLY USED TO ENCLOSE.

| ENCLOSURE HERE USED AS NATIONAL BOUNDARIES | COUNTRY... AUTHORITY OF KING 王 WITHIN THE NATIONAL BOUNDARIES JME 79 | JADE (SEAL) OF THE KING REPRESENTING HIS CONTROL, AUTHORITY (JME 64) | THE DOT ` INCREASES CONTROL BY THE KING 王 THROUGH THE SEAL 王 | THE KING JME 49 (MEDIATES FROM EARTH TO HEAVEN FOR HIS PEOPLE) |
|---|---|---|---|---|

| JME 80 | Stroke 11 | Rad 203 |
|---|---|---|

KOKU; KURO, (GURO), KUROI, BLACK.

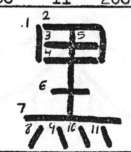

BLACK 黒 IS A COMPOSITE. THE FOUR STROKES BELOW 灬 REPRESENT A FIRE 火 JME 13 IN A COMPONENT FORM. OVER THE FIRE 灬 IS A STOVE OF EARTH 土 (LIKE ADOBE). THE VERTICAL FLUE | LEADS TO A GRATED 田 CHIMNEY WHERE THE BLACK 黒 SOOT COLLECTS. THE BLACKNESS IS EMPHASIZED BY TURNING THE TOP OF THE GRATE TO US. SOOT WAS USED AS AN INGREDIENT OF BLACK CHINESE INK.

| VERTICAL FLUE AND GRATE (NOTE MOUTHS) FOR BLACK SOOT TO MAKE THE BLACK INK | BLACK... EMPHASIS ON THE SOOT OF THE GRATE | EARTH JME 17 OF WHICH STOVE IS MADE | FIRE JME 13 UNDER THE EARTHEN STOVE | FIRE AS A COMPONENT JME 13 |
|---|---|---|---|---|

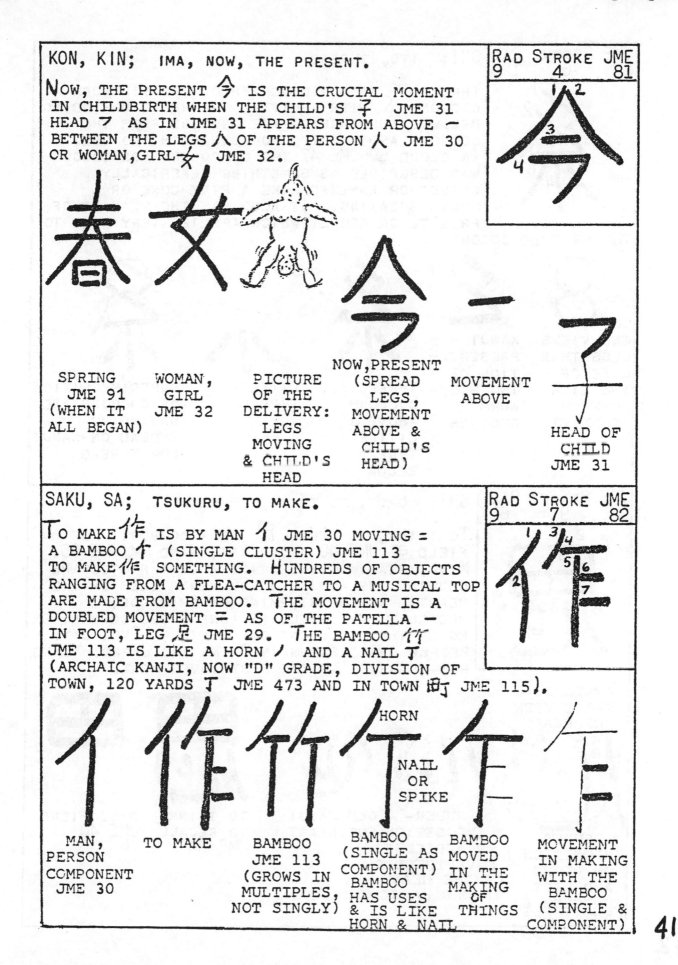

KON, KIN;   IMA, NOW, THE PRESENT.

NOW, THE PRESENT 今 IS THE CRUCIAL MOMENT
IN CHILDBIRTH WHEN THE CHILD'S 子 JME 31
HEAD フ AS IN JME 31 APPEARS FROM ABOVE ー
BETWEEN THE LEGS 人 OF THE PERSON 人 JME 30
OR WOMAN, GIRL 女 JME 32.

| RAD | STROKE | JME |
|-----|--------|-----|
| 9 | 4 | 81 |

SPRING
JME 91
(WHEN IT
ALL BEGAN)

WOMAN,
GIRL
JME 32

PICTURE
OF THE
DELIVERY:
LEGS
MOVING
& CHILD'S
HEAD

NOW, PRESENT
(SPREAD
LEGS,
MOVEMENT
ABOVE &
CHILD'S
HEAD)

MOVEMENT
ABOVE

HEAD OF
CHILD
JME 31

SAKU, SA;  TSUKURU, TO MAKE.

TO MAKE 作 IS BY MAN 亻 JME 30 MOVING =
A BAMBOO 乍 (SINGLE CLUSTER) JME 113
TO MAKE 作 SOMETHING. HUNDREDS OF OBJECTS
RANGING FROM A FLEA-CATCHER TO A MUSICAL TOP
ARE MADE FROM BAMBOO. THE MOVEMENT IS A
DOUBLED MOVEMENT = AS OF THE PATELLA ー
IN FOOT, LEG 足 JME 29. THE BAMBOO 竹
JME 113 IS LIKE A HORN ノ AND A NAIL 丁
(ARCHAIC KANJI, NOW "D" GRADE, DIVISION OF
TOWN, 120 YARDS 丁 JME 473 AND IN TOWN 町 JME 115).

| RAD | STROKE | JME |
|-----|--------|-----|
| 9 | 7 | 82 |

MAN,
PERSON
COMPONENT
JME 30

TO MAKE

BAMBOO
JME 113
(GROWS IN
MULTIPLES,
NOT SINGLY)

BAMBOO
(SINGLE AS
COMPONENT)
BAMBOO
HAS USES
& IS LIKE
HORN & NAIL

HORN

NAIL
OR
SPIKE

BAMBOO
MOVED
IN THE
MAKING
OF
THINGS

MOVEMENT
IN MAKING
WITH THE
BAMBOO
(SINGLE &
COMPONENT)

| JME 83 | Stroke 6 | Rad 120 |
|--------|----------|---------|

SHI; ITO, THREAD.

THREAD 糸 IS A PICTOGRAPH OF TWO SILKWORM COCOONS 8 WITH A LITTLE 小 THREAD UNWINDING BELOW. THE THREADS ARE UNWOUND FROM THE COCOONS AND TWISTED FOR STRENGTH AND USE. IN CLOUD 雲 JME 47 THE COMPONENT FOR COCOON WAS DESCRIBED AS SOMETHING GENERICALLY COILED OR LAYERED LIKE A PINE CONE OR A MOUTH SPEAKING. IT ALSO HAS THE MEANING OF PRIVATE OR SECRET WHICH APPLIES VERY WELL TO THE WRAPPED COCOON.

END VIEWS LESS THAN LIFE OF TWO SILK-WORM COCOONS

KANJI RE-PRESENTA-TION OF TWO SILK-WORM COCOONS

THREAD.... COCOONS ABOVE & LITTLE THREAD BELOW

LITTLE THREAD

SUPERIMPOSITION OF COCOONS AND UNWINDING THREAD ON KANJI FOR THREAD

| JME 84 | Stroke 9 | Rad 61 |
|--------|----------|--------|

SHI; OMOU, TO THINK, TO RECALL.

TO THINK, TO RECALL 思 IS A COMPOSITE OF FIELD 田 JME 40 AND HEART, MIND 心 JME 95. MIND, HEART 心 WAS ORIGINALLY A PICTOGRAPH SHOWING THE AURICLES AND VENTRICLES OF THE HEART. THE HEART, MIND 心 THINK OF, RECALL 思. THE FIELD 田 (ONE'S OLD COUNTRY HOME, THE FIELD ONE OWNS, ETC.) EVEN CITY PEOPLE OWNED FARMS IN CHINA AND JAPAN. LAND WAS REGARDED AS THE BEST INVESTMENT.

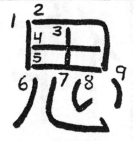

ANATOMICAL FRONT VIEW OF HEART

SUPER-IMPOSITION ON RIGHT AND LEFT AURICLES & VENTRICLES

SUPER-IMPOSITION ON AURICLES & VENTRICLES OF THE HEART IN OLD KANJI

OLD KANJI FOR HEART

TO THINK, TO RECALL JME 84

RICE FIELD JME 40

SHI; KAMI, (GAMI), PAPER.

PAPER 紙 IS A COMPOSITE OF THREAD 糸 (SILK) JME 83, AND FAMILY, CLAN 氏 JME 620. FAMILY, CLAN 氏 ORIGINATES FROM A KANJI FOR THE FLOATING PATTERN OF A WATER PLANT WITH MANY BRANCHES AND PARTS WHICH THUS RESEMBLES THE FAMILY TREE OF A GREAT PATRIARCHAL FAMILY OR CLAN 氏. TO MAKE PAPER 紙 THE PARTICLES OF WASTE SILK MADE OF THREADS 糸 ARE PLACED IN A SOLUTION. AT THIS STAGE THEY RESEMBLE THE BRANCHED WATER PLANT LIKE A GREAT CLAN WITH ITS MANY PARTS AND PARTICLES (INDIVIDUAL MEMBERS). ORIGINALLY SILK WAS USED FOR WRITING. SILK THREADS 糸 SPREAD IN THE WARP AND WOOF OF THE SILK MATERIAL LIKE THE RAMIFICATIONS OF THE CLAN RELATIONSHIP LINES IN A GENEALOGICAL CHART.

| Rad 120 | Stroke 10 | JME 85 |
|---|---|---|

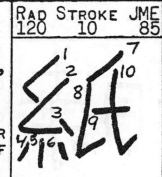

OLD MEANING OF THIS KANJI WAS SILK

REPRESENTS A FLOATING WATER PLANT SPREAD OUT ON THE SURFACE OF THE WATER

THREAD JME 83  PAPER JME 85  FAMILY, CLAN JME 620

---

JI, IDEOGRAPH, WORD, LETTER; AZA, (VILLAGE) SECTION.

IDEOGRAPH, WORD, LETTER 字 IS A COMPOSITE OF ROOF ウ (JME 53 HAS ANOTHER EXAMPLE) AND CHILD 子 JME 31. WITH THOUSANDS OF KANJI TO LEARN, THE ORIENTAL CHILD 子 UNDER THE ROOF ウ (NOT OUT WORKING OR PLAYING) IS NATURALLY STUDYING IDEOGRAPHS, WORDS, LETTERS 字. JI, IDEOGRAPH 字 IS THE LAST PART OF THE COMPOUND WORD KAN-JI. KAN IS JAPANESE FOR HAN (HAN DYNASTY) AND KAN-JI MEANS HAN OR KAN IDEOGRAPHS.

| Rad 40 | Stroke 6 | JME 86 |
|---|---|---|

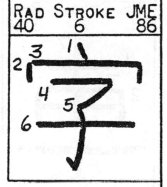

SUPERIMPOSED

CHILD JME 31

IDEOGRAPH, WORD, LETTER JME 86 ROOF OVER CHILD

ROOF..... AS IN HOUSE, HOME JME 53

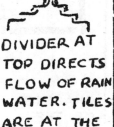
DIVIDER AT TOP DIRECTS FLOW OF RAIN WATER. TILES ARE AT THE ENDS.

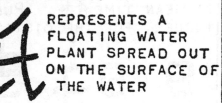

| JME 87 | STROKE 10 | RAD 72 |
|---|---|---|

**JI; TOKI, (DOKI), TIME.**

TIME 時 HAS ON THE LOWER RIGHT A HAND 寸, ORIGINALLY 屮, WITH A DOT · ADDED, TO CHANGE THE MEANING TO PULSE 寸. THE PULSE IS AN EXTENSION OF THE HAND'S ABILITY TO GRASP OR CONTROL SINCE THE PULSE KEEPS TIME FOR THE BODY AND REGULATES HEALTH. THE LOGIC OF THE ADDED DOT IS SIMILAR TO DOG 犬 JME 66 AND JADE 玉 (SEAL) JME 64. OVER PULSE 寸 IS THE COMPONENT FOR EARTH 土 JME 17. THE COMPOSITE OF EARTH 土 OVER PULSE 寸 MEANS TEMPLE 寺 SINCE THE TEMPLE IS THE PULSE OR TIMEKEEPER OF THE EARTH (LAND) SCHEDULING RELIGIOUS EVENTS AND STRIKING THE BELL AT VARIOUS HOURS FOR PRAYERS, ETC. THE SUN 日 JME 11, ANOTHER TIME REGULATOR, IS PLACED TO THE LEFT OF TEMPLE TO MEAN TIME 時. PULSE 寸 IS NOW A UNIT OF LENGTH, 1.93 INCHES, FOR THE DISTANCE OF THE PULSE FROM THE HAND.

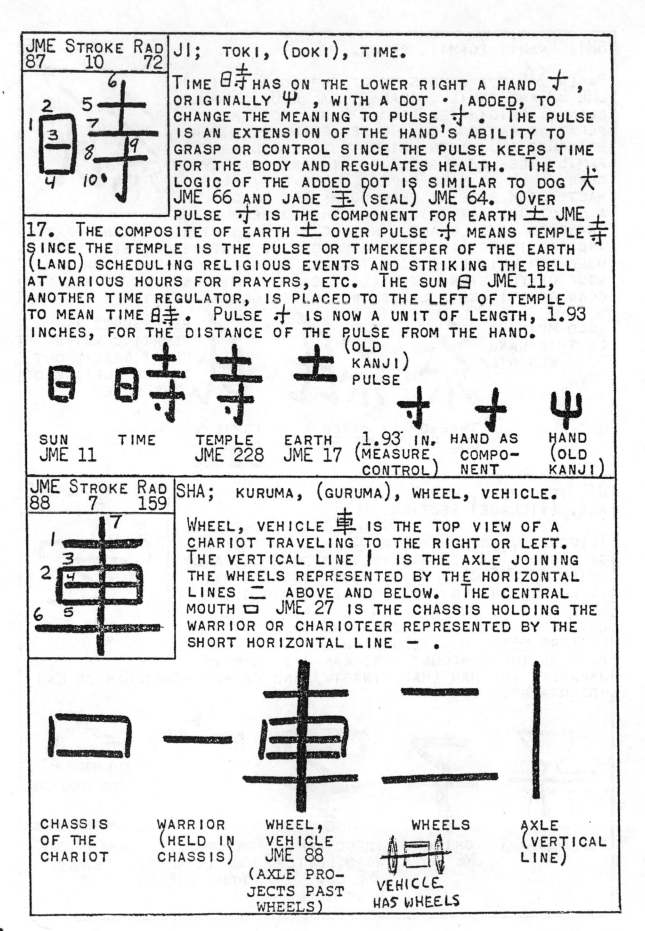

SUN JME 11    TIME    TEMPLE JME 228    EARTH JME 17    1.93 IN. (MEASURE CONTROL)    HAND AS COMPONENT    HAND (OLD KANJI)

(OLD KANJI) PULSE

| JME 88 | STROKE 7 | RAD 159 |
|---|---|---|

**SHA; KURUMA, (GURUMA), WHEEL, VEHICLE.**

WHEEL, VEHICLE 車 IS THE TOP VIEW OF A CHARIOT TRAVELING TO THE RIGHT OR LEFT. THE VERTICAL LINE | IS THE AXLE JOINING THE WHEELS REPRESENTED BY THE HORIZONTAL LINES 二 ABOVE AND BELOW. THE CENTRAL MOUTH 口 JME 27 IS THE CHASSIS HOLDING THE WARRIOR OR CHARIOTEER REPRESENTED BY THE SHORT HORIZONTAL LINE 一 .

CHASSIS OF THE CHARIOT    WARRIOR (HELD IN CHASSIS)    WHEEL, VEHICLE JME 88 (AXLE PROJECTS PAST WHEELS)    WHEELS / VEHICLE HAS WHEELS    AXLE (VERTICAL LINE)

SHŪ; AKI, FALL, AUTUMN.

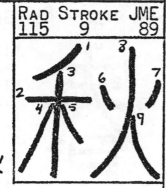

FALL, AUTUMN 秋 IS A COMPOSITE OF A STALK OF RIPE RICE 禾 ON THE LEFT AND FIRE 火 JME 13 ON THE RIGHT. IN RICE 禾 , THE OBLIQUE LINE AT THE TOP ノ IS THE HEAVY GRAIN FILLED HEAD. THE VERTICAL LINE | IS THE STEM. THE LATERAL SHOOTS ARE THE HORIZONTAL LINE ー . THE SLANTING LOWER LINES 八 ARE THE ROOTS. IN FALL, AUTUMN 秋 THE RICE 禾 IS RIPENED BY THE FIERY 火 HEAT.

| TREE, WOOD JME 15 NOTE SIMILARITY TO RICE EXCEPT FOR HEAD | RICE AS RIPENED IN THE PADDY (FIELD) | FALL, AUTUMN JME 89 RICE ON LEFT IS RIPENED BY FIERY HEAT | FIRE JME 13 | PICTURE |

SHUTSU, SUI; DERU, TO COME OUT, TO EMERGE; DASU, TO PUT OUT, TO TAKE OUT, TO PULL OUT.

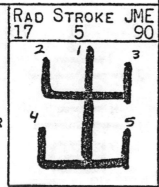

TO COME OUT, TO EMERGE, TO PUT OUT, TO TAKE OUT, TO PULL OUT 出 IS A COMPOSITE OF A VERTICAL LINE FOR MOVEMENT UP | AND A DOUBLING 凵 OF THE SYMBOL FOR OPEN VESSEL OR RECEPTACLE 凵 . THUS SOMETHING IS COMING OUT, EMERGING, BEING PUT OUT, TAKEN OUT, OR PULLED OUT 出 OF THE VESSELS OR RECEPTACLES WHICH ARE SHOWN DOUBLE 凵 .

 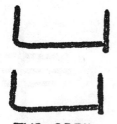 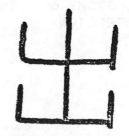

| OPEN VESSEL, RECEPTACLE | TWO OPEN VESSELS OR RECEPTACLES ONE OVER THE OTHER | TO COME OUT, TO EMERGE, TO PUT OUT, TO TAKE OUT, TO PULL OUT JME 90 | VERTICAL LINE WHICH HERE SHOWS THE DIRECTION (UP) BY WHICH SOMETHING COMES OUT, IS PUT OUT |

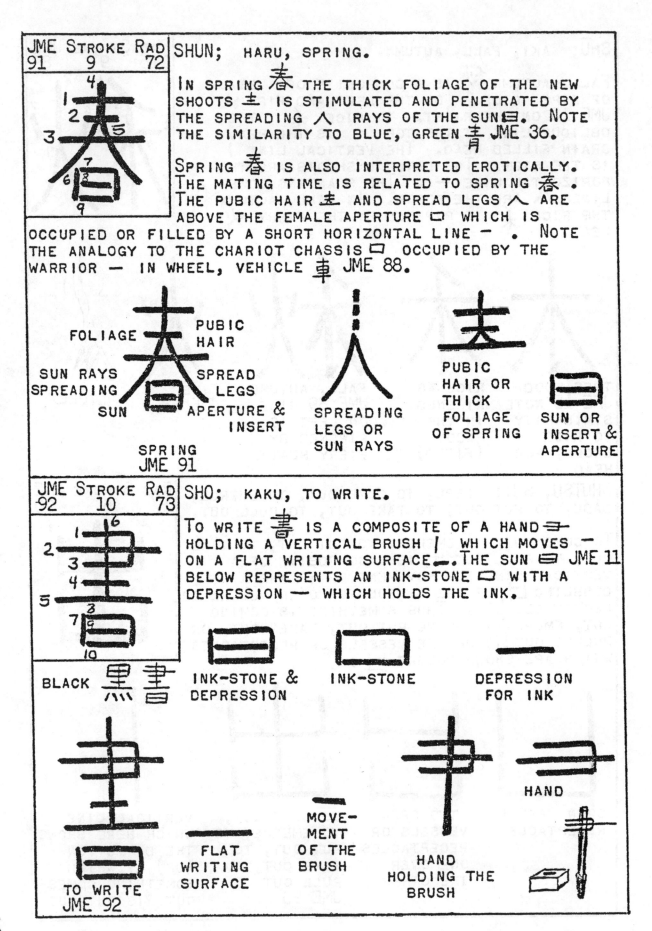

| JME 91 | Stroke 9 | Rad 72 |
|---|---|---|

SHUN; HARU, SPRING.

IN SPRING 春 THE THICK FOLIAGE OF THE NEW SHOOTS 主 IS STIMULATED AND PENETRATED BY THE SPREADING 人 RAYS OF THE SUN 日. NOTE THE SIMILARITY TO BLUE, GREEN 青 JME 36.

SPRING 春 IS ALSO INTERPRETED EROTICALLY. THE MATING TIME IS RELATED TO SPRING 春. THE PUBIC HAIR 主 AND SPREAD LEGS 人 ARE ABOVE THE FEMALE APERTURE 口 WHICH IS OCCUPIED OR FILLED BY A SHORT HORIZONTAL LINE — . NOTE THE ANALOGY TO THE CHARIOT CHASSIS 口 OCCUPIED BY THE WARRIOR — IN WHEEL, VEHICLE 車 JME 88.

FOLIAGE / PUBIC HAIR
SUN RAYS SPREADING / SPREAD LEGS
SUN / APERTURE & INSERT

SPRING JME 91

SPREADING LEGS OR SUN RAYS

PUBIC HAIR OR THICK FOLIAGE OF SPRING

SUN OR INSERT & APERTURE

| JME 92 | Stroke 10 | Rad 73 |
|---|---|---|

SHO; KAKU, TO WRITE.

TO WRITE 書 IS A COMPOSITE OF A HAND 彐 HOLDING A VERTICAL BRUSH | WHICH MOVES — ON A FLAT WRITING SURFACE —. THE SUN 日 JME 11 BELOW REPRESENTS AN INK-STONE 口 WITH A DEPRESSION — WHICH HOLDS THE INK.

BLACK 黒 書

INK-STONE & DEPRESSION

INK-STONE

DEPRESSION FOR INK

TO WRITE JME 92

FLAT WRITING SURFACE

MOVE-MENT OF THE BRUSH

HAND HOLDING THE BRUSH

HAND

SHŌ; SUKOSHI, SUKUNAI, LITTLE, FEW, SCARCE.

| RAD | STROKE | JME |
|-----|--------|-----|
| 42  | 4      | 93  |

LITTLE, FEW, SCARCE 少 IS A LITTLE 小 JME 24 CARRIED AS ON A SLANTED STICK ノ, BOARD OR BACK, SHOULDERS. THE SLANTED STICK SYMBOL ノ APPEARED IN TO THINK, IDEA, THOUGHT, OPINION 考 JME 74. THE CONCEPT OF A LITTLE 小 ONE NECESSARILY BEING CARRIED SEEMS THE BASIS FOR LITTLE, FEW, SCARCE 少.

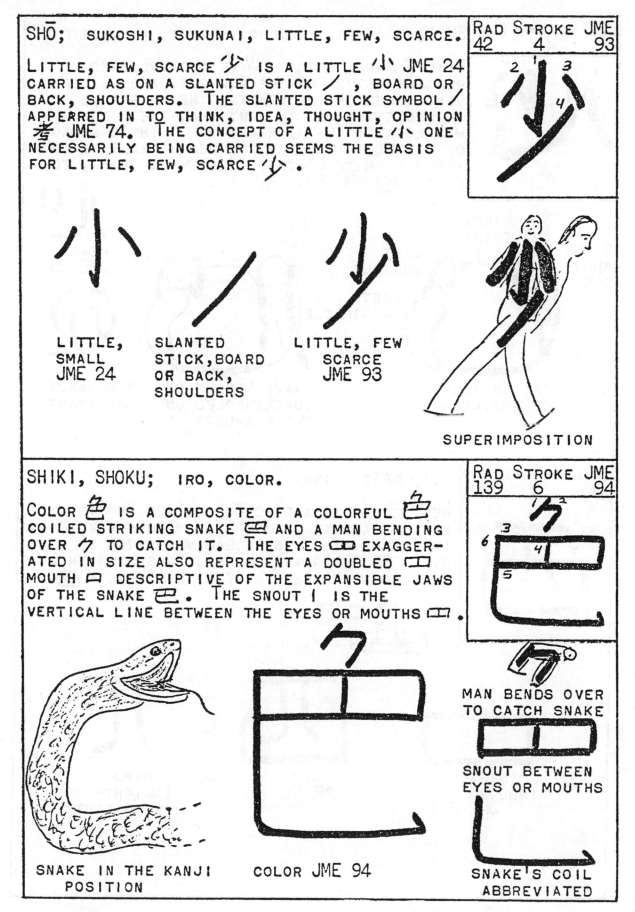

LITTLE, SMALL JME 24

SLANTED STICK, BOARD OR BACK, SHOULDERS

LITTLE, FEW SCARCE JME 93

SUPERIMPOSITION

SHIKI, SHOKU; IRO, COLOR.

| RAD | STROKE | JME |
|-----|--------|-----|
| 139 | 6      | 94  |

COLOR 色 IS A COMPOSITE OF A COLORFUL 色 COILED STRIKING SNAKE 巴 AND A MAN BENDING OVER ク TO CATCH IT. THE EYES ⊂⊃ EXAGGERATED IN SIZE ALSO REPRESENT A DOUBLED ⊂⊃ MOUTH ⊐ DESCRIPTIVE OF THE EXPANSIBLE JAWS OF THE SNAKE 巴. THE SNOUT I IS THE VERTICAL LINE BETWEEN THE EYES OR MOUTHS ⊂⊃.

MAN BENDS OVER TO CATCH SNAKE

SNOUT BETWEEN EYES OR MOUTHS

SNAKE IN THE KANJI POSITION

COLOR JME 94

SNAKE'S COIL ABBREVIATED

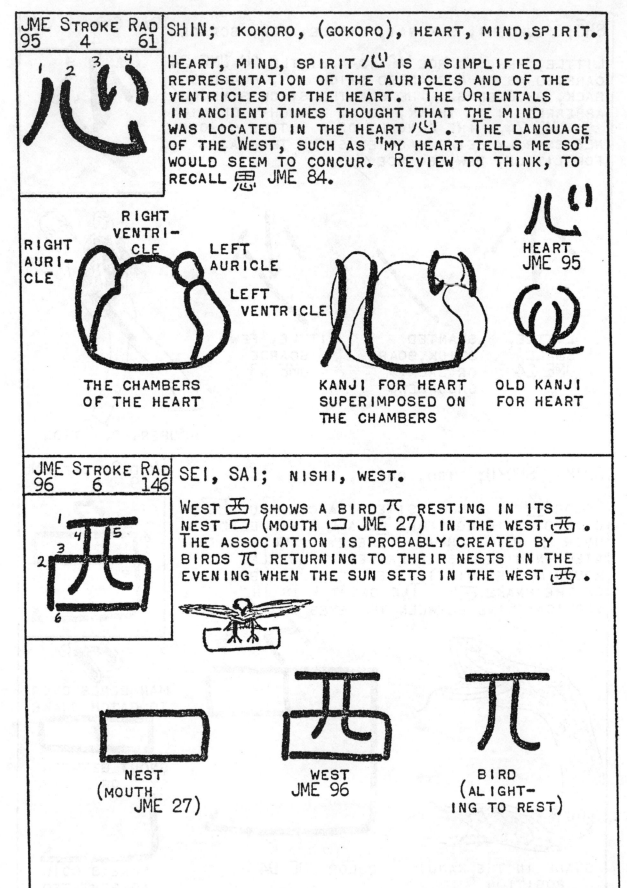

| JME 95 | Stroke 4 | Rad 61 |
| --- | --- | --- |

SHIN; KOKORO, (GOKORO), HEART, MIND, SPIRIT.

HEART, MIND, SPIRIT 心 IS A SIMPLIFIED REPRESENTATION OF THE AURICLES AND OF THE VENTRICLES OF THE HEART. THE ORIENTALS IN ANCIENT TIMES THOUGHT THAT THE MIND WAS LOCATED IN THE HEART 心. THE LANGUAGE OF THE WEST, SUCH AS "MY HEART TELLS ME SO" WOULD SEEM TO CONCUR. REVIEW TO THINK, TO RECALL 思 JME 84.

RIGHT AURI-CLE

RIGHT VENTRI-CLE

LEFT AURICLE

LEFT VENTRICLE

THE CHAMBERS OF THE HEART

KANJI FOR HEART SUPERIMPOSED ON THE CHAMBERS

HEART JME 95

OLD KANJI FOR HEART

| JME 96 | Stroke 6 | Rad 146 |
| --- | --- | --- |

SEI, SAI; NISHI, WEST.

WEST 西 SHOWS A BIRD 兀 RESTING IN ITS NEST 口 (MOUTH 口 JME 27) IN THE WEST 西. THE ASSOCIATION IS PROBABLY CREATED BY BIRDS 兀 RETURNING TO THEIR NESTS IN THE EVENING WHEN THE SUN SETS IN THE WEST 西.

NEST (MOUTH JME 27)

WEST JME 96

BIRD (ALIGHT-ING TO REST)

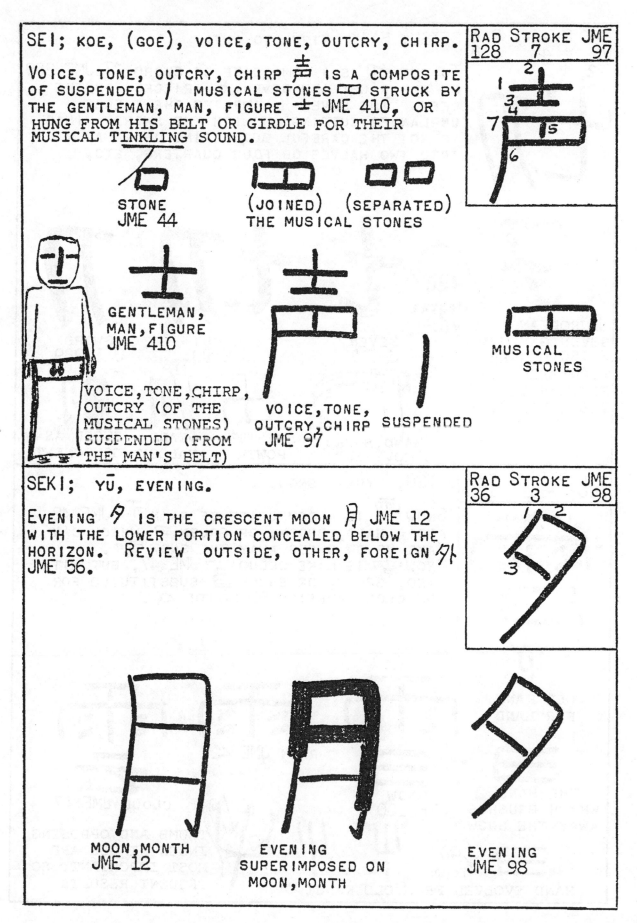

SEI; KOE, (GOE), VOICE, TONE, OUTCRY, CHIRP.

VOICE, TONE, OUTCRY, CHIRP 声 IS A COMPOSITE OF SUSPENDED / MUSICAL STONES 口口 STRUCK BY THE GENTLEMAN, MAN, FIGURE 士 JME 410, OR HUNG FROM HIS BELT OR GIRDLE FOR THEIR MUSICAL TINKLING SOUND.

| RAD | STROKE | JME |
|-----|--------|-----|
| 128 | 7 | 97 |

STONE
JME 44

(JOINED)   (SEPARATED)
THE MUSICAL STONES

GENTLEMAN,
MAN, FIGURE
JME 410

MUSICAL
STONES

VOICE, TONE, CHIRP,
OUTCRY (OF THE
MUSICAL STONES)
SUSPENDED (FROM
THE MAN'S BELT)

VOICE, TONE,
OUTCRY, CHIRP SUSPENDED
JME 97

SEKI; YŪ, EVENING.

EVENING 夕 IS THE CRESCENT MOON 月 JME 12 WITH THE LOWER PORTION CONCEALED BELOW THE HORIZON. REVIEW OUTSIDE, OTHER, FOREIGN 外 JME 56.

| RAD | STROKE | JME |
|-----|--------|-----|
| 36 | 3 | 98 |

MOON, MONTH
JME 12

EVENING
SUPERIMPOSED ON
MOON, MONTH

EVENING
JME 98

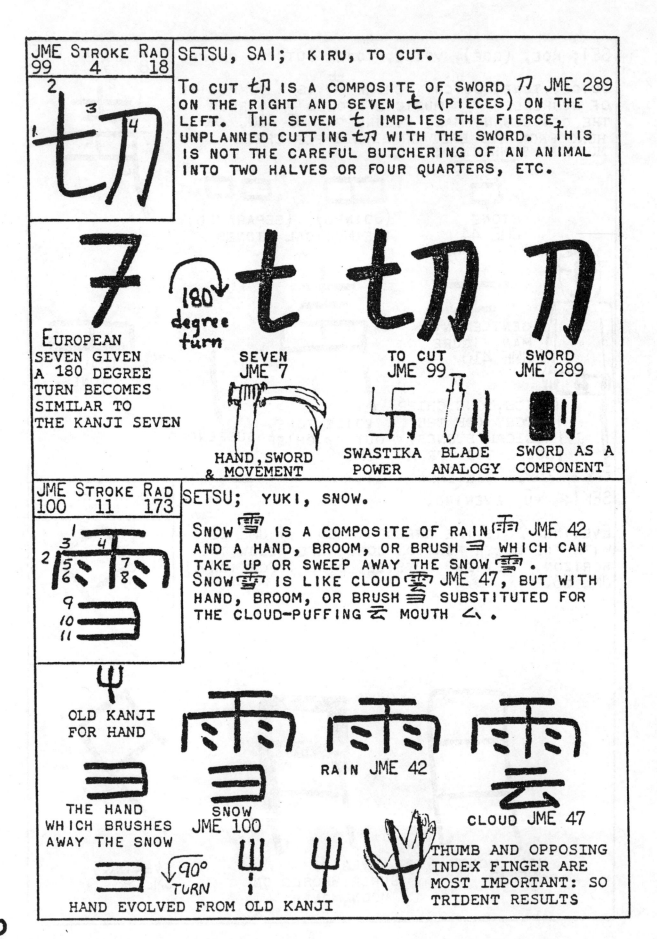

| JME | Stroke | Rad |
|-----|--------|-----|
| 99 | 4 | 18 |

SETSU, SAI; KIRU, TO CUT.

To cut 切 IS A COMPOSITE OF SWORD, 刀 JME 289 ON THE RIGHT AND SEVEN 七 (PIECES) ON THE LEFT. THE SEVEN 七 IMPLIES THE FIERCE, UNPLANNED CUTTING 切 WITH THE SWORD. THIS IS NOT THE CAREFUL BUTCHERING OF AN ANIMAL INTO TWO HALVES OR FOUR QUARTERS, ETC.

EUROPEAN SEVEN GIVEN A 180 DEGREE TURN BECOMES SIMILAR TO THE KANJI SEVEN

180 degree turn

SEVEN JME 7

TO CUT JME 99

SWORD JME 289

HAND, SWORD & MOVEMENT

SWASTIKA POWER

BLADE ANALOGY

SWORD AS A COMPONENT

| JME | Stroke | Rad |
|-----|--------|-----|
| 100 | 11 | 173 |

SETSU; YUKI, SNOW.

SNOW 雪 IS A COMPOSITE OF RAIN 雨 JME 42 AND A HAND, BROOM, OR BRUSH ⺕ WHICH CAN TAKE UP OR SWEEP AWAY THE SNOW 雪. SNOW 雪 IS LIKE CLOUD 雲 JME 47, BUT WITH HAND, BROOM, OR BRUSH ⺕ SUBSTITUTED FOR THE CLOUD-PUFFING 云 MOUTH ム.

OLD KANJI FOR HAND

THE HAND WHICH BRUSHES AWAY THE SNOW

SNOW JME 100

RAIN JME 42

CLOUD JME 47

90° TURN

HAND EVOLVED FROM OLD KANJI

THUMB AND OPPOSING INDEX FINGER ARE MOST IMPORTANT: SO TRIDENT RESULTS

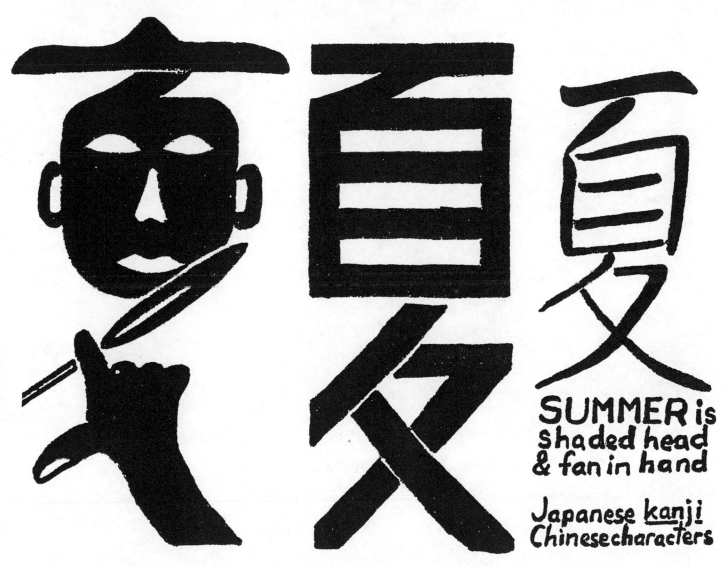

SUMMER is
shaded head
& fan in hand

Japanese <u>kanji</u>
Chinese characters

SEN, (ZEN); CHI, THOUSAND.

| RAD | STROKE | JME |
|-----|--------|-----|
| 24  | 3      | 101 |

THOUSAND 千 IS REPRESENTED BY THE OFFICER WITH THE HORNED ノ CREST WHO COMMANDS TEN 十 HUNDREDS OR A THOUSAND 千 MEN. CENTRAL ASIAN ARMIES USED THE DECIMAL SYSTEM. THE MILLENION OVER A THOUSAND MEN COMMANDED TEN 十 HORNS (BUGLES) ノ OR CENTURIONS.

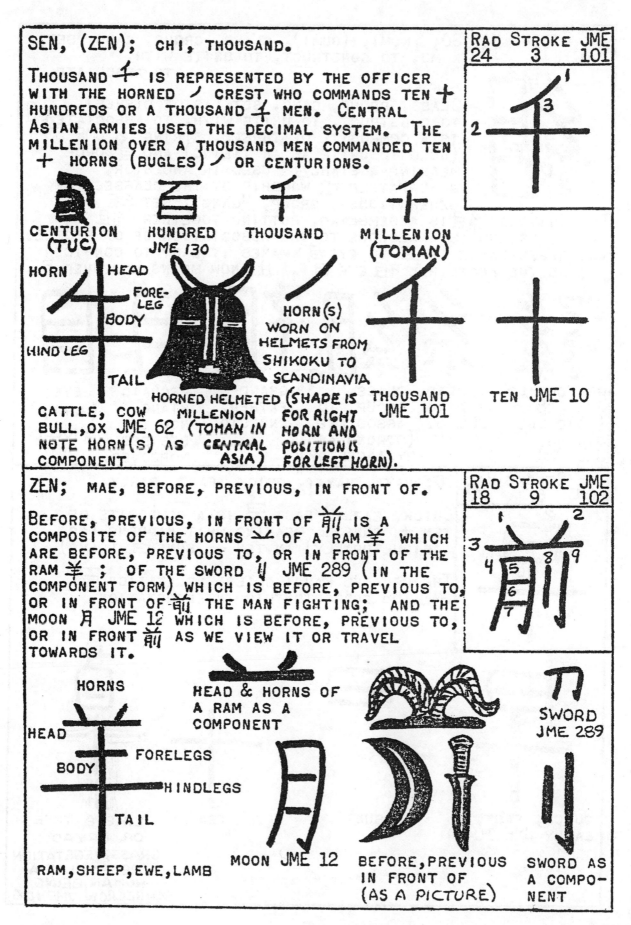

CENTURION (TUC)

HUNDRED JME 130

THOUSAND

MILLENION (TOMAN)

HORN   HEAD
FORE-LEG
BODY
HIND LEG
TAIL

CATTLE, COW BULL, OX JME 62 NOTE HORN(S) AS COMPONENT

HORNED HELMETED MILLENION (TOMAN IN CENTRAL ASIA)

HORN(S) WORN ON HELMETS FROM SHIKOKU TO SCANDINAVIA (SHAPE IS FOR RIGHT HORN AND POSITION IS FOR LEFT HORN).

THOUSAND JME 101

TEN JME 10

ZEN; MAE, BEFORE, PREVIOUS, IN FRONT OF.

| RAD | STROKE | JME |
|-----|--------|-----|
| 18  | 9      | 102 |

BEFORE, PREVIOUS, IN FRONT OF 前 IS A COMPOSITE OF THE HORNS ⃗ OF A RAM 羊 WHICH ARE BEFORE, PREVIOUS TO, OR IN FRONT OF THE RAM 羊; OF THE SWORD 刂 JME 289 (IN THE COMPONENT FORM) WHICH IS BEFORE, PREVIOUS TO, OR IN FRONT OF 前 THE MAN FIGHTING; AND THE MOON 月 JME 12 WHICH IS BEFORE, PREVIOUS TO, OR IN FRONT 前 AS WE VIEW IT OR TRAVEL TOWARDS IT.

HORNS
HEAD
BODY   FORELEGS
HINDLEGS
TAIL

RAM, SHEEP, EWE, LAMB

HEAD & HORNS OF A RAM AS A COMPONENT

MOON JME 12

BEFORE, PREVIOUS IN FRONT OF (AS A PICTURE)

SWORD JME 289

SWORD AS A COMPONENT

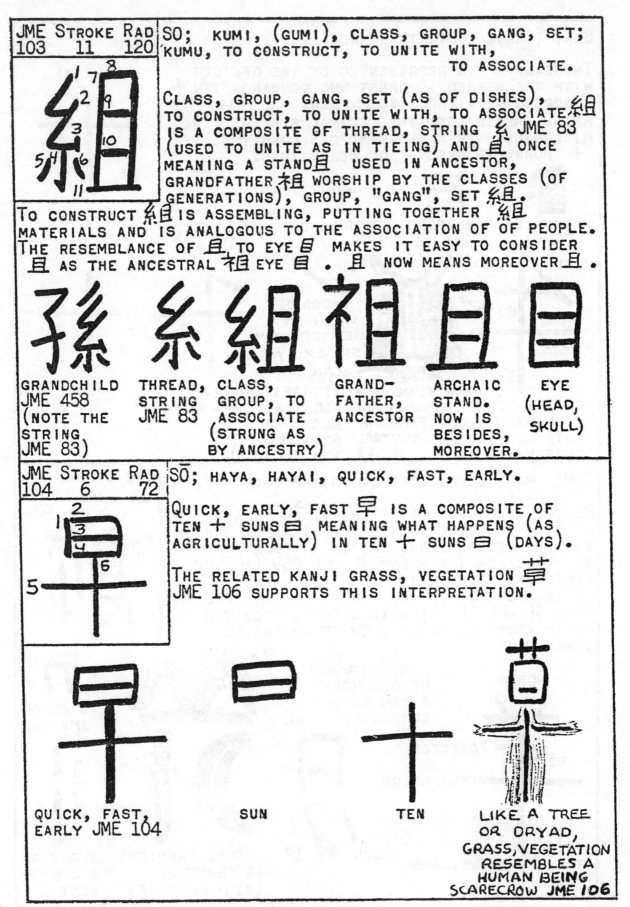

| JME 103 | Stroke 11 | Rad 120 |
|---------|-----------|---------|

SO; KUMI, (GUMI), CLASS, GROUP, GANG, SET; KUMU, TO CONSTRUCT, TO UNITE WITH, TO ASSOCIATE.

CLASS, GROUP, GANG, SET (AS OF DISHES), TO CONSTRUCT, TO UNITE WITH, TO ASSOCIATE 組 IS A COMPOSITE OF THREAD, STRING 糸 JME 83 (USED TO UNITE AS IN TIEING) AND 且 ONCE MEANING A STAND 且 USED IN ANCESTOR, GRANDFATHER 祖 WORSHIP BY THE CLASSES (OF GENERATIONS), GROUP, "GANG", SET 組.

TO CONSTRUCT 組 IS ASSEMBLING, PUTTING TOGETHER 組 MATERIALS AND IS ANALOGOUS TO THE ASSOCIATION OF OF PEOPLE. THE RESEMBLANCE OF 且 TO EYE 目 MAKES IT EASY TO CONSIDER 且 AS THE ANCESTRAL 祖 EYE 目. 且 NOW MEANS MOREOVER 且.

GRANDCHILD JME 458 (NOTE THE STRING JME 83)

THREAD, STRING JME 83

CLASS, GROUP, TO ASSOCIATE (STRUNG AS BY ANCESTRY)

GRAND-FATHER, ANCESTOR

ARCHAIC STAND. NOW IS BESIDES, MOREOVER.

EYE (HEAD, SKULL)

| JME 104 | Stroke 6 | Rad 72 |
|---------|----------|--------|

SŌ; HAYA, HAYAI, QUICK, FAST, EARLY.

QUICK, EARLY, FAST 早 IS A COMPOSITE OF TEN 十 SUNS 日 MEANING WHAT HAPPENS (AS AGRICULTURALLY) IN TEN 十 SUNS 日 (DAYS).

THE RELATED KANJI GRASS, VEGETATION 草 JME 106 SUPPORTS THIS INTERPRETATION.

QUICK, FAST, EARLY JME 104

SUN

TEN

LIKE A TREE OR DRYAD, GRASS, VEGETATION RESEMBLES A HUMAN BEING SCARECROW JME 106

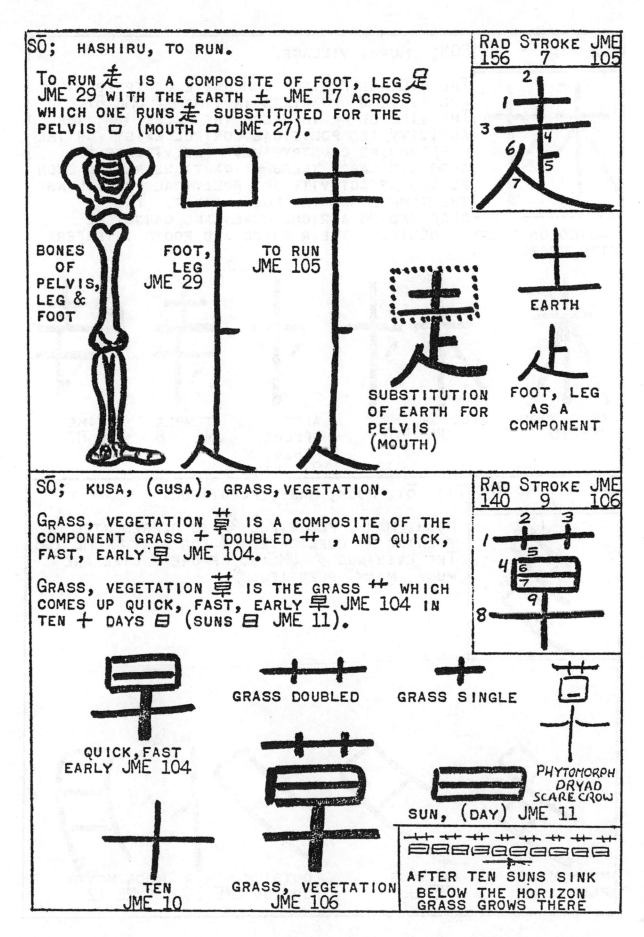

SŌ; HASHIRU, TO RUN.

TO RUN 走 IS A COMPOSITE OF FOOT, LEG 足 JME 29 WITH THE EARTH 土 JME 17 ACROSS WHICH ONE RUNS 走 SUBSTITUTED FOR THE PELVIS 口 (MOUTH 口 JME 27).

| RAD | STROKE | JME |
|-----|--------|-----|
| 156 | 7 | 105 |

BONES OF PELVIS, LEG & FOOT

FOOT, LEG JME 29

TO RUN JME 105

SUBSTITUTION OF EARTH FOR PELVIS (MOUTH)

EARTH

FOOT, LEG AS A COMPONENT

SŌ; KUSA, (GUSA), GRASS, VEGETATION.

GRASS, VEGETATION 草 IS A COMPOSITE OF THE COMPONENT GRASS + DOUBLED ++ , AND QUICK, FAST, EARLY 早 JME 104.

GRASS, VEGETATION 草 IS THE GRASS ++ WHICH COMES UP QUICK, FAST, EARLY 早 JME 104 IN TEN 十 DAYS 日 (SUNS 日 JME 11).

| RAD | STROKE | JME |
|-----|--------|-----|
| 140 | 9 | 106 |

QUICK, FAST EARLY JME 104

GRASS DOUBLED

GRASS SINGLE

PHYTOMORPH DRYAD SCARECROW

SUN, (DAY) JME 11

TEN JME 10

GRASS, VEGETATION JME 106

AFTER TEN SUNS SINK BELOW THE HORIZON GRASS GROWS THERE

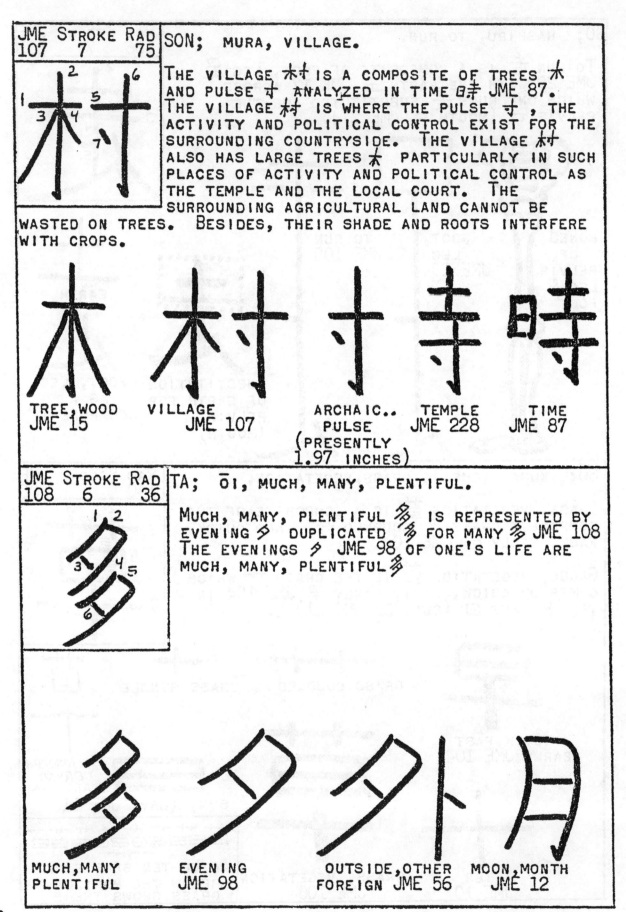

| JME 107 | STROKE 7 | RAD 75 |
|---|---|---|

SON; MURA, VILLAGE.

THE VILLAGE 村 IS A COMPOSITE OF TREES 木 AND PULSE 寸 ANALYZED IN TIME 日寺 JME 87. THE VILLAGE 村 IS WHERE THE PULSE 寸, THE ACTIVITY AND POLITICAL CONTROL EXIST FOR THE SURROUNDING COUNTRYSIDE. THE VILLAGE 村 ALSO HAS LARGE TREES 木 PARTICULARLY IN SUCH PLACES OF ACTIVITY AND POLITICAL CONTROL AS THE TEMPLE AND THE LOCAL COURT. THE SURROUNDING AGRICULTURAL LAND CANNOT BE WASTED ON TREES. BESIDES, THEIR SHADE AND ROOTS INTERFERE WITH CROPS.

TREE, WOOD JME 15

VILLAGE JME 107

ARCHAIC.. PULSE (PRESENTLY 1.97 INCHES)

TEMPLE JME 228

TIME JME 87

| JME 108 | STROKE 6 | RAD 36 |
|---|---|---|

TA; ŌI, MUCH, MANY, PLENTIFUL.

MUCH, MANY, PLENTIFUL 多 IS REPRESENTED BY EVENING 夕 DUPLICATED 多 FOR MANY 多 JME 108 THE EVENINGS 夕 JME 98 OF ONE'S LIFE ARE MUCH, MANY, PLENTIFUL 多

MUCH, MANY PLENTIFUL

EVENING JME 98

OUTSIDE, OTHER FOREIGN JME 56

MOON, MONTH JME 12

DAN, NAN;  OTOKO, MAN, MALE.

| RAD | STROKE | JME |
|-----|--------|-----|
| 102 | 7 | 109 |

THE MAN, MALE 男 IS THE STRENGTH 力 JME 148
OF THE RICE FIELD 田 JME 40 FROM AN AGRI-
CULTURAL STANDPOINT.  STRENGTH 力 MAY BE
VISUALIZED AS THE SET AND STRAINING LEGS
OF A MAN 男 CARRYING THE RICE FIELD 田.
STRENGTH IS ALSO A QUARTER OR QUADRANT OF
THE SWASTIKA 卐 WHICH IS THE EMBODIMENT OF
THE JUGGERNAUT OF ROLLING CRUSHING STRENGTH
力 JME 148.

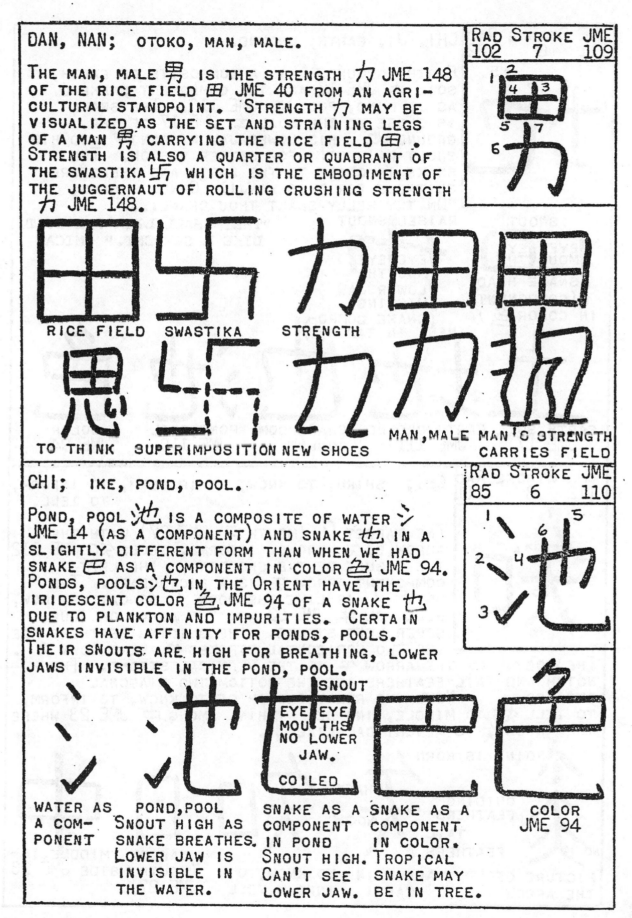

RICE FIELD   SWASTIKA   STRENGTH

TO THINK   SUPERIMPOSITION NEW SHOES

MAN, MALE MAN'S STRENGTH
CARRIES FIELD

CHI;  IKE, POND, POOL.

| RAD | STROKE | JME |
|-----|--------|-----|
| 85 | 6 | 110 |

POND, POOL 池 IS A COMPOSITE OF WATER 氵
JME 14 (AS A COMPONENT) AND SNAKE 也 IN A
SLIGHTLY DIFFERENT FORM THAN WHEN WE HAD
SNAKE 巴 AS A COMPONENT IN COLOR 色 JME 94.
PONDS, POOLS 氵也 IN THE ORIENT HAVE THE
IRIDESCENT COLOR 色 JME 94 OF A SNAKE 也
DUE TO PLANKTON AND IMPURITIES.  CERTAIN
SNAKES HAVE AFFINITY FOR PONDS, POOLS.
THEIR SNOUTS ARE HIGH FOR BREATHING, LOWER
JAWS INVISIBLE IN THE POND, POOL.

SNOUT
EYE EYE
MOUTHS
NO LOWER
JAW.

COILED

WATER AS
A COM-
PONENT

POND, POOL
SNOUT HIGH AS
SNAKE BREATHES.
LOWER JAW IS
INVISIBLE IN
THE WATER.

SNAKE AS A
COMPONENT
IN POND
SNOUT HIGH.
CAN'T SEE
LOWER JAW.

SNAKE AS A
COMPONENT
IN COLOR.
TROPICAL
SNAKE MAY
BE IN TREE.

COLOR
JME 94

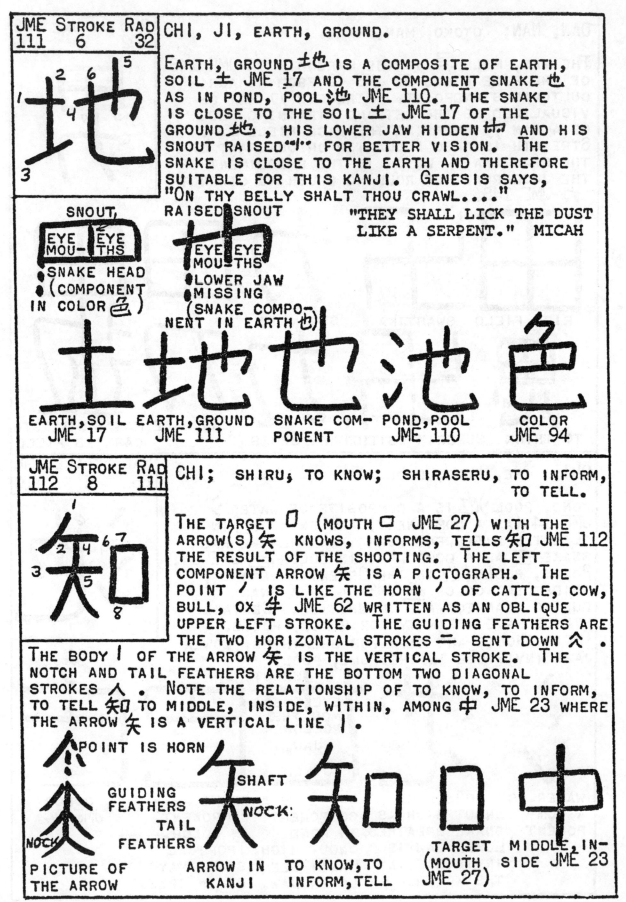

| JME 111 | Stroke 6 | Rad 32 |
|---|---|---|

CHI, JI, EARTH, GROUND.

EARTH, GROUND 地 IS A COMPOSITE OF EARTH, SOIL 土 JME 17 AND THE COMPONENT SNAKE 也 AS IN POND, POOL 池 JME 110. THE SNAKE IS CLOSE TO THE SOIL 土 JME 17 OF THE GROUND 地, HIS LOWER JAW HIDDEN 曲 AND HIS SNOUT RAISED "✓" FOR BETTER VISION. THE SNAKE IS CLOSE TO THE EARTH AND THEREFORE SUITABLE FOR THIS KANJI. GENESIS SAYS, "ON THY BELLY SHALT THOU CRAWL...."

"THEY SHALL LICK THE DUST LIKE A SERPENT." MICAH

RAISED SNOUT

SNOUT, EYE EYE MOUTHS
SNAKE HEAD (COMPONENT IN COLOR 色)

EYE EYE MOUTHS
LOWER JAW MISSING (SNAKE COMPONENT IN EARTH 也)

| 土 | 地 | 也 | 池 | 色 |
|---|---|---|---|---|
| EARTH,SOIL JME 17 | EARTH,GROUND JME 111 | SNAKE COMPONENT | POND,POOL JME 110 | COLOR JME 94 |

| JME 112 | Stroke 8 | Rad 111 |
|---|---|---|

CHI; SHIRU, TO KNOW; SHIRASERU, TO INFORM, TO TELL.

THE TARGET ロ (MOUTH ロ JME 27) WITH THE ARROW(S) 矢 KNOWS, INFORMS, TELLS 知 JME 112 THE RESULT OF THE SHOOTING. THE LEFT COMPONENT ARROW 矢 IS A PICTOGRAPH. THE POINT ✓ IS LIKE THE HORN ✓ OF CATTLE, COW, BULL, OX 牛 JME 62 WRITTEN AS AN OBLIQUE UPPER LEFT STROKE. THE GUIDING FEATHERS ARE THE TWO HORIZONTAL STROKES 二 BENT DOWN 스. THE BODY | OF THE ARROW 矢 IS THE VERTICAL STROKE. THE NOTCH AND TAIL FEATHERS ARE THE BOTTOM TWO DIAGONAL STROKES 人. NOTE THE RELATIONSHIP OF TO KNOW, TO INFORM, TO TELL 知 TO MIDDLE, INSIDE, WITHIN, AMONG 中 JME 23 WHERE THE ARROW 矢 IS A VERTICAL LINE |.

POINT IS HORN

GUIDING FEATHERS
TAIL FEATHERS
NOCK

PICTURE OF THE ARROW

SHAFT
NOCK
ARROW IN KANJI

知
TO KNOW,TO INFORM,TELL

口
TARGET (MOUTH JME 27)

中
MIDDLE, INSIDE JME 23

CHIKU; TAKE, (DAKE), BAMBOO.

| RAD | STROKE | JME |
|-----|--------|-----|
| 118 | 6 | 113 |

BAMBOO 竹 SHOWS TWO CLUSTERS OF BAMBOO LEAVES TO LEFT 𥫗 AND TO RIGHT 𥫗 . THE BAMBOO HAS A CHARACTERISTIC LEAF PATTERN PAINTED AS A CLUSTER OF THREE STROKES, ONE FOR EACH OF THREE LEAVES.

Also note pattern in <u>Nandina domestica</u>, Heavenly Bamboo.

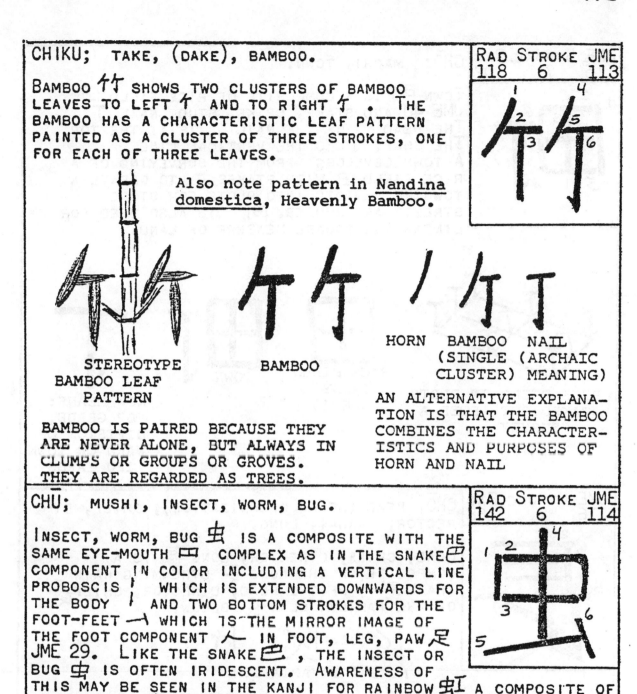

STEREOTYPE BAMBOO LEAF PATTERN

BAMBOO

HORN (SINGLE CLUSTER)

BAMBOO

NAIL (ARCHAIC MEANING)

BAMBOO IS PAIRED BECAUSE THEY ARE NEVER ALONE, BUT ALWAYS IN CLUMPS OR GROUPS OR GROVES. THEY ARE REGARDED AS TREES.

AN ALTERNATIVE EXPLANATION IS THAT THE BAMBOO COMBINES THE CHARACTERISTICS AND PURPOSES OF HORN AND NAIL

CHŪ; MUSHI, INSECT, WORM, BUG.

| RAD | STROKE | JME |
|-----|--------|-----|
| 142 | 6 | 114 |

INSECT, WORM, BUG 虫 IS A COMPOSITE WITH THE SAME EYE-MOUTH 口 COMPLEX AS IN THE SNAKE 巴 COMPONENT IN COLOR INCLUDING A VERTICAL LINE PROBOSCIS ❘ WHICH IS EXTENDED DOWNWARDS FOR THE BODY ❘ AND TWO BOTTOM STROKES FOR THE FOOT-FEET ㇟ WHICH IS THE MIRROR IMAGE OF THE FOOT COMPONENT ㇏ IN FOOT, LEG, PAW 足 JME 29. LIKE THE SNAKE 巴 , THE INSECT OR BUG 虫 IS OFTEN IRIDESCENT. AWARENESS OF THIS MAY BE SEEN IN THE KANJI FOR RAINBOW 虹 A COMPOSITE OF INSECT, BUG 虫 ON THE LEFT AND WORKER, ENGINEERING, CONSTRUCTION 工 TO THE RIGHT. THE EYE-MOUTH 口 COMPLEX SHOWS BUG-EYEDNESS AND VORACIOUSNESS.

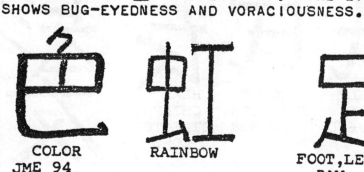

COLOR
JME 94

RAINBOW

FOOT, LEG
PAW
JME 229

INSECT
WORM, BUG

SUPER-
IMPOSED
INSECT

| JME 115 | Stroke 7 | Rad 102 |
|---|---|---|

CHŌ; MACHI, TOWN.

TOWN 町 IS A COMPOSITE OF RICE FIELD 田 JME 40 AND STAKE, SPIKE, STUD, NAIL 丁. THE HEAD ‾ OF THE NAIL 丁 IS AT THE TOP. THE SHAFT 亅 IS THE VERTICAL LINE. A TOWN DEVELOPS FROM THE SURVEYING OF A RICE FIELD 田 WITH STAKES 丁 TO CREATE A TOWN 町 DIVIDED INTO PLOTS FOR STORES, STREETS AND HOUSES. 町 IS ALSO USED FOR LINEAR AND SQUARE MEASURE OF LAND.

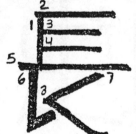

RICE FIELD IN PLOTS
STAKED OUT AFTER A
SURVEY

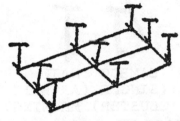

RICE FIELD
PADDY
JME 40

TOWN

NOW MEANS:
"D" GRADE,
DIVISION OF
A WARD OR TOWN,
120 YARDS
JME 473

| JME 116 | Stroke 8 | Rad 168 |
|---|---|---|

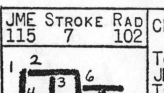

CHŌ, HEAD (OF AN ORGANIZATION), CHIEF, DIRECTOR; NAGAI, LONG.

HEAD, CHIEF, DIRECTOR, LONG 長 IS A COMPOSITE OF THE LONG 長 STREAMING HAIR (HAIR 髟) OF THE HEAD, DIRECTOR, CHIEF 長 OF THE FAMILY, CLAN 氏 BELOW.

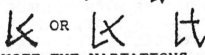

NOTE THE VARIATIONS

PAPER
JME 85

FAMILY
CLAN
JME 620

PEOPLE
SUBJECTS
JME 518

HEAD
CHIEF
DIRECTOR
LONG

HAIR

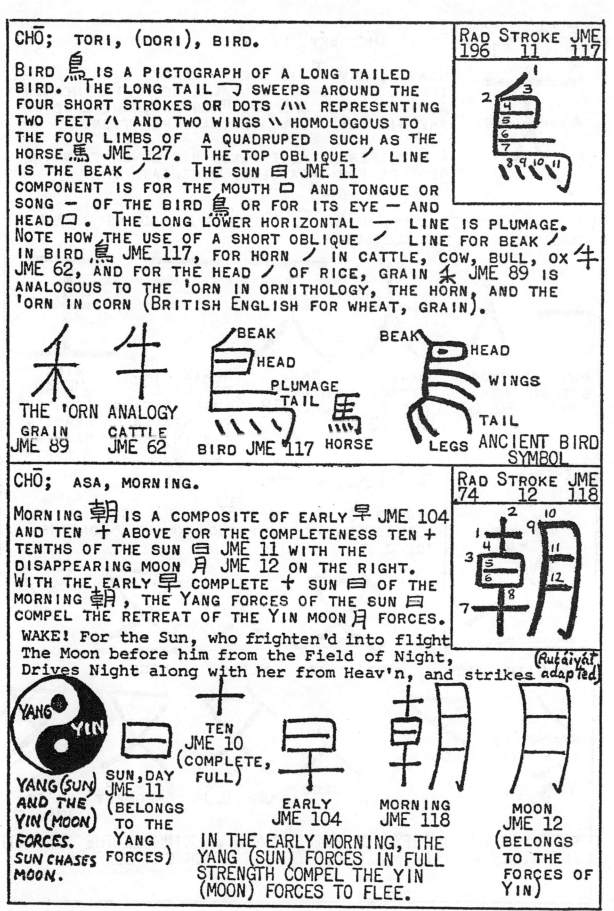

CHŌ; TORI, (DORI), BIRD.

BIRD 鳥 IS A PICTOGRAPH OF A LONG TAILED BIRD. THE LONG TAIL ⁊ SWEEPS AROUND THE FOUR SHORT STROKES OR DOTS /\\\ REPRESENTING TWO FEET /\ AND TWO WINGS \\ HOMOLOGOUS TO THE FOUR LIMBS OF A QUADRUPED SUCH AS THE HORSE 馬 JME 127. THE TOP OBLIQUE / LINE IS THE BEAK /. THE SUN 日 JME 11 COMPONENT IS FOR THE MOUTH 口 AND TONGUE OR SONG — OF THE BIRD 鳥 OR FOR ITS EYE — AND HEAD 口. THE LONG LOWER HORIZONTAL — LINE IS PLUMAGE. NOTE HOW THE USE OF A SHORT OBLIQUE / LINE FOR BEAK / IN BIRD 鳥 JME 117, FOR HORN / IN CATTLE, COW, BULL, OX 牛 JME 62, AND FOR THE HEAD / OF RICE, GRAIN 禾 JME 89 IS ANALOGOUS TO THE 'ORN IN ORNITHOLOGY, THE HORN, AND THE 'ORN IN CORN (BRITISH ENGLISH FOR WHEAT, GRAIN).

THE 'ORN ANALOGY
GRAIN JME 89    CATTLE JME 62

BEAK  HEAD  PLUMAGE  TAIL
BIRD JME 117    HORSE

BEAK  HEAD  WINGS  TAIL  LEGS  ANCIENT BIRD SYMBOL

CHŌ; ASA, MORNING.

MORNING 朝 IS A COMPOSITE OF EARLY 早 JME 104 AND TEN 十 ABOVE FOR THE COMPLETENESS TEN 十 TENTHS OF THE SUN 日 JME 11 WITH THE DISAPPEARING MOON 月 JME 12 ON THE RIGHT. WITH THE EARLY 早 COMPLETE 十 SUN 日 OF THE MORNING 朝, THE YANG FORCES OF THE SUN 日 COMPEL THE RETREAT OF THE YIN MOON 月 FORCES.

WAKE! For the Sun, who frighten'd into flight
The Moon before him from the Field of Night,
Drives Night along with her from Heav'n, and strikes
(Rubáiyát adapted)

YANG (SUN) AND THE YIN (MOON) FORCES. SUN CHASES MOON.

SUN, DAY JME 11 (BELONGS TO THE YANG FORCES)

TEN JME 10 (COMPLETE, FULL)

EARLY JME 104

MORNING JME 118

MOON JME 12 (BELONGS TO THE FORCES OF YIN)

IN THE EARLY MORNING, THE YANG (SUN) FORCES IN FULL STRENGTH COMPEL THE YIN (MOON) FORCES TO FLEE.

| RAD | STROKE | JME |
|---|---|---|
| 196 | 11 | 117 |

| RAD | STROKE | JME |
|---|---|---|
| 74 | 12 | 118 |

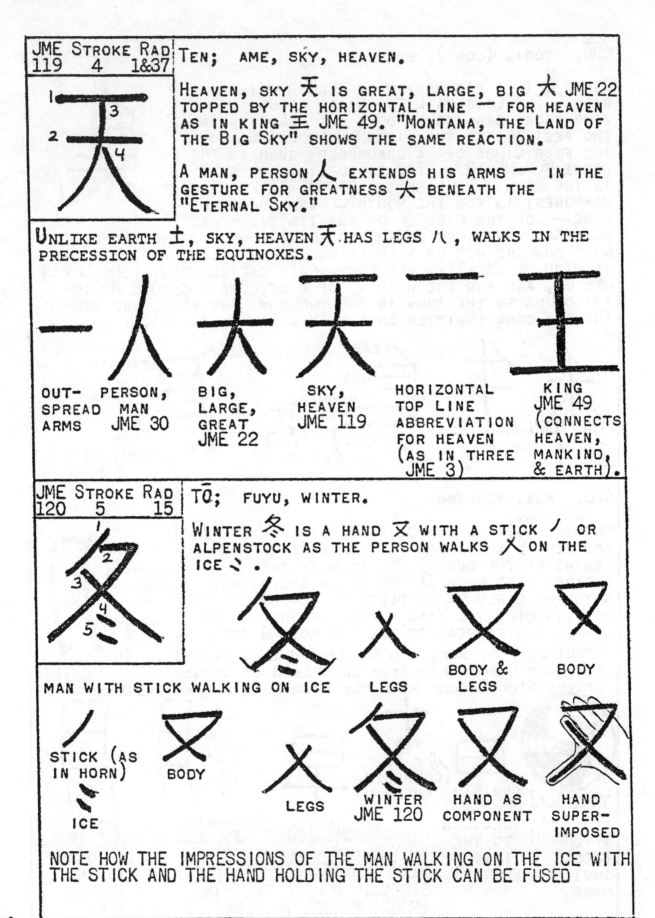

| JME 119 | Stroke 4 | Rad 1&37 |
|---|---|---|

TEN; AME, SKY, HEAVEN.

HEAVEN, SKY 天 IS GREAT, LARGE, BIG 大 JME 22 TOPPED BY THE HORIZONTAL LINE 一 FOR HEAVEN AS IN KING 王 JME 49. "MONTANA, THE LAND OF THE BIG SKY" SHOWS THE SAME REACTION.

A MAN, PERSON 人 EXTENDS HIS ARMS 一 IN THE GESTURE FOR GREATNESS 大 BENEATH THE "ETERNAL SKY."

UNLIKE EARTH 土, SKY, HEAVEN 天 HAS LEGS 八, WALKS IN THE PRECESSION OF THE EQUINOXES.

一　人　大　天　一　王

OUT-SPREAD ARMS

PERSON, MAN    JME 30

BIG, LARGE, GREAT JME 22

SKY, HEAVEN JME 119

HORIZONTAL TOP LINE ABBREVIATION FOR HEAVEN (AS IN THREE JME 3)

KING JME 49 (CONNECTS HEAVEN, MANKIND, & EARTH).

| JME 120 | Stroke 5 | Rad 15 |
|---|---|---|

TŌ; FUYU, WINTER.

WINTER 冬 IS A HAND 又 WITH A STICK ノ OR ALPENSTOCK AS THE PERSON WALKS 人 ON THE ICE 冫.

MAN WITH STICK WALKING ON ICE

LEGS

BODY & LEGS

BODY

STICK (AS IN HORN)
ICE

BODY

LEGS

WINTER JME 120

HAND AS COMPONENT

HAND SUPER-IMPOSED

NOTE HOW THE IMPRESSIONS OF THE MAN WALKING ON THE ICE WITH THE STICK AND THE HAND HOLDING THE STICK CAN BE FUSED

TO; HIGASHI, EAST.

East 東 IS A COMPOSITE OF THE SUN 日 JME 11 RISING BEHIND A TREE 木 JME 15. THE EASTERN PROVINCES OF CHINA WERE HEAVILY FORESTED.

| Rad | Stroke | JME |
|-----|--------|-----|
| 75  | 8      | 121 |

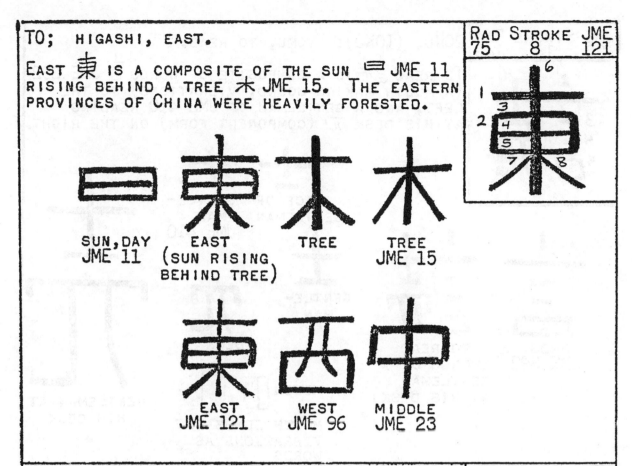

SUN, DAY
JME 11

EAST
(SUN RISING
BEHIND TREE)

TREE

TREE
JME 15

EAST
JME 121

WEST
JME 96

MIDDLE
JME 23

DŌ; MICHI, ROAD, WAY, PATH.

| Rad | Stroke | JME |
|-----|--------|-----|
| 162 | 12     | 122 |

ROAD, WAY, PATH 道 IS A COMPOSITE OF THE ELEVATED ANIMAL HORNS  FUSED ON THE RIGHT WITH THE KANJI COMPONENT FOR HEAD 百, AND ON THE LEFT THE COMPONENT 辶 MEANING TO GO FAST AND STOP SUDDENLY 辶 AND REPRESENTING A ROAD COMMENCING WITH THE DOT(S) ON THE UPPER LEFT AND WINDING ITS WAY TO THE LOWER RIGHT 辶. THE HEAD 百 (LEADER) ELK 丷 GOES FAST AND STOPS SUDDENLY 辶 ON THE ROAD, WAY, PATH 道 (AS DESCENDING THE CLIFF). MOST ROADS ORIGINATE AS ANIMAL TRAILS SUCH AS THE NARROW CROOKED COWPATH STREETS OF BOSTON.

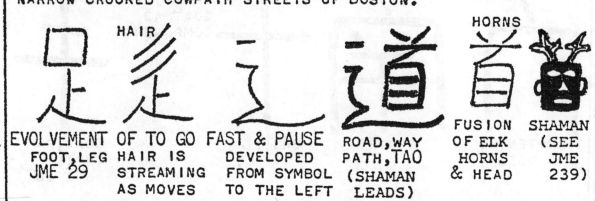

HAIR

HORNS

EVOLVEMENT OF
FOOT, LEG
JME 29

TO GO
HAIR IS
STREAMING
AS MOVES

FAST & PAUSE
DEVELOPED
FROM SYMBOL
TO THE LEFT

ROAD, WAY
PATH, TAO
(SHAMAN
LEADS)

FUSION
OF ELK
HORNS
& HEAD

SHAMAN
(SEE
JME
239)

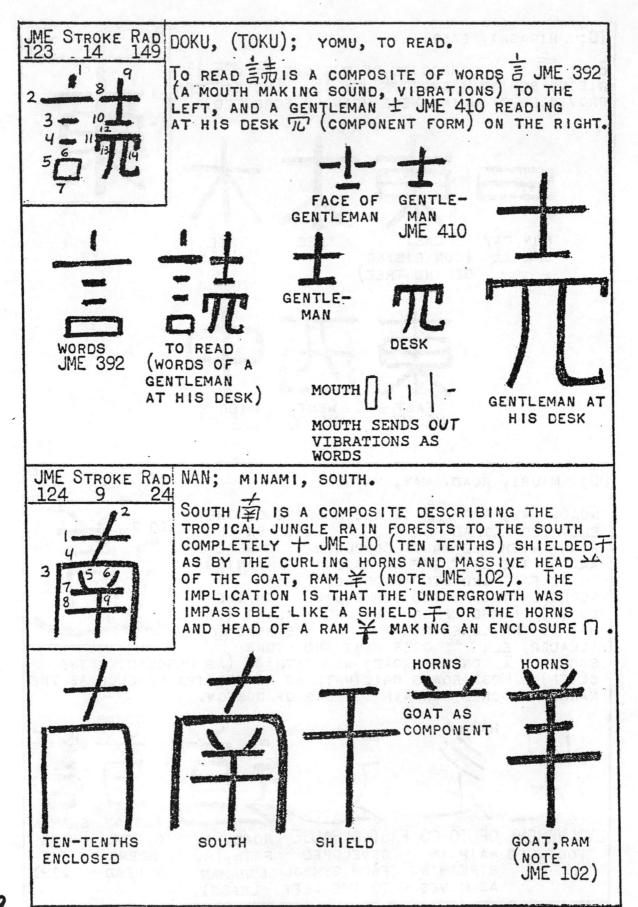

| JME | Stroke | Rad |
|-----|--------|-----|
| 123 | 14 | 149 |

DOKU, (TOKU); YOMU, TO READ.

TO READ 読 IS A COMPOSITE OF WORDS 言 JME 392 (A MOUTH MAKING SOUND, VIBRATIONS) TO THE LEFT, AND A GENTLEMAN 士 JME 410 READING AT HIS DESK 几 (COMPONENT FORM) ON THE RIGHT.

FACE OF GENTLEMAN

GENTLE-MAN JME 410

WORDS JME 392

TO READ (WORDS OF A GENTLEMAN AT HIS DESK)

GENTLE-MAN

DESK

MOUTH

MOUTH SENDS OUT VIBRATIONS AS WORDS

GENTLEMAN AT HIS DESK

| JME | Stroke | Rad |
|-----|--------|-----|
| 124 | 9 | 24 |

NAN; MINAMI, SOUTH.

SOUTH 南 IS A COMPOSITE DESCRIBING THE TROPICAL JUNGLE RAIN FORESTS TO THE SOUTH COMPLETELY 十 JME 10 (TEN TENTHS) SHIELDED 干 AS BY THE CURLING HORNS AND MASSIVE HEAD ㅗ OF THE GOAT, RAM 羊 (NOTE JME 102). THE IMPLICATION IS THAT THE UNDERGROWTH WAS IMPASSIBLE LIKE A SHIELD 干 OR THE HORNS AND HEAD OF A RAM 羊 MAKING AN ENCLOSURE ⌂.

HORNS

HORNS

GOAT AS COMPONENT

TEN-TENTHS ENCLOSED

SOUTH

SHIELD

GOAT, RAM (NOTE JME 102)

NYŪ; IRI, ENTERING, ATTENDANCE;
IRU, TO GO IN, TO ENTER; IRERU, TO PUT IN.

ENTERING, ATTENDANCE, TO GO IN, TO ENTER,
TO PUT IN 入 SHOWS A SINGLE LINE 丿 FORKING
INTO TWO LINES 八 , AS WHEN ONE STREAM
GOES IN, ENTERS, IS PUT IN 入 THE LUNGS 八 .
THE MAN IN ATTENDANCE 人 USED TO INHALE WITH A
SOFTLY SIBILANT SOUND.     TO GO IN, TO ENTER
入 IS THE MIRROR IMAGE OF MAN, PERSON 人 .
IN MAN 人 THE LONG STROKE IS TO THE LEFT 丿 .
IN TO GO IN, TO ENTER 入 THE LONG STROKE IS ON THE RIGHT 乀 .
THIS IS APT BECAUSE IT IS MAN, PERSON 人 THAT IS CONCERNED
WITH THE GOING IN, ENTERING, INHALING 入 OF THE AIR.

MIRROR IMAGES

人  人  入  入

| MAN, PERSON JME 30 | MAN, PERSON (LONG STROKE TO THE LEFT) | TO ENTER (LONG STROKE TO RIGHT) | ENTERING, ATTENDANCE, TO GO IN, TO ENTER | SUPERIMPOSITION OF GO IN AND LUNGS |

NEN; TOSHI, YEAR.

YEAR 年 IS A FUSION OF THE ZODIAC OR THE
CALENDAR HORSE 午 JME 207 AND AN ARCHAIC
KANJI FOR TOOTH 开 . THE ZODIAC HORSE'S
TEETH 开 TELL HIS YEAR 年 (YEARLING) OR AGE.
"DON'T LOOK A GIFT HORSE IN THE MOUTH".
THE ZODIAC HORSE 午 CURRENTLY MEANS NOON 午
JME 207 (THE HOUR OF THE HORSE: NOON HOUR).
THE CURRENT KANJI FOR HORSE IS 馬 JME 127.
THE CURRENT KANJI FOR TOOTH IS 歯 JME 414.
KEEP UP WITH THE TIMES.

午  年  开  牙

CROWN
VISIBLE TOOTH
GUM LINE
ROOTS

TOOTH
EQUINE PERMANENT
INCISORS APPEAR
AT 2.5 TO 3 YEARS.
AGE MAY BE APPRAISED IF YOU
CHECK TEETH SURFACE WEAR.

馬
HORSE
JME 127

歯
TOOTH, TEETH
JME 414

| (ZODIAC HORSE) NOON JME 207 | YEAR JME 126 | TOOTH AS COMPONENT | EQUINE PERMANENT INCISORS ... |

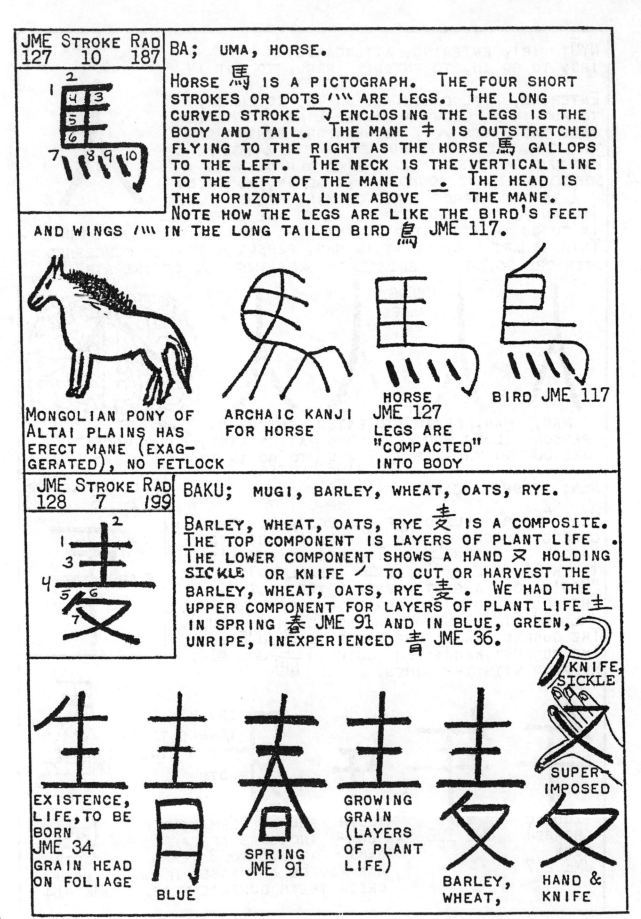

| JME | STROKE | RAD |
|-----|--------|-----|
| 127 | 10 | 187 |

BA;  UMA, HORSE.

HORSE 馬 IS A PICTOGRAPH. THE FOUR SHORT STROKES OR DOTS ⺣ ARE LEGS. THE LONG CURVED STROKE ⁊ ENCLOSING THE LEGS IS THE BODY AND TAIL. THE MANE ≠ IS OUTSTRETCHED FLYING TO THE RIGHT AS THE HORSE 馬 GALLOPS TO THE LEFT. THE NECK IS THE VERTICAL LINE TO THE LEFT OF THE MANE | . THE HEAD IS THE HORIZONTAL LINE ABOVE ⎯ THE MANE. NOTE HOW THE LEGS ARE LIKE THE BIRD'S FEET AND WINGS ⺣ IN THE LONG TAILED BIRD 鳥 JME 117.

MONGOLIAN PONY OF ALTAI PLAINS HAS ERECT MANE (EXAGGERATED), NO FETLOCK

ARCHAIC KANJI FOR HORSE

HORSE JME 127 LEGS ARE "COMPACTED" INTO BODY

BIRD JME 117

| JME | STROKE | RAD |
|-----|--------|-----|
| 128 | 7 | 199 |

BAKU;  MUGI, BARLEY, WHEAT, OATS, RYE.

BARLEY, WHEAT, OATS, RYE 麦 IS A COMPOSITE. THE TOP COMPONENT IS LAYERS OF PLANT LIFE . THE LOWER COMPONENT SHOWS A HAND 又 HOLDING SICKLE OR KNIFE ⁄ TO CUT OR HARVEST THE BARLEY, WHEAT, OATS, RYE 麦. WE HAD THE UPPER COMPONENT FOR LAYERS OF PLANT LIFE 主 IN SPRING 春 JME 91 AND IN BLUE, GREEN, UNRIPE, INEXPERIENCED 青 JME 36.

EXISTENCE, LIFE, TO BE BORN JME 34 GRAIN HEAD ON FOLIAGE

BLUE

SPRING JME 91

GROWING GRAIN (LAYERS OF PLANT LIFE)

BARLEY, WHEAT,

KNIFE, SICKLE

SUPERIMPOSED

HAND & KNIFE

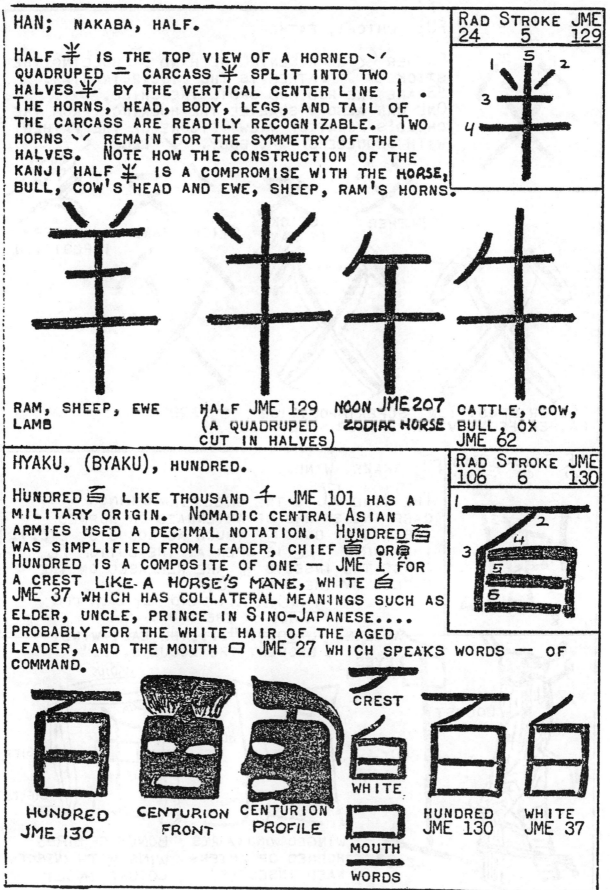

HAN; NAKABA, HALF.

HALF 半 IS THE TOP VIEW OF A HORNED ∨ QUADRUPED = CARCASS 半 SPLIT INTO TWO HALVES 半 BY THE VERTICAL CENTER LINE | . THE HORNS, HEAD, BODY, LEGS, AND TAIL OF THE CARCASS ARE READILY RECOGNIZABLE. TWO HORNS ∨ REMAIN FOR THE SYMMETRY OF THE HALVES. NOTE HOW THE CONSTRUCTION OF THE KANJI HALF 半 IS A COMPROMISE WITH THE HORSE, BULL, COW'S HEAD AND EWE, SHEEP, RAM'S HORNS.

| Rad | Stroke | JME |
|-----|--------|-----|
| 24  | 5      | 129 |

RAM, SHEEP, EWE LAMB

HALF JME 129 (A QUADRUPED CUT IN HALVES)

NOON JME 207 ZODIAC HORSE

CATTLE, COW, BULL, OX JME 62

HYAKU, (BYAKU), HUNDRED.

HUNDRED 百 LIKE THOUSAND 千 JME 101 HAS A MILITARY ORIGIN. NOMADIC CENTRAL ASIAN ARMIES USED A DECIMAL NOTATION. HUNDRED 百 WAS SIMPLIFIED FROM LEADER, CHIEF 首 OR 首 HUNDRED IS A COMPOSITE OF ONE — JME 1 FOR A CREST LIKE A HORSE'S MANE, WHITE 白 JME 37 WHICH HAS COLLATERAL MEANINGS SUCH AS ELDER, UNCLE, PRINCE IN SINO-JAPANESE.... PROBABLY FOR THE WHITE HAIR OF THE AGED LEADER, AND THE MOUTH 口 JME 27 WHICH SPEAKS WORDS — OF COMMAND.

| Rad | Stroke | JME |
|-----|--------|-----|
| 106 | 6      | 130 |

HUNDRED JME 130

CENTURION FRONT

CENTURION PROFILE

CREST

WHITE

MOUTH

WORDS

HUNDRED JME 130

WHITE JME 37

| JME | Stroke | Rad |
|-----|--------|-----|
| 131 | 4 | 88 |

FU; CHICHI, FATHER.

FATHER 父 REPRESENTS THE HAND 又 HOLDING THE STICK ∕. FATHER IS THE DISCIPLINARIAN. "SPARE THE ROD AND SPOIL THE CHILD." ONE CAN ALSO VISUALIZE THE HULKING (FROM THE CHILD'S POINT OF VIEW) FIGURE OF THE FATHER WITH SHOULDERS ⌢, BODY, ∨ LEGS ∧.

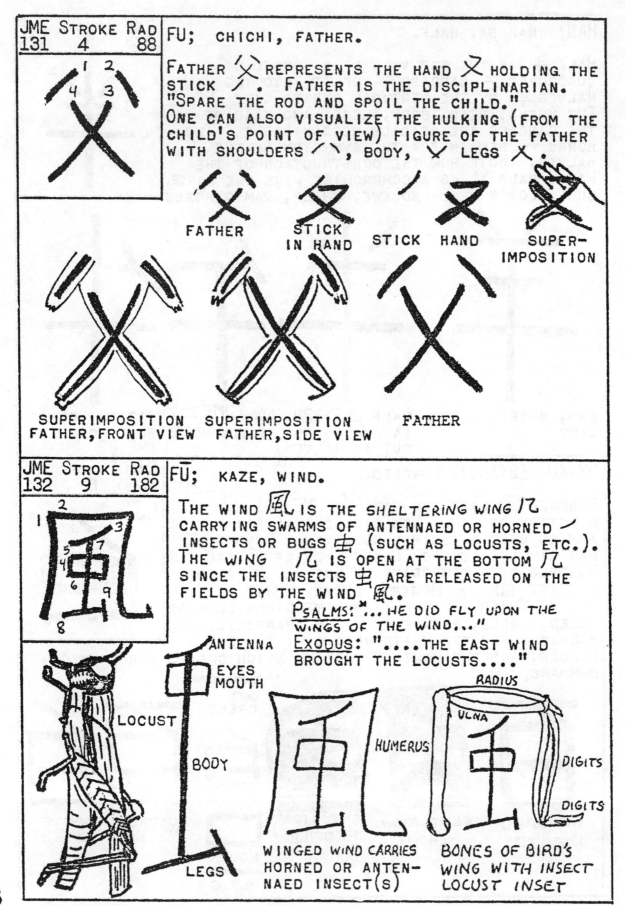

FATHER    STICK IN HAND    STICK    HAND    SUPER-IMPOSITION

SUPERIMPOSITION FATHER, FRONT VIEW    SUPERIMPOSITION FATHER, SIDE VIEW    FATHER

| JME | Stroke | Rad |
|-----|--------|-----|
| 132 | 9 | 182 |

FŪ; KAZE, WIND.

THE WIND 風 IS THE SHELTERING WING 几 CARRYING SWARMS OF ANTENNAED OR HORNED ∕ INSECTS OR BUGS 虫 (SUCH AS LOCUSTS, ETC.). THE WING 几 IS OPEN AT THE BOTTOM 几 SINCE THE INSECTS 虫 ARE RELEASED ON THE FIELDS BY THE WIND 風.

PSALMS: "... HE DID FLY UPON THE WINGS OF THE WIND..."
EXODUS: "....THE EAST WIND BROUGHT THE LOCUSTS...."

ANTENNA
EYES
MOUTH
LOCUST
BODY
LEGS

WINGED WIND CARRIES HORNED OR ANTEN-NAED INSECT(S)

RADIUS
ULNA
HUMERUS
DIGITS
DIGITS

BONES OF BIRD'S WING WITH INSECT LOCUST INSET

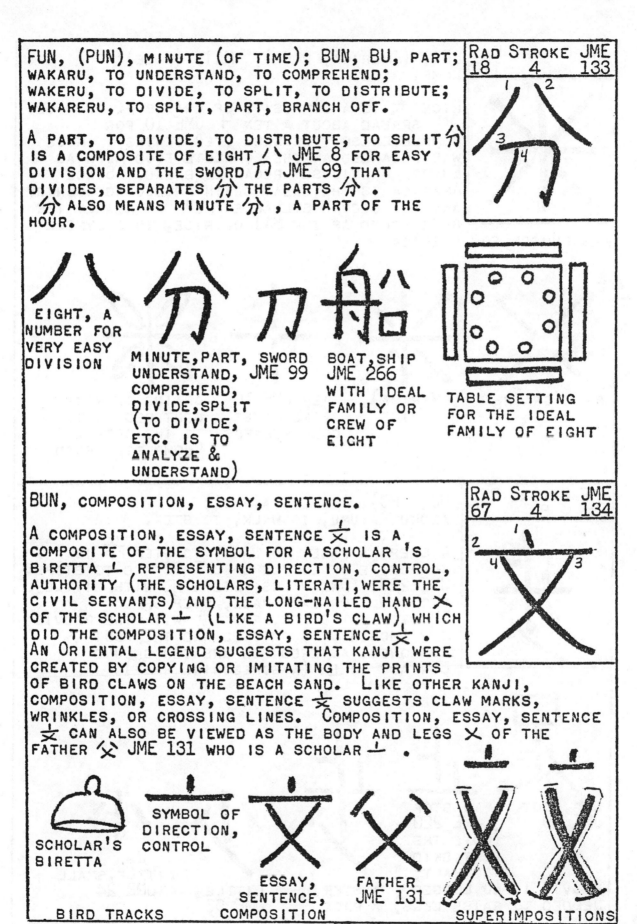

FUN, (PUN), MINUTE (OF TIME); BUN, BU, PART; WAKARU, TO UNDERSTAND, TO COMPREHEND; WAKERU, TO DIVIDE, TO SPLIT, TO DISTRIBUTE; WAKARERU, TO SPLIT, PART, BRANCH OFF.

A PART, TO DIVIDE, TO DISTRIBUTE, TO SPLIT 分 IS A COMPOSITE OF EIGHT 八 JME 8 FOR EASY DIVISION AND THE SWORD 刀 JME 99 THAT DIVIDES, SEPARATES 分 THE PARTS 分 . 分 ALSO MEANS MINUTE 分 , A PART OF THE HOUR.

| Rad | Stroke | JME |
|---|---|---|
| 18 | 4 | 133 |

EIGHT, A NUMBER FOR VERY EASY DIVISION

MINUTE, PART, UNDERSTAND, COMPREHEND, DIVIDE, SPLIT (TO DIVIDE, ETC. IS TO ANALYZE & UNDERSTAND)

SWORD JME 99

BOAT, SHIP JME 266 WITH IDEAL FAMILY OR CREW OF EIGHT

TABLE SETTING FOR THE IDEAL FAMILY OF EIGHT

BUN, COMPOSITION, ESSAY, SENTENCE.

A COMPOSITION, ESSAY, SENTENCE 文 IS A COMPOSITE OF THE SYMBOL FOR A SCHOLAR'S BIRETTA ⊥ REPRESENTING DIRECTION, CONTROL, AUTHORITY (THE SCHOLARS, LITERATI, WERE THE CIVIL SERVANTS) AND THE LONG-NAILED HAND X OF THE SCHOLAR ⊥ (LIKE A BIRD'S CLAW), WHICH DID THE COMPOSITION, ESSAY, SENTENCE 文. AN ORIENTAL LEGEND SUGGESTS THAT KANJI WERE CREATED BY COPYING OR IMITATING THE PRINTS OF BIRD CLAWS ON THE BEACH SAND. LIKE OTHER KANJI, COMPOSITION, ESSAY, SENTENCE 文 SUGGESTS CLAW MARKS, WRINKLES, OR CROSSING LINES. COMPOSITION, ESSAY, SENTENCE 文 CAN ALSO BE VIEWED AS THE BODY AND LEGS X OF THE FATHER 父 JME 131 WHO IS A SCHOLAR ⊥ .

| Rad | Stroke | JME |
|---|---|---|
| 67 | 4 | 134 |

SCHOLAR'S BIRETTA

SYMBOL OF DIRECTION, CONTROL

ESSAY, SENTENCE, COMPOSITION

FATHER JME 131

BIRD TRACKS      SUPERIMPOSITIONS

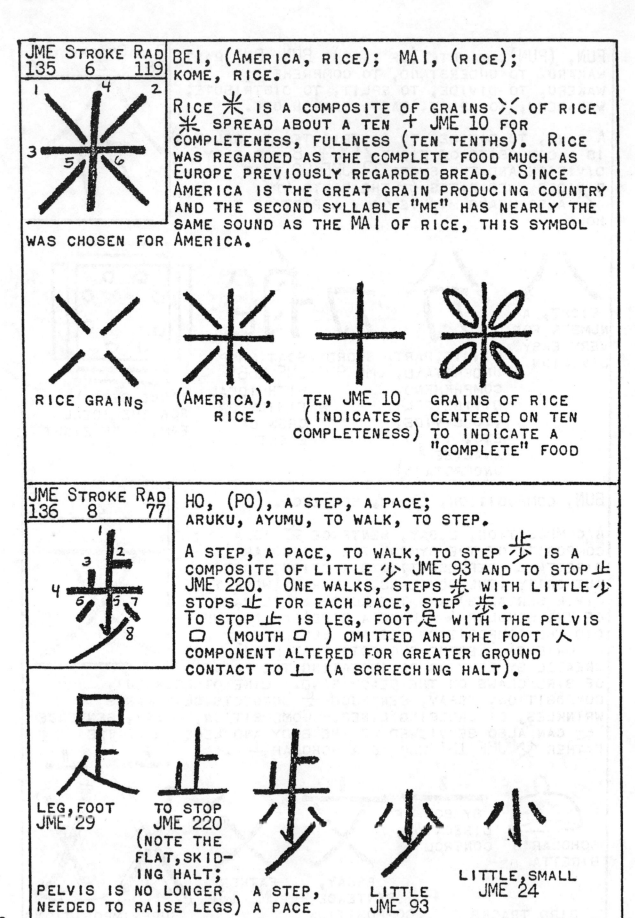

| JME 135 | Stroke 6 | Rad 119 |
|---|---|---|

BEI, (AMERICA, RICE); MAI, (RICE); KOME, RICE.

RICE 米 IS A COMPOSITE OF GRAINS 丷 OF RICE 米 SPREAD ABOUT A TEN 十 JME 10 FOR COMPLETENESS, FULLNESS (TEN TENTHS). RICE WAS REGARDED AS THE COMPLETE FOOD MUCH AS EUROPE PREVIOUSLY REGARDED BREAD. SINCE AMERICA IS THE GREAT GRAIN PRODUCING COUNTRY AND THE SECOND SYLLABLE "ME" HAS NEARLY THE SAME SOUND AS THE MAI OF RICE, THIS SYMBOL WAS CHOSEN FOR AMERICA.

RICE GRAINS

(AMERICA), RICE

TEN JME 10 (INDICATES COMPLETENESS)

GRAINS OF RICE CENTERED ON TEN TO INDICATE A "COMPLETE" FOOD

| JME 136 | Stroke 8 | Rad 77 |
|---|---|---|

HO, (PO), A STEP, A PACE; ARUKU, AYUMU, TO WALK, TO STEP.

A STEP, A PACE, TO WALK, TO STEP 歩 IS A COMPOSITE OF LITTLE 少 JME 93 AND TO STOP 止 JME 220. ONE WALKS, STEPS 歩 WITH LITTLE 少 STOPS 止 FOR EACH PACE, STEP 歩. TO STOP 止 IS LEG, FOOT 足 WITH THE PELVIS 口 (MOUTH 口) OMITTED AND THE FOOT 人 COMPONENT ALTERED FOR GREATER GROUND CONTACT TO ⊥ (A SCREECHING HALT).

LEG, FOOT JME 29

TO STOP JME 220 (NOTE THE FLAT, SKIDING HALT; PELVIS IS NO LONGER NEEDED TO RAISE LEGS)

A STEP, A PACE

LITTLE JME 93

LITTLE, SMALL JME 24

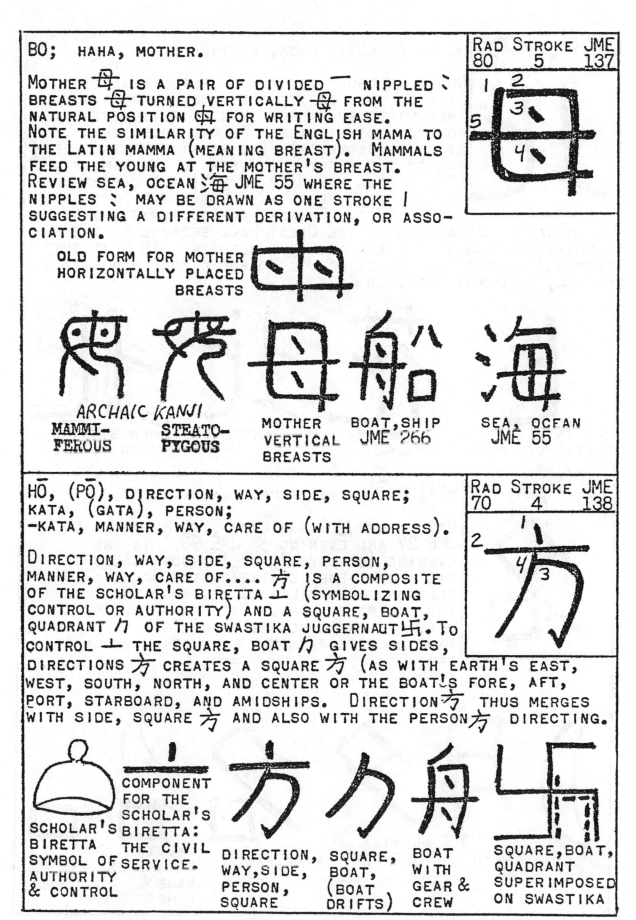

| RAD | STROKE | JME |
|-----|--------|-----|
| 80  | 5      | 137 |

BO;  HAHA, MOTHER.

MOTHER 母 IS A PAIR OF DIVIDED ⼀ NIPPLED ∶
BREASTS 母 TURNED VERTICALLY 母 FROM THE
NATURAL POSITION 毌 FOR WRITING EASE.
NOTE THE SIMILARITY OF THE ENGLISH MAMA TO
THE LATIN MAMMA (MEANING BREAST). MAMMALS
FEED THE YOUNG AT THE MOTHER'S BREAST.
REVIEW SEA, OCEAN 海 JME 55 WHERE THE
NIPPLES ∶ MAY BE DRAWN AS ONE STROKE |
SUGGESTING A DIFFERENT DERIVATION, OR ASSO-
CIATION.

OLD FORM FOR MOTHER
HORIZONTALLY PLACED
BREASTS

ARCHAIC KANJI
MAMMI-FEROUS     STEATO-PYGOUS     MOTHER VERTICAL BREASTS     BOAT, SHIP JME 266     SEA, OCEAN JME 55

| RAD | STROKE | JME |
|-----|--------|-----|
| 70  | 4      | 138 |

HŌ, (PŌ), DIRECTION, WAY, SIDE, SQUARE;
KATA, (GATA), PERSON;
-KATA, MANNER, WAY, CARE OF (WITH ADDRESS).

DIRECTION, WAY, SIDE, SQUARE, PERSON,
MANNER, WAY, CARE OF.... 方 IS A COMPOSITE
OF THE SCHOLAR'S BIRETTA 亠 (SYMBOLIZING
CONTROL OR AUTHORITY) AND A SQUARE, BOAT,
QUADRANT 勹 OF THE SWASTIKA JUGGERNAUT 卐. TO
CONTROL 亠 THE SQUARE, BOAT 勹 GIVES SIDES,
DIRECTIONS 方 CREATES A SQUARE 方 (AS WITH EARTH'S EAST,
WEST, SOUTH, NORTH, AND CENTER OR THE BOAT'S FORE, AFT,
PORT, STARBOARD, AND AMIDSHIPS. DIRECTION 方 THUS MERGES
WITH SIDE, SQUARE 方 AND ALSO WITH THE PERSON 方 DIRECTING.

SCHOLAR'S BIRETTA SYMBOL OF AUTHORITY & CONTROL     COMPONENT FOR THE SCHOLAR'S BIRETTA: THE CIVIL SERVICE.     DIRECTION, WAY, SIDE, PERSON, SQUARE     SQUARE, BOAT, (BOAT DRIFTS)     BOAT WITH GEAR & CREW     SQUARE, BOAT, QUADRANT SUPERIMPOSED ON SWASTIKA

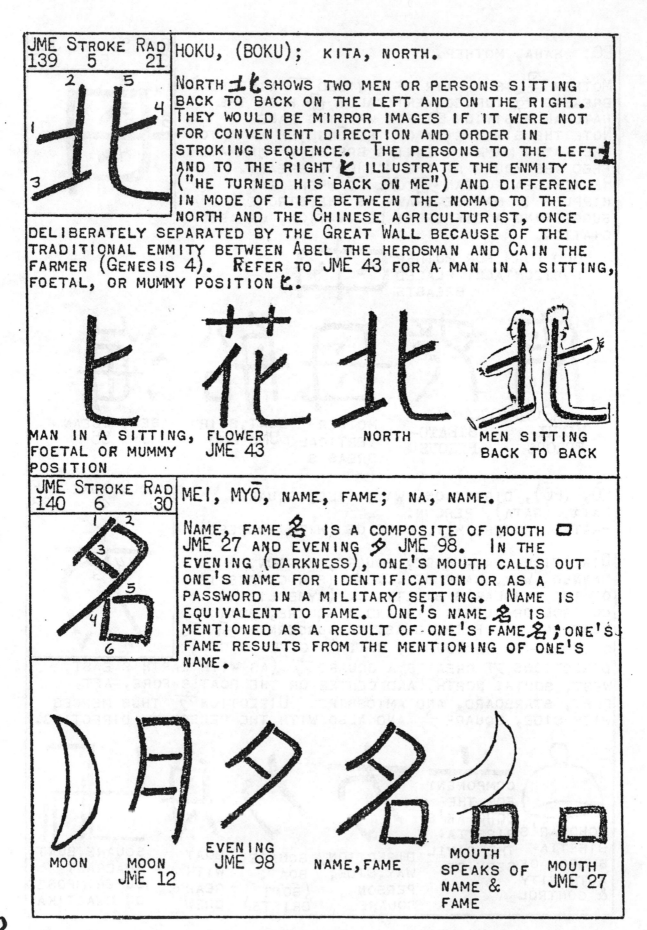

| JME | Stroke | Rad |
|-----|--------|-----|
| 139 | 5 | 21 |

HOKU, (BOKU); KITA, NORTH.

NORTH 北 SHOWS TWO MEN OR PERSONS SITTING BACK TO BACK ON THE LEFT AND ON THE RIGHT. THEY WOULD BE MIRROR IMAGES IF IT WERE NOT FOR CONVENIENT DIRECTION AND ORDER IN STROKING SEQUENCE. THE PERSONS TO THE LEFT 土 AND TO THE RIGHT ヒ ILLUSTRATE THE ENMITY ("HE TURNED HIS BACK ON ME") AND DIFFERENCE IN MODE OF LIFE BETWEEN THE NOMAD TO THE NORTH AND THE CHINESE AGRICULTURIST, ONCE DELIBERATELY SEPARATED BY THE GREAT WALL BECAUSE OF THE TRADITIONAL ENMITY BETWEEN ABEL THE HERDSMAN AND CAIN THE FARMER (GENESIS 4). REFER TO JME 43 FOR A MAN IN A SITTING, FOETAL, OR MUMMY POSITION ヒ.

MAN IN A SITTING, FOETAL OR MUMMY POSITION

FLOWER JME 43

NORTH

MEN SITTING BACK TO BACK

| JME | Stroke | Rad |
|-----|--------|-----|
| 140 | 6 | 30 |

MEI, MYŌ, NAME, FAME; NA, NAME.

NAME, FAME 名 IS A COMPOSITE OF MOUTH 口 JME 27 AND EVENING 夕 JME 98. IN THE EVENING (DARKNESS), ONE'S MOUTH CALLS OUT ONE'S NAME FOR IDENTIFICATION OR AS A PASSWORD IN A MILITARY SETTING. NAME IS EQUIVALENT TO FAME. ONE'S NAME 名 IS MENTIONED AS A RESULT OF ONE'S FAME 名; ONE'S FAME RESULTS FROM THE MENTIONING OF ONE'S NAME.

MOON

MOON JME 12

EVENING JME 98

NAME, FAME

MOUTH SPEAKS OF NAME & FAME

MOUTH JME 27

MEI, MYŌ, (BRIGHT); AKARUI, LIGHT, BRIGHT; AKIRAKA, BRIGHT, CLEAR; AKERU, TO DAWN.

BRIGHT, LIGHT, CLEAR, TO DAWN 明 IS A COMPOSITE OF SUN 日 AND MOON 月 AS THE BRIGHT 明 HEAVENLY BODIES WHICH MAKE BRIGHT, CLEAR 明. WITH THE MEANING OF BRIGHT, BRILLIANT, 明 IS THE MING 明 (1368-1644) DYNASTY OF CHINA AND MEIJI 明 (1868-1912) (ERA) OF JAPAN.

| Rad 72 | Stroke 8 | JME 141 |
|---|---|---|

明

日
SUN, DAY
JME 11

明
LIGHT, BRIGHT, CLEAR, TO DAWN UNITES THE SUN AND MOON, THE SYMBOL WAS CHOSEN FOR THE MEIJI (ERA) OF JAPAN AND THE MING DYNASTY OF CHINA

月
MOON, MONTH
JME 12

MOON

---

MŌ; KE, HAIR, WOOL, FUR, FEATHERS.

HAIR, WOOL, FUR, FEATHERS 毛 IS A PICTOGRAPH OF A FEATHER (MUCH LIKE A HAND WITH THE FEATHER'S BARBS, ETC. AS FINGERS), BUT WITH THE LOWER END CURVED TO SHOW IT IS ROOTED OR CLINGING LIKE A SNAKE'S 色 TAIL レ. HAIR, WOOL, FUR, FEATHERS 毛 CAN ALSO BE INTER-PRETED AS A HAND 手 CARESSING THE SINUOUS SNAKY 色 (MEDUSA) HAIR 毛.

| Rad 82 | Stroke 4 | JME 142 |
|---|---|---|

毛

手
HAND
JME 28

毛
HAIR, WOOL, FUR, FEATHERS

地
EARTH, GROUND
JME 111

色
COLOR
JME 94

(NOTE ANALOGOUS FORM OF SNAKES' TAILS & FEATHER)

牛
COW, BULL
JME 62

毛
HAIR, WOOL, FUR, FEATHERS

羊
SHEEP

Ψ
OLD SYMBOL FOR HAND

FEATHER

| JME Stroke Rad |
|---|
| 143    8    169 |

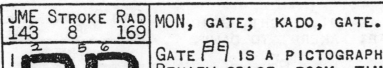

MON, GATE; KADO, GATE.

GATE 門 IS A PICTOGRAPH OF DOUBLE DOORS 吅. REVIEW SPACE, ROOM, TIME, INTERVAL, DISTANCE 間 JME 58. THE GATE 門 MAY BE VISUALIZED AS SWINGING BAR DOORS. THE GATE COMPOSED OF DOUBLE DOORS WAS TRADITIONALLY THE ENTRANCE THROUGH THE COMPOUND WALL. THE ORIENTAL ARCHITECTURAL STYLE LIKE THE SPANISH ENCLOSED ITS LIVING AREAS AND BUILDINGS.

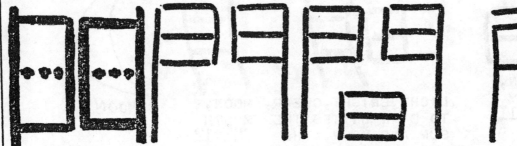

| PICTURE OF A GATE TO SHOW MODIFICATION FOR THE KANJI | GATE (PAIRED OR DOUBLE DOORS) | SPACE, ROOM, TIME, INTERVAL, DISTANCE JME 58 (NOTE HOW GATE JME 143 IS A COMPONENT HERE) | DOOR JME 69  戸  DOOR JME 69 |

| JME Stroke Rad |
|---|
| 144    8    36 |

YA; YO, YORU,

EVENING, NIGHT 夜 IS A COMPOSITE OF THE SCHOLAR'S BIRETTA 亠 (FOR SCHOLAR OR DIRECTION), A MAN 亻, EVENING 夕 (AS A SIMPLER KANJI 夕 JME 98), MOON 夕, AND A MAN, PERSON WALKING 夂. IN THE ORIENT, MOON-VIEWING WAS A CULTURAL, SOCIAL, AND EVEN RELIGIOUS AFFAIR WITH A RITUALISTIC OVERTONE. EVENING, NIGHT 夜 SHOWS THE SCHOLAR 亠 OR MAN 亻 STROLLING 夂 IN THE EVENING 夕 VIEWING THE MOON 夕.

| 亠 SCHOLAR'S BIRETTA | 亻 PERSON, MAN (AS COMPONENT) | 夜 EVENING, NIGHT | 夂 MAN WALKING | 夕 MOON JME 12 | 夕 EVENING JME 98 |

THE SCHOLAR OR MAN IS WALKING ON A MOONLIGHT EVENING
....a braw moonlicht nicht.

YŪ; TOMO, FRIEND.

| Rad | Stroke | JME |
|-----|--------|-----|
| 29 | 4 | 145 |

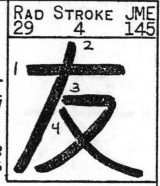

FRIEND 友 IS A COMPOSITE OF CLASPED HANDS, ONE HAND TO THE LOWER RIGHT 又, AND THE OTHER TO THE UPPER LEFT ナ . THE UPPER LEFT HAND ナ WAS IN LEFT 左 JME 18 AND IN RIGHT 右 JME 19. THE LOWER RIGHT COMPONENT 又 IN FRIEND 友 IS THE HAND THAT USUALLY HOLDS SOMETHING AS IN BARLEY 麦 JME 128 AND SUMMER 夏 JME 52. THE CLASPING OF HANDS INDICATES FRIENDSHIP BETWEEN FRIENDS 友 .

OLD SYMBOL FOR HAND    HAND AS A COMPONENT (THREE FINGERS CLOSED)    FRIEND    HAND AS A COMPONENT    THERE IS A SUGGESTION OF WALKING WHILE HAND IN HAND

YŌ, BUSINESS; MOCHIIRU, TO USE.

| Rad | Stroke | JME |
|-----|--------|-----|
| 101 | 5 | 146 |

BUSINESS, TO USE 用 REPRESENTS THE GUTS OR INTESTINES ‡ IN THE ABDOMINAL CAVITY 冂 . THE INTESTINES ‡ IN THE CAVITY 冂 USE 用 THE FOOD TO OUR BENEFIT. THE COMPLEXITY OF THE COILED INTESTINES IS SIMILAR TO THE COMPLEXITY OF BUSINESS 用 . IN ENGLISH, WE MAY TELL A LITTLE CHILD, "DO YOUR BUSINESS," WHEN ENCOURAGING HIM TO EMPTY HIS BOWELS OR INTESTINES. WHEN FOOD IS PRESENT, THE SMALL INTESTINE MOVES AND CHURNS WITH CONTRACTIONS, RELAXATIONS.

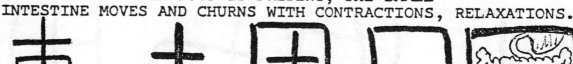

WHEEL, VEHICLE JME 88    INTESTINES COILING & TURNING LIKE THE WHEELS OF A VEHICLE    BUSINESS, TO USE    ABDOMINAL CAVITY OR ENCLOSURE    ABDOMINAL CAVITY WITH COLON AND SMALL INTESTINE

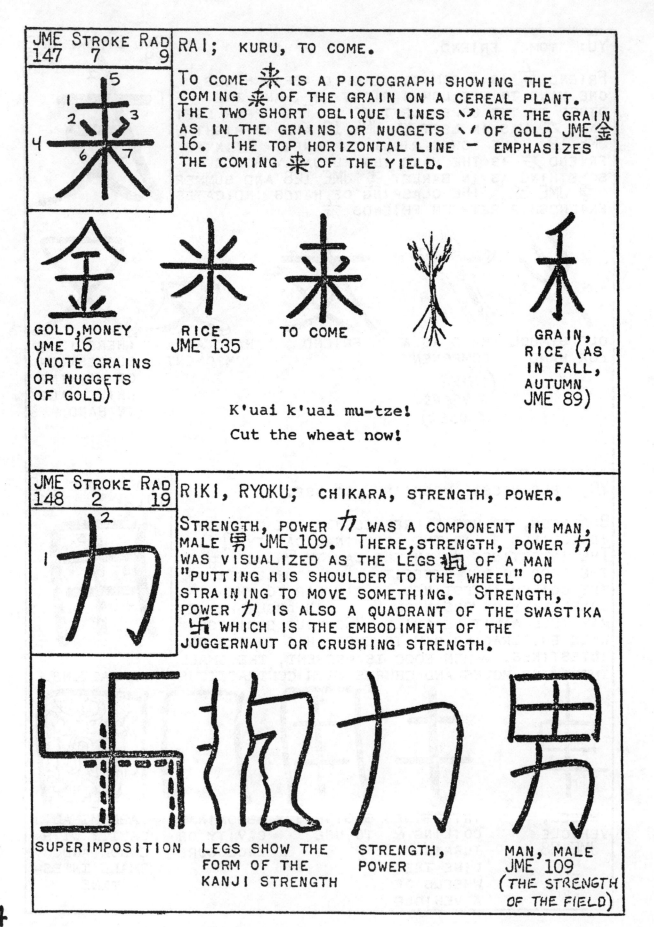

| JME<br>147 | Stroke<br>7 | Rad<br>9 |
| --- | --- | --- |

RAI; KURU, TO COME.

TO COME 来 IS A PICTOGRAPH SHOWING THE COMING 来 OF THE GRAIN ON A CEREAL PLANT. THE TWO SHORT OBLIQUE LINES ゛ ARE THE GRAIN AS IN THE GRAINS OR NUGGETS ゛ OF GOLD JME 金 16. THE TOP HORIZONTAL LINE ー EMPHASIZES THE COMING 来 OF THE YIELD.

GOLD, MONEY
JME 16
(NOTE GRAINS
OR NUGGETS
OF GOLD)

RICE
JME 135

TO COME

GRAIN,
RICE (AS
IN FALL,
AUTUMN
JME 89)

K'uai k'uai mu-tze!

Cut the wheat now!

| JME<br>148 | Stroke<br>2 | Rad<br>19 |
| --- | --- | --- |

RIKI, RYOKU; CHIKARA, STRENGTH, POWER.

STRENGTH, POWER 力 WAS A COMPONENT IN MAN, MALE 男 JME 109. THERE, STRENGTH, POWER 力 WAS VISUALIZED AS THE LEGS 𠤎 OF A MAN "PUTTING HIS SHOULDER TO THE WHEEL" OR STRAINING TO MOVE SOMETHING. STRENGTH, POWER 力 IS ALSO A QUADRANT OF THE SWASTIKA 卐 WHICH IS THE EMBODIMENT OF THE JUGGERNAUT OR CRUSHING STRENGTH.

SUPERIMPOSITION

LEGS SHOW THE
FORM OF THE
KANJI STRENGTH

STRENGTH,
POWER

MAN, MALE
JME 109
(THE STRENGTH
OF THE FIELD)

149-150

RITSU; TATSU, TACHI, (DACHI), TO STAND.

TO STAND 立 IS A PERSON 亢 WITH HEAD ` ,
ARMS —, AND LEGS \/ CLEARLY DELINEATED
STANDING 立 ON THE HORIZONTAL BASELINE —.
REVIEW SIX 六 JME 6 AND SOUND 音 JME 50.

| Rad | Stroke | JME |
|-----|--------|-----|
| 117 | -8 | 149 |

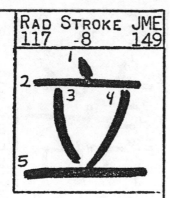

OLD SYMBOLS FOR MAN | SIX<br>JME 6<br>AS IT MAY<br>DERIVE FROM<br>MAN | TO STAND | BASELINE<br>OR EARTH<br>(AS IN<br>THREE<br>JME 3)

RIN; HAYASHI, (BAYASHI), GROVE, WOODS.

GROVE, WOODS 林 IS A DOUBLING OF THE KANJI
FOR WOOD, TREE 木 JME 15. A KANJI MAY BE
DOUBLED TO INDICATE INCREASE IN QUANTITY
(NUMBERS) OR QUALITY (SIZE, ETC.). TREE,
WOOD 木 JME 15 WAS TRIPLED TO BECOME FOREST
森 JME 41.

| Rad | Stroke | JME |
|-----|--------|-----|
| 75 | 8 | 150 |

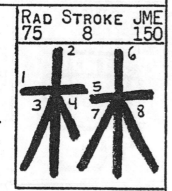

TREE, WOOD<br>JME 15 | GROVE, WOODS<br>JME 150 | FOREST<br>JME 41

| JME 151 | Stroke 13 | Rad 149 |
|---|---|---|

WA; HANASHI, (BANASHI), STORY; HANASU, TO SPEAK.

STORY, TO SPEAK 話 IS A COMPOSITE. THE LEFT COMPONENT MEANS SPEECH, WORDS, TO SAY 言 JME 392. IT HAS A MOUTH 口 BELOW AND SPEECH VIBRATIONS ≡ ABOVE. THE RIGHT COMPONENT IS TONGUE 舌 JME 827. TONGUE HAS A MOUTH 口 BELOW, A VERTICAL LINE FOR THE BODY | OF THE TONGUE, A SHORT HORIZONTAL LINE FOR THE MOVEMENT — OF THE TONGUE, AND A TOP OBLIQUE LINE FOR THE TIP ノ OF THE TONGUE (ANALOGOUS TO THE POINT ノ OF THE ARROW 矢 JME 112; THE HORN ノ OF THE BULL, COW 牛 JME 62; ETC.).

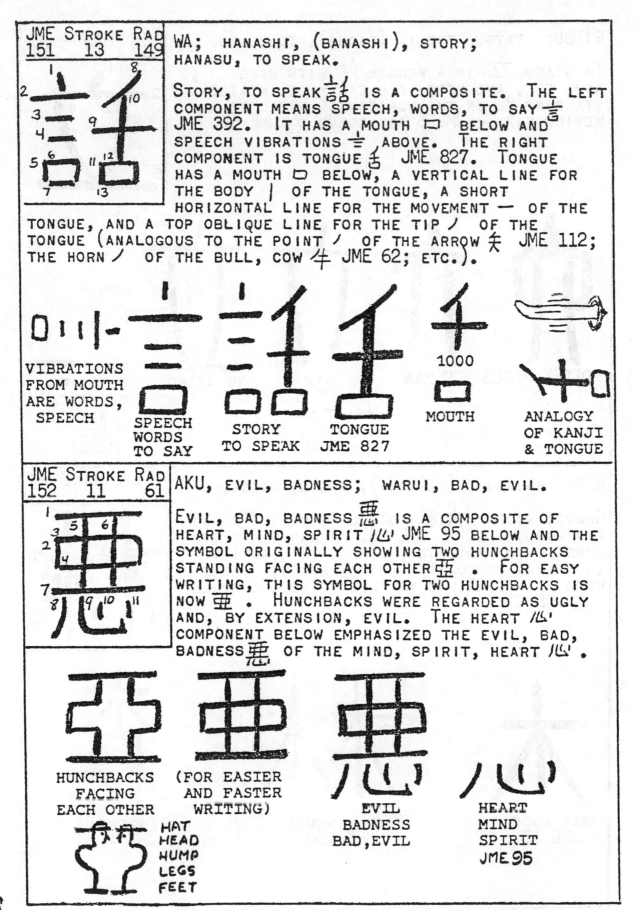

VIBRATIONS FROM MOUTH ARE WORDS, SPEECH

SPEECH WORDS TO SAY

STORY TO SPEAK

TONGUE JME 827

1000 MOUTH

ANALOGY OF KANJI & TONGUE

| JME 152 | Stroke 11 | Rad 61 |
|---|---|---|

AKU, EVIL, BADNESS; WARUI, BAD, EVIL.

EVIL, BAD, BADNESS 悪 IS A COMPOSITE OF HEART, MIND, SPIRIT 心 JME 95 BELOW AND THE SYMBOL ORIGINALLY SHOWING TWO HUNCHBACKS STANDING FACING EACH OTHER 亞 . FOR EASY WRITING, THIS SYMBOL FOR TWO HUNCHBACKS IS NOW 亜 . HUNCHBACKS WERE REGARDED AS UGLY AND, BY EXTENSION, EVIL. THE HEART 心 COMPONENT BELOW EMPHASIZED THE EVIL, BAD, BADNESS 悪 OF THE MIND, SPIRIT, HEART 心 .

HUNCHBACKS FACING EACH OTHER

HAT HEAD HUMP LEGS FEET

(FOR EASIER AND FASTER WRITING)

EVIL BADNESS BAD, EVIL

HEART MIND SPIRIT JME 95

AN; YASUI, INEXPENSIVE, EASY.

INEXPENSIVE, EASY 安 IS A COMPOSITE OF A WOMAN 女 JME 32 UNDER A ROOF 宀. THE DOMESTIC LIFE WITH A WOMAN 女 UNDER A ROOF 宀 IS SUPPOSED TO BE INEXPENSIVE, EASY 安 COMPARED TO THAT OF A SPENDTHRIFT BACHELOR. WE HAD ROOF 宀 AS A COMPONENT IN HOUSE, HOME 家 JME 53 AND IN IDEOGRAPH, LETTER, WORD 字 JME 86.

| Rad | Stroke | JME |
|-----|--------|-----|
| 40 | 6 | 153 |

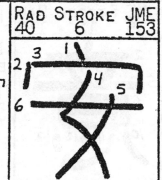

ROOF.......
AS IN HOUSE,
HOME JME 53

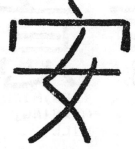

INEXPENSIVE,
EASY JME 153

WOMAN, GIRL,
FEMALE JME 32

SUPERIMPOSITION

---

AN; KURAI, DARK.

DARK 暗 IS THE STANDING 立 OF A SUN 日 OR HEAVENLY BODY OVER ANOTHER SUN 日 OR HEAVENLY BODY PRODUCING DARKNESS 日暗 (OR ECLIPSE). ONE SUN 日 OR HEAVENLY BODY STANDS 立 OVER (OR SHUTS OFF) THE SOUND 音 (OR EFFECT) OF THE OTHER HEAVENLY BODY.

| Rad | Stroke | JME |
|-----|--------|-----|
| 72 | 13 | 154 |

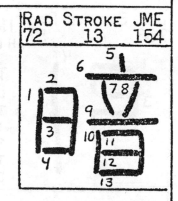

SUN
JME 11

DARK
JME 154

SOUND
JME 50

DARK
(AS FROM AN ECLIPSE)

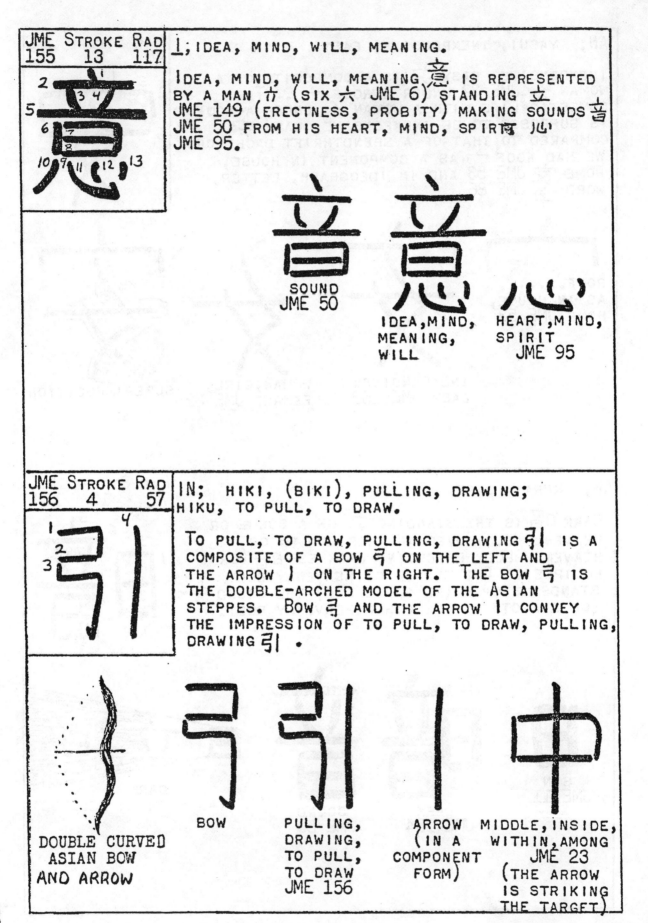

| JME | STROKE | RAD |
|-----|--------|-----|
| 155 | 13 | 117 |

意

1; IDEA, MIND, WILL, MEANING.

IDEA, MIND, WILL, MEANING 意 IS REPRESENTED BY A MAN 六 (SIX 六 JME 6) STANDING 立 JME 149 (ERECTNESS, PROBITY) MAKING SOUNDS 音 JME 50 FROM HIS HEART, MIND, SPIRIT 心 JME 95.

音
SOUND
JME 50

意
IDEA, MIND,
MEANING,
WILL

心
HEART, MIND,
SPIRIT
JME 95

| JME | STROKE | RAD |
|-----|--------|-----|
| 156 | 4 | 57 |

引

IN; HIKI, (BIKI), PULLING, DRAWING; HIKU, TO PULL, TO DRAW.

TO PULL, TO DRAW, PULLING, DRAWING 引 IS A COMPOSITE OF A BOW 弓 ON THE LEFT AND THE ARROW 丨 ON THE RIGHT. THE BOW 弓 IS THE DOUBLE-ARCHED MODEL OF THE ASIAN STEPPES. BOW 弓 AND THE ARROW 丨 CONVEY THE IMPRESSION OF TO PULL, TO DRAW, PULLING, DRAWING 引 .

DOUBLE CURVED
ASIAN BOW
AND ARROW

弓
BOW

引
PULLING,
DRAWING,
TO PULL,
TO DRAW
JME 156

丨
ARROW
(IN A
COMPONENT
FORM)

中
MIDDLE, INSIDE,
WITHIN, AMONG
JME 23
(THE ARROW
IS STRIKING
THE TARGET)

UN, LUCK; HAKOBU, TO CARRY, TO TRANSPORT.

LUCK, TO CARRY, TO TRANSPORT 運 IS A COMPOSITE OF A CANOPIED 冖 WAGON, VEHICLE, CHARIOT 車 JME 88 TRAVELLING FROM THE DISTANCE INTO THE FOREGROUND ⻌ (UPPER LEFT TO FRONT RIGHT). TO CARRY, TO TRANSPORT 運 IS LUCK 運 FOR THE PERSON INVOLVED (WHETHER IT IS HIS PACK, LUGGAGE, OR PERSON). THE MOVEMENT COMPONENT ⻌ WAS PART OF ROAD, WAY, PATH 道 JME 122.

| RAD 162 | STROKE 12 | JME 157 |
|---|---|---|

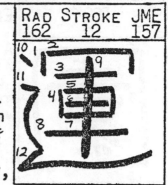

"AND THE CAISSONS GO ROLLING ALONG"

(A CAISSON IS A BOX OR CHEST FOR AMMUNITION OR A TWO-WHEELED VEHICLE FOR ARTILLERY AMMUNITION).

⻌ TO GO AND TO PAUSE, TO STOP & GO, MOVEMENT

運 TO TRANSPORT, TO CARRY, LUCK JME 157

車 CANOPY / CANOPIED WAGON, VEHICLE, CHARIOT (SURREY WITH A FRINGE, COVERED WAGON)

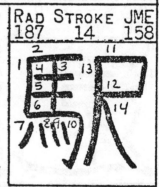
CHINESE WAR CHARIOT

CAISSONS

EKI, STATION.

STATION 駅 IS A COMPOSITE OF HORSE 馬 JME 127 ON THE LEFT AND SHAKU 尺 REPRESENTING A FOOT ON THE RIGHT. (SHAKU, 尺 IS A LINEAR MEASURE EQUAL TO .995 FEET). THE STATION (ORIGINALLY A GOVERNMENT POST-STATION OR RELAY STATION WITH HORSES) WAS WHERE FRESH HORSES 馬 WAITED AT A CERTAIN DISTANCE IN SHAKU 尺 (FEET). A SHAKU IS A PICTOGRAPH OF A BODY STEPPING OUT TO MEASURE (AS IN PACES).

| RAD 187 | STROKE 14 | JME 158 |
|---|---|---|

馬 HORSE JME 127

駅 STATION

尺 SHAKU (.995 FEET)

尺 BODY STEPS OUT AS FOR THE MEASUREMENT IN PACES

尸 HUMAN BODY AS OF THE MERCHANT, SHOPKEEPER (SEE SHOP 屋 JME 161)

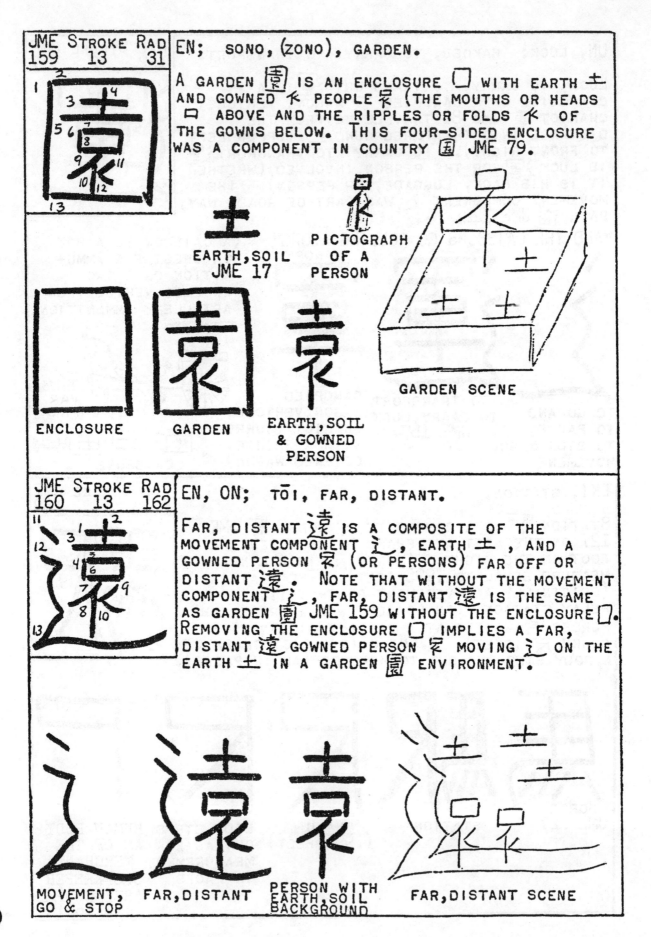

| JME 159 | Stroke 13 | Rad 31 |
|---|---|---|

EN; SONO, (ZONO), GARDEN.

A GARDEN 園 IS AN ENCLOSURE □ WITH EARTH 土 AND GOWNED 衣 PEOPLE 袁 (THE MOUTHS OR HEADS 口 ABOVE AND THE RIPPLES OR FOLDS 衣 OF THE GOWNS BELOW. THIS FOUR-SIDED ENCLOSURE WAS A COMPONENT IN COUNTRY 国 JME 79.

土
EARTH, SOIL
JME 17

PICTOGRAPH
OF A
PERSON

GARDEN SCENE

ENCLOSURE        GARDEN        EARTH, SOIL
                                & GOWNED
                                PERSON

| JME 160 | Stroke 13 | Rad 162 |
|---|---|---|

EN, ON; TŌI, FAR, DISTANT.

FAR, DISTANT 遠 IS A COMPOSITE OF THE MOVEMENT COMPONENT 辶, EARTH 土, AND A GOWNED PERSON 袁 (OR PERSONS) FAR OFF OR DISTANT 遠. NOTE THAT WITHOUT THE MOVEMENT COMPONENT 辶, FAR, DISTANT 遠 IS THE SAME AS GARDEN 園 JME 159 WITHOUT THE ENCLOSURE □. REMOVING THE ENCLOSURE □ IMPLIES A FAR, DISTANT 遠 GOWNED PERSON 袁 MOVING 辶 ON THE EARTH 土 IN A GARDEN 園 ENVIRONMENT.

MOVEMENT,        FAR, DISTANT        PERSON WITH        FAR, DISTANT SCENE
GO & STOP                           EARTH, SOIL
                                    BACKGROUND

OKU; YA, SHOP.

SHOP 屋 IS A COMPOSITE OF HUMAN BODY 尸 AND TO REACH, TO ARRIVE 至 JME 796. GOODS REACH OR ARRIVE 至 AT THE SHOP 屋 WHERE THE HUMAN BODY 尸 LAYS 一 (THEM HORIZONTALLY) SECRETLY AND PRIVATELY 厶 (AS IN A COCOON) ON THE SOIL OR EARTH 土 (FLOOR). THE HUMAN BODY 尸 (OF THE SHOPKEEPER) HAS A MOUTH OR HEAD 口 ABOVE A VERTICAL LINE / FOR THE BODY. THE BODY 尸 ALSO SUGGESTS A DOOR 戸 AS FOR THE SHOP 屋. SHOPKEEPER'S BODY 尸 STANDS IN DOOR 戸 WAY. HE SAYS, "COME IN!"

| RAD | STROKE | JME |
|---|---|---|
| 44 | 9 | 161 |

DOOR
JME 69

HUMAN BODY
(AS OF THE SHOPKEEPER OR CORPSE IN A COFFIN)

SUPER-IMPOSITION
(DOOR HAS PINS IN SOCKETS, NOT HINGES)

SHOP

TO REACH, ARRIVE
JME 796

CORPSE IN THE COFFIN (SUPER-IMPOSED)

ON, (WARM).

WARM 温 IS A COMPOSITE OF THE SUN 日 WARMING 温 WATER 氵 IN A DISH 皿. THE TWO VERTICAL LINES IN THE CENTRAL PART OF THE DISH 皿 INDICATE A TROUGH OR CONCAVITY || FOR HOLDING WATER 氵 ETC.

| RAD | STROKE | JME |
|---|---|---|
| 85 | 12 | 162 |

WATER
(COMPONENT)

WARM

SUN OVER DISH

PICTURE OF SUN WARMING WATER IN A DISH

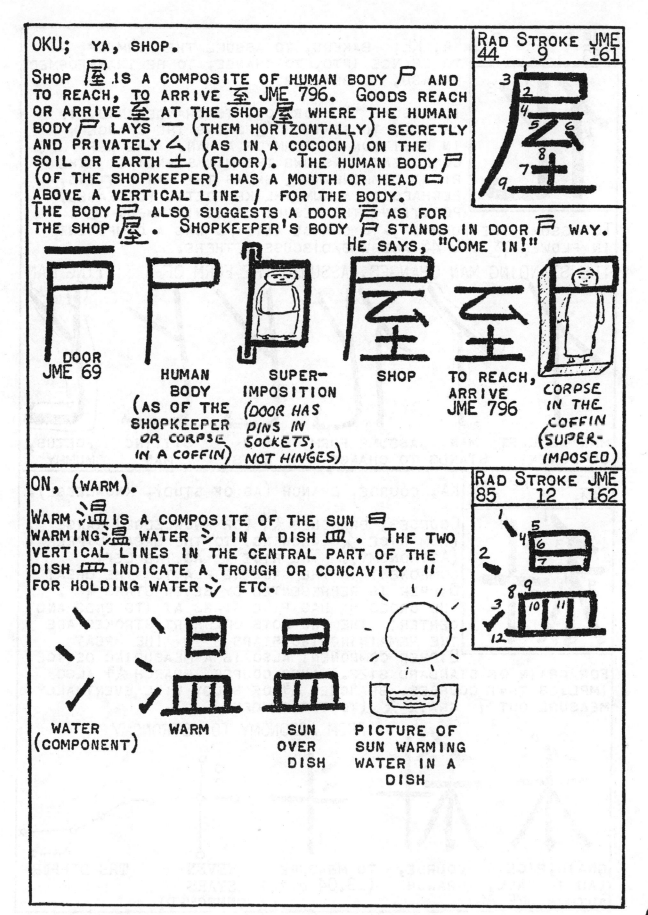

| JME 163 | Stroke 4 | Rad 21 |
|---|---|---|

化

KA, KE; BAKERU, TO ASSUME THE FORM OF, TO CHANGE INTO, TO CHANGE, TO BE TRANSFORMED; BAKASU, TO BEWITCH.

TO ASSUME THE FORM OF, TO CHANGE INTO, TO CHANGE, TO BEWITCH 化 SHOWS THE CHANGE IN POSITION OR FORM OF A MAN. THE LEFT COMPONENT イ SHOWS THE MAN STANDING; THE RIGHT COMPONENT ヒ SHOWS THE MAN SITTING, PERHAPS IN A MUMMY-LIKE FOETAL (DECEASED) POSITION, THE RESULT OF BEWITCHMENT ヒ.

TO ASSUME THE FORM OF, TO CHANGE INTO 化 WAS A COMPONENT IN FLOWER 花 JME 43 AND WAS DISCUSSED THERE.

THE STANDING MAN CHANGES, ASSUMES THE FORM OF A SITTING MAN

| MAN AS LEFT COMPONENT | MAN STANDS | ASSUME FORM, TO CHANGE | MAN SITS | SITTING MAN | FOETUS, MUMMY |
|---|---|---|---|---|---|

| JME 164 | Stroke 9 | Rad 115 |
|---|---|---|

科

KA, COURSE, BRANCH (AS OF STUDY, KNOWLEDGE).

COURSES, BRANCHES 科 (OF KNOWLEDGE) RANGE FROM RICE 禾 (GROWING) TO THE GREAT DIPPER 斗 (ASTRONOMY). THE RICE 禾 AS THE LEFT COMPONENT IS THE GROWING PLANT. THE GREAT DIPPER IS REPRESENTED BY SEVEN STARS 斗. THE CROSS 十 HAS FIVE STARS AT ITS ENDS AND CENTER; THE TWO DOTS OR SHORT STROKES ARE THE REMAINING TWO STARS ⠄. THE GREAT DIPPER COMPONENT ALSO IS A MEASURING DEVICE FOR GRAIN OF STANDARD SIZE. THUS COURSE, BRANCH 科 ALSO IMPLIES THAT COURSES, BRANCHES 科 OF STUDY WILL EVENTUALLY MEASURE OUT 斗 GRAIN 禾 (TO THE STUDENT).

FROM AGRONOMY TO ASTRONOMY

| GRAIN, RICE (AS IN FALL, AUTUMN JME 89) | COURSE, BRANCH | TO MEASURE (19.04 QTS.) | SEVEN STARS (CONNECTED) | THE DIPPER |
|---|---|---|---|---|

KA;  NI, LOAD, BURDEN.

LOAD, BURDEN 荷 IS REPRESENTED BY A MAN 亻
WHOSE MOUTH 口 IS EXCLAIMING 丁 IN THE
CUSTOMARY CADENCE (UNDER A LOAD OF
GRASS 艹 (STRAW). REVIEW WHAT, HOW MANY 何
JME 51. ORIENTAL FARMERS, PORTERS, ETC.
CHANTED WHILE CARRYING LOADS.

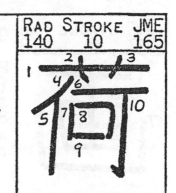

Rad | Stroke | JME
140 | 10 | 165

荷        亻        荷        可        艹

LOAD,
BURDEN

MAN AS
LEFT
COMPONENT

LOAD,
BURDEN

MOUTH
EXCLAIMING
IN CADENCE

GRASS
(STRAW,
HAY AS A
LOAD)

---

KA;  UTA, SONG;  UTAU, TO SING.

SONG, TO SING 歌 IS A COMPOSITE OF A MOUTH 口
EXCLAIMING 丁 IN CADENCE DOUBLED 哥 (REVIEW
LOAD, BURDEN 荷 JME 165), AND A MAN, PERSON
INHALING INTO A COVER 欠 (LUNGS). THUS THE
MAN 人 INHALES INTO THE COVER, WRAPPER 勹
(LUNGS) SO HIS MOUTH 口 CAN EXCLAIM 丁 IN
SONG 歌. THE COMPONENT MAN 人 MAY HAVE
BEEN ENTER 入 JME 125 FOR THE AIR ENTERING 入
THE MAN'S 人 LUNGS 勹 SINCE THE COMPONENT 入
ENTER IS SOMETIMES WRITTEN MAN 人 AS AN ERROR OR AMBIGUITY.
OR THE MAN 人 MAY HAVE A WRAPPER, COVER 勹 AS HE WALKS AND
SINGS 歌.

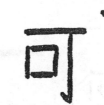

Rad | Stroke | JME
76 | 14 | 166

 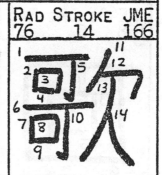

 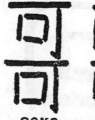   

WHAT?,
HOW MANY?
JME 51

SONG,
ELDER
BROTHER

SONG,
TO SING

LACK, WANT
(AIR ENTERS
LUNGS FOR
SINGING)

LUNGS
WANT,
LACK
AIR FOR
SINGING

AS
HE
SINGS,
MAN WALKS
UNDER COVER

| JME 167 | Stroke 8 | Rad 102 |
|---|---|---|

GA, (PICTURE); KAKU, STROKE (OF A KANJI).

PICTURE 画 IS A COMPOSITE OF A FIELD 田 (LANDSCAPE) FRAMED ⊔ (BY THE SURROUNDING STROKES) AND HUNG | (VERTICAL STROKE). STROKES 画 CREATE A PICTURE 画 (SOMETIMES A KANJI) WHICH MAY BE REGARDED AS QUARTERED 田, FRAMED ⊔ , AND HUNG | .

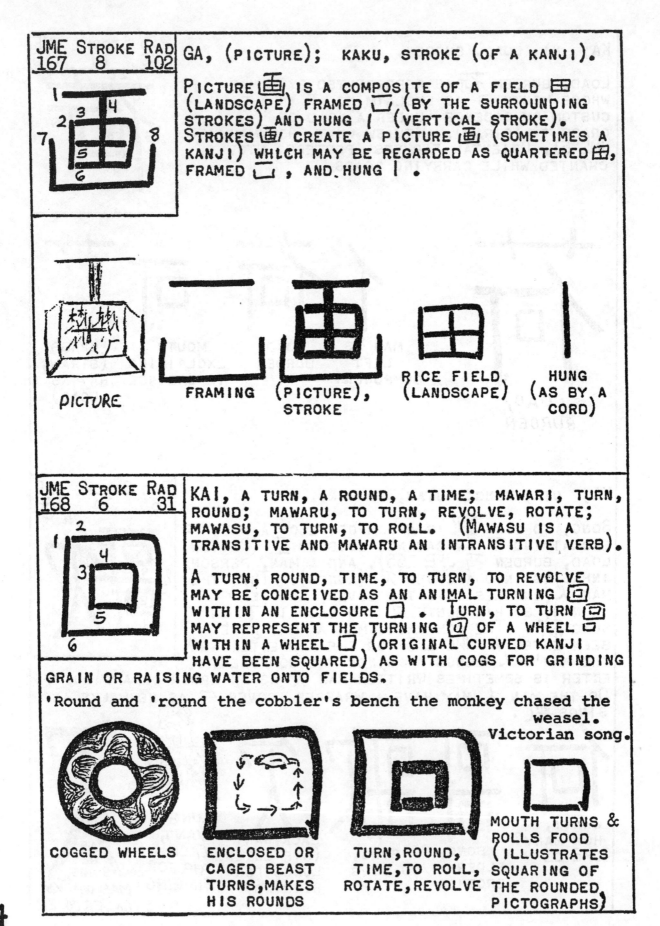

PICTURE        FRAMING (PICTURE), STROKE        RICE FIELD (LANDSCAPE)        HUNG (AS BY A CORD)

| JME 168 | Stroke 6 | Rad 31 |
|---|---|---|

KAI, A TURN, A ROUND, A TIME; MAWARI, TURN, ROUND; MAWARU, TO TURN, REVOLVE, ROTATE; MAWASU, TO TURN, TO ROLL. (MAWASU IS A TRANSITIVE AND MAWARU AN INTRANSITIVE VERB).

A TURN, ROUND, TIME, TO TURN, TO REVOLVE MAY BE CONCEIVED AS AN ANIMAL TURNING 回 WITHIN AN ENCLOSURE ☐ . TURN, TO TURN 回 MAY REPRESENT THE TURNING 回 OF A WHEEL ☐ WITHIN A WHEEL ☐ , (ORIGINAL CURVED KANJI HAVE BEEN SQUARED) AS WITH COGS FOR GRINDING GRAIN OR RAISING WATER ONTO FIELDS.

'Round and 'round the cobbler's bench the monkey chased the weasel.
Victorian song.

COGGED WHEELS        ENCLOSED OR CAGED BEAST TURNS, MAKES HIS ROUNDS        TURN, ROUND, TIME, TO ROLL, ROTATE, REVOLVE        MOUTH TURNS & ROLLS FOOD (ILLUSTRATES SQUARING OF THE ROUNDED PICTOGRAPHS)

KAI, (GAI), SEA SHELL.

THE SEA SHELL 貝 IS AN EYE 目 (WHICH IT OFTEN RESEMBLES) MOUNTED ON SHORT LEGS (TO SHOW MOBILITY).

AS A KANJI COMPONENT, SEA SHELL 貝 MEANS MONEY. SHELLS 貝, ESPECIALLY COWRIE, WERE WIDELY USED IN THE ANCIENT WORLD AS A MEDIUM OF EXCHANGE. WE STILL SPEAK OF "SHELLING OUT" MONEY AND OF "CLAMS" AS UNITS OF VALUE.

| Rad | Stroke | JME |
|-----|--------|-----|
| 154 | 7 | 169 |

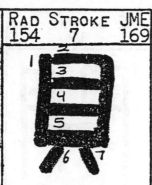

LITTLE LEGS, PERHAPS OF CRAB TENANT, CIRCULATE THE COWRIE

EAR

EAR
JME 26
("CONCHA"
MEANS THE
EXTERNAL EAR)

EYE
JME 25

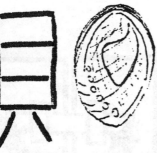
SEA SHELL
(THE EAR-
SHELL IS A
FLATTENED
UNIVALVE SHELL)

ABALONE
IS AN
EAR-SHELL
(GENUS
HALIOTIS)

KAI, (WORLD).

WORLD 界 IS A FIELD 田 OR EXPANSE (AS MEASURED OUT OR WITH LATITUDE AND LONGITUDE LINES) WHICH SEPARATE 八 PEOPLE ||.
WORLD 界 ALSO SUGGESTS THE FIELD 田 (OF THE WORLD) BALANCED ACCORDING TO ANCIENT LEGEND ON A MOUNTAIN PEAK OR A GREAT TORTOISE 介.
(Tectonic plates contain the earth just as the hexagonal plates of the carapace and rectangular plates of the plastron contain the tortoise.)

| Rad | Stroke | JME |
|-----|--------|-----|
| 102 | 9 | 170 |

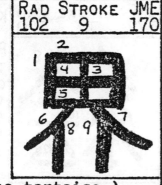

RICE FIELD
(MAY ALSO
REPRESENT
DIAGRAMMED
TORTOISE
SHELL OR
CARAPACE)

WORLD

MAY
REPRESENT A
GREAT TOR-
TOISE OR A
MOUNTAIN

FIELD OR EXPANSE OF THE
WORLD BALANCED ON THE
GREAT TORTOISE OR THE
MOUNTAIN

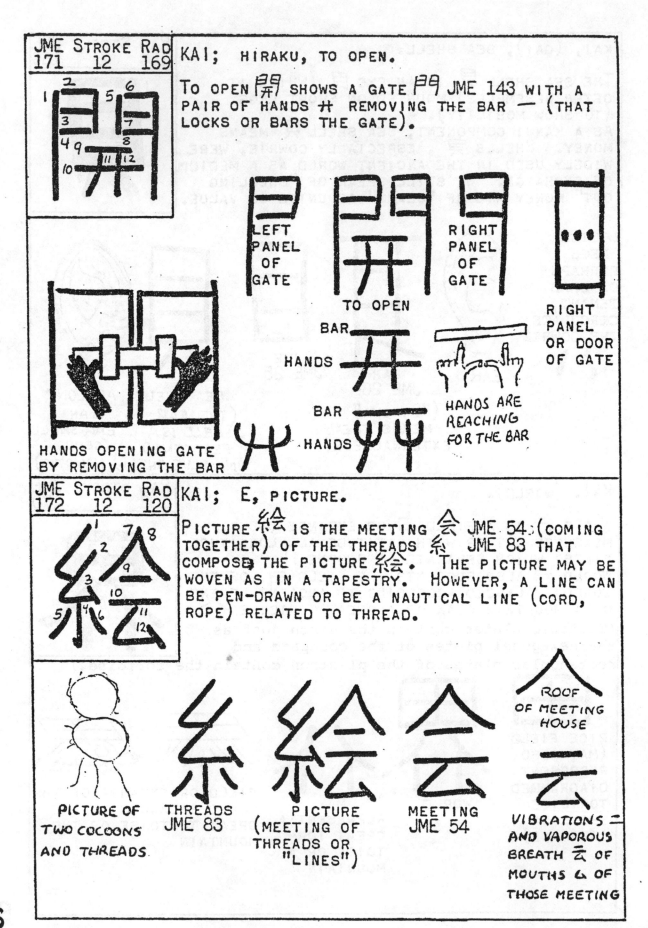

| JME 171 | Stroke 12 | Rad 169 |
|---|---|---|

KAI; HIRAKU, TO OPEN.

TO OPEN 開 SHOWS A GATE 門 JME 143 WITH A PAIR OF HANDS 廾 REMOVING THE BAR 一 (THAT LOCKS OR BARS THE GATE).

LEFT PANEL OF GATE

TO OPEN

RIGHT PANEL OF GATE

RIGHT PANEL OR DOOR OF GATE

BAR

HANDS

BAR

HANDS

HANDS ARE REACHING FOR THE BAR

HANDS OPENING GATE BY REMOVING THE BAR

| JME 172 | Stroke 12 | Rad 120 |
|---|---|---|

KAI; E, PICTURE.

PICTURE 絵 IS THE MEETING 会 JME 54 (COMING TOGETHER) OF THE THREADS 糸 JME 83 THAT COMPOSE THE PICTURE 絵. THE PICTURE MAY BE WOVEN AS IN A TAPESTRY. HOWEVER, A LINE CAN BE PEN-DRAWN OR BE A NAUTICAL LINE (CORD, ROPE) RELATED TO THREAD.

PICTURE OF TWO COCOONS AND THREADS

THREADS JME 83

PICTURE (MEETING OF THREADS OR "LINES")

MEETING JME 54

ROOF OF MEETING HOUSE

VIBRATIONS = AND VAPOROUS BREATH 云 OF MOUTHS 厶 OF THOSE MEETING

KAKU, ANGLE; TSUNO, HORN (ANIMAL HORN).

ANGLE, HORN 角 IS A PICTOGRAPH OF A STRIATED 土 HORN 角 (LIKE AN ENCLOSURE: 冂 EMPTY INSIDE) WITH A MAN BENDING OVER 勹 (AS TO INSPECT OR DEHORN). THE BASE OF THE HORN 角 IS LEFT OPEN TO SUGGEST THE HORN IS HOLLOW (AND USED FOR POURING, AS A CONTAINER AND DRINKING-HORN). NOTE THE SIMILARITY OF THE BODY OF THE HORN 用 TO THE BODY OF THE FISH 田 JME 190 WHOSE SCALES ARE RELATED TO HORN. A MAN IS ALSO BENDING OVER 勹 THE FISH 魚 AND OVER 勹 THE SNAKE COMPONENT 巴 IN COLOR 色 JME 94. A HORN IS USUALLY IN AN ANGLED POSITION: THUS ALSO MEANS ANGLE 角. NOTE THE RELATIONSHIP OF CORNER (THE MEETING PLACE OF ANGLES) AND HORN.

| Rad | Stroke | JME |
|-----|--------|-----|
| 148 | 7 | 173 |

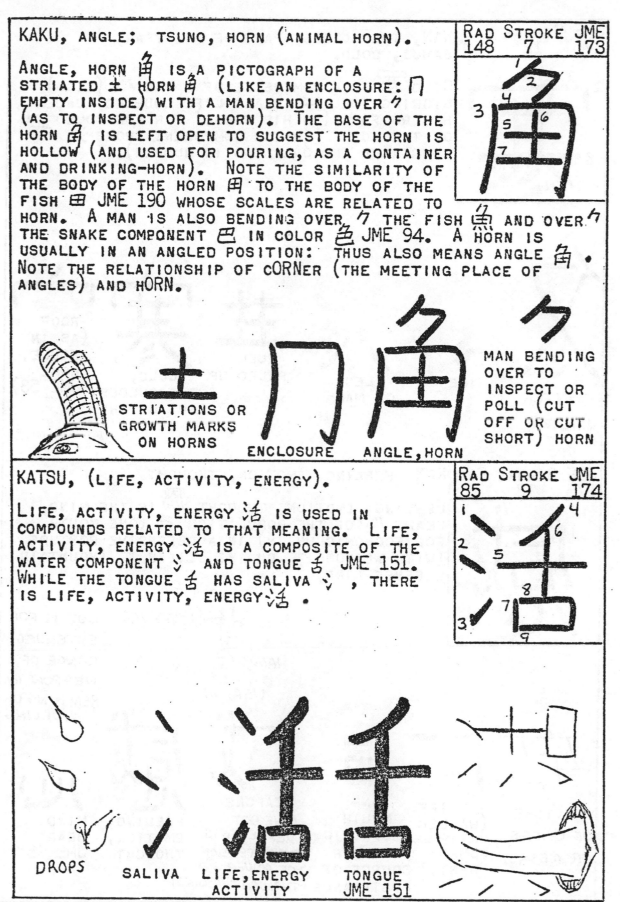

STRIATIONS OR GROWTH MARKS ON HORNS

ENCLOSURE    ANGLE, HORN

MAN BENDING OVER TO INSPECT OR POLL (CUT OFF OR CUT SHORT) HORN

KATSU, (LIFE, ACTIVITY, ENERGY).

LIFE, ACTIVITY, ENERGY 活 IS USED IN COMPOUNDS RELATED TO THAT MEANING. LIFE, ACTIVITY, ENERGY 活 IS A COMPOSITE OF THE WATER COMPONENT 氵 AND TONGUE 舌 JME 151. WHILE THE TONGUE 舌 HAS SALIVA 氵, THERE IS LIFE, ACTIVITY, ENERGY 活.

| Rad | Stroke | JME |
|-----|--------|-----|
| 85 | 9 | 174 |

DROPS    SALIVA    LIFE, ENERGY ACTIVITY    TONGUE JME 151

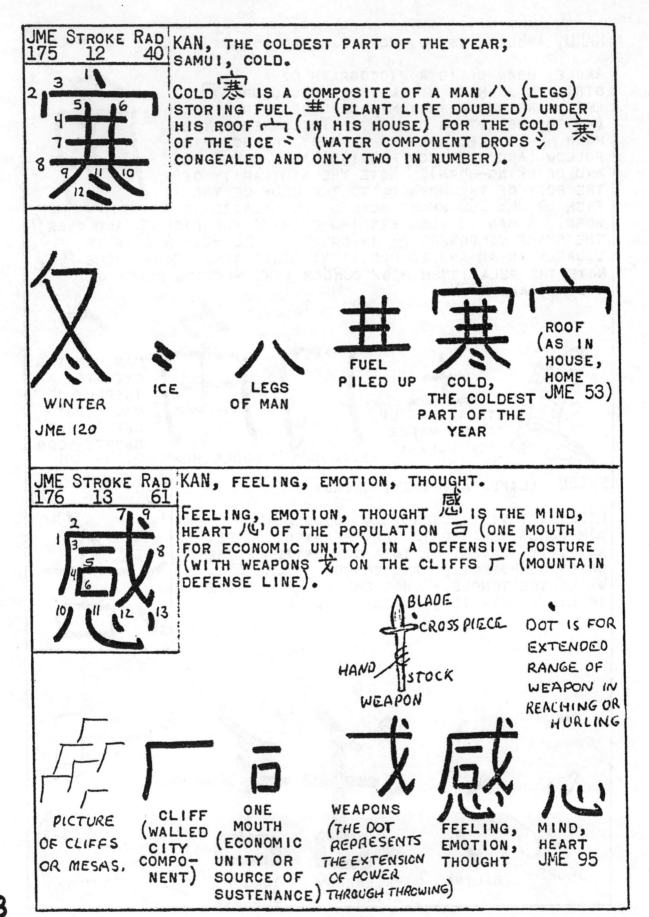

| JME 175 | Stroke 12 | Rad 40 |
|---|---|---|

KAN, THE COLDEST PART OF THE YEAR; SAMUI, COLD.

COLD 寒 IS A COMPOSITE OF A MAN 八 (LEGS) STORING FUEL 丰 (PLANT LIFE DOUBLED) UNDER HIS ROOF 宀 (IN HIS HOUSE) FOR THE COLD 寒 OF THE ICE 冫 (WATER COMPONENT DROPS 氵 CONGEALED AND ONLY TWO IN NUMBER).

冬
WINTER
JME 120

冫
ICE

八
LEGS OF MAN

丰
FUEL PILED UP

寒
COLD, THE COLDEST PART OF THE YEAR

宀
ROOF (AS IN HOUSE, HOME JME 53)

| JME 176 | Stroke 13 | Rad 61 |
|---|---|---|

KAN, FEELING, EMOTION, THOUGHT.

FEELING, EMOTION, THOUGHT 感 IS THE MIND, HEART 心 OF THE POPULATION 口 (ONE MOUTH FOR ECONOMIC UNITY) IN A DEFENSIVE POSTURE (WITH WEAPONS 戈 ON THE CLIFFS 厂 (MOUNTAIN DEFENSE LINE).

BLADE
CROSS PIECE
HAND
STOCK
WEAPON

DOT IS FOR EXTENDED RANGE OF WEAPON IN REACHING OR HURLING

PICTURE OF CLIFFS OR MESAS.

厂
CLIFF (WALLED CITY COMPONENT)

口
ONE MOUTH (ECONOMIC UNITY OR SOURCE OF SUSTENANCE)

戈
WEAPONS (THE DOT REPRESENTS THE EXTENSION OF POWER THROUGH THROWING)

感
FEELING, EMOTION, THOUGHT

心
MIND, HEART JME 95

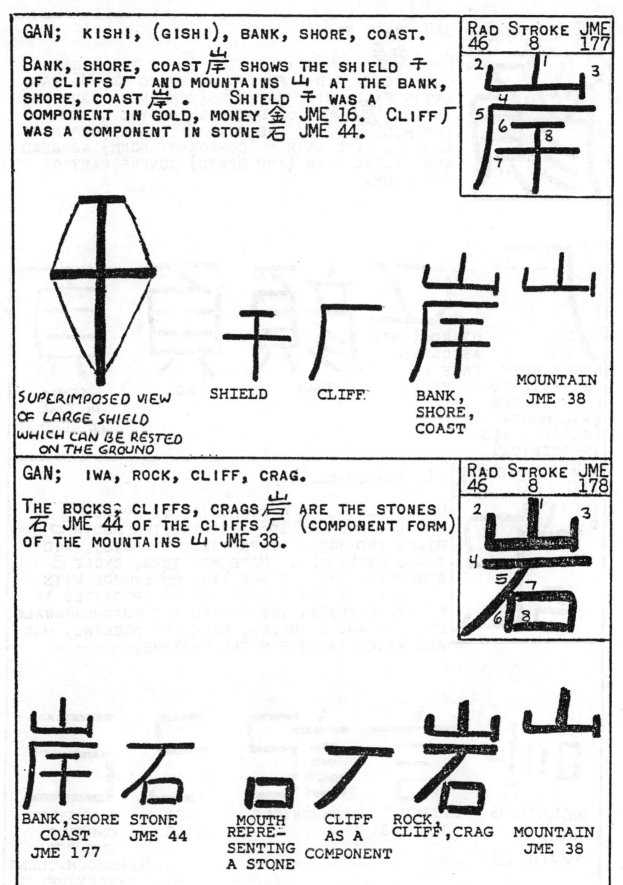

GAN; KISHI, (GISHI), BANK, SHORE, COAST.

BANK, SHORE, COAST 岸 SHOWS THE SHIELD 干
OF CLIFFS 厂 AND MOUNTAINS 山 AT THE BANK,
SHORE, COAST 岸.　SHIELD 干 WAS A
COMPONENT IN GOLD, MONEY 金 JME 16.　CLIFF 厂
WAS A COMPONENT IN STONE 石 JME 44.

RAD 46　STROKE 8　JME 177

SUPERIMPOSED VIEW
OF LARGE SHIELD
WHICH CAN BE RESTED
ON THE GROUND

SHIELD

CLIFF

BANK,
SHORE,
COAST

MOUNTAIN
JME 38

GAN; IWA, ROCK, CLIFF, CRAG.

THE ROCKS, CLIFFS, CRAGS 岩 ARE THE STONES
石 JME 44 OF THE CLIFFS 厂 (COMPONENT FORM)
OF THE MOUNTAINS 山 JME 38.

RAD 46　STROKE 8　JME 178

BANK, SHORE
COAST
JME 177

STONE
JME 44

MOUTH
REPRE-
SENTING
A STONE

CLIFF
AS A
COMPONENT

ROCK,
CLIFF, CRAG

MOUNTAIN
JME 38

| JME 179 | Stroke 18 | Rad 181 |
|---|---|---|

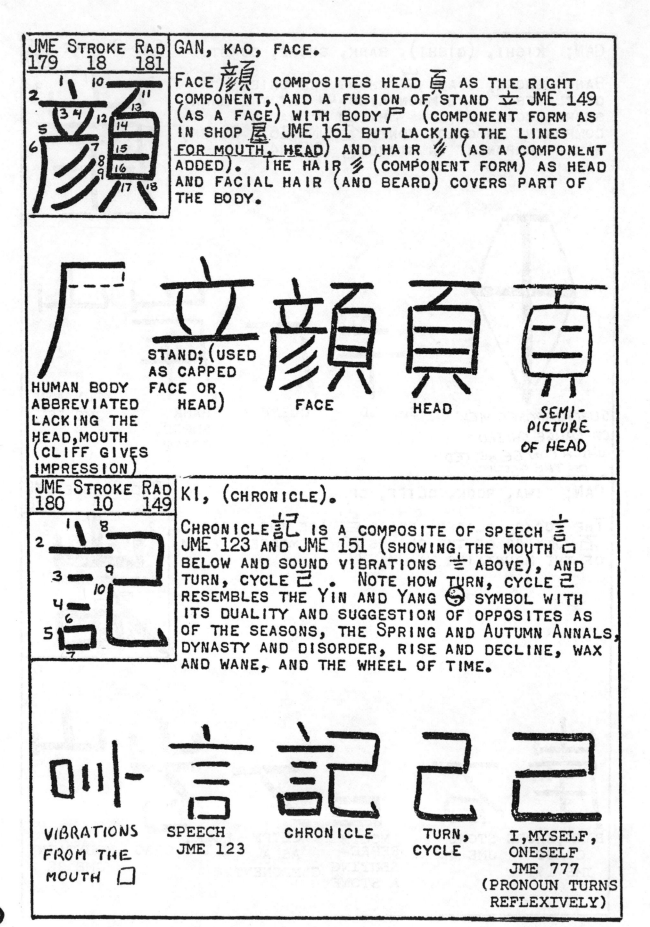

**GAN, KAO, FACE.**

FACE 顔 COMPOSITES HEAD 頁 AS THE RIGHT COMPONENT, AND A FUSION OF STAND 立 JME 149 (AS A FACE) WITH BODY 尸 (COMPONENT FORM AS IN SHOP 屋 JME 161 BUT LACKING THE LINES FOR MOUTH, HEAD) AND HAIR 彡 (AS A COMPONENT ADDED). THE HAIR 彡 (COMPONENT FORM) AS HEAD AND FACIAL HAIR (AND BEARD) COVERS PART OF THE BODY.

**HUMAN BODY ABBREVIATED LACKING THE HEAD, MOUTH (CLIFF GIVES IMPRESSION)**

**STAND; (USED AS CAPPED FACE OR HEAD)**

**FACE**

**HEAD**

**SEMI-PICTURE OF HEAD**

| JME 180 | Stroke 10 | Rad 149 |
|---|---|---|

**KI, (CHRONICLE).**

CHRONICLE 記 IS A COMPOSITE OF SPEECH 言 JME 123 AND JME 151 (SHOWING THE MOUTH 口 BELOW AND SOUND VIBRATIONS 三 ABOVE), AND TURN, CYCLE 己. NOTE HOW TURN, CYCLE 己 RESEMBLES THE YIN AND YANG ☯ SYMBOL WITH ITS DUALITY AND SUGGESTION OF OPPOSITES AS OF THE SEASONS, THE SPRING AND AUTUMN ANNALS, DYNASTY AND DISORDER, RISE AND DECLINE, WAX AND WANE, AND THE WHEEL OF TIME.

**VIBRATIONS FROM THE MOUTH 口**

**SPEECH JME 123**

**CHRONICLE**

**TURN, CYCLE**

**I, MYSELF, ONESELF JME 777 (PRONOUN TURNS REFLEXIVELY)**

KI; OKIRU, TO GET UP, TO RISE; OKOSU, TO RAISE, SET UPRIGHT, (TRANSITIVE VERB).

TO GET UP, TO RISE, TO RAISE, TO SET UPRIGHT 起 COMPOSITES TO RUN 走 JME 105 AS THE LEFT COMPONENT, AND TURN, CYCLE 己 AS THE RIGHT COMPONENT. ONE GETS UP, RISES, RAISES, SETS UPRIGHT 起 ON TURNING 己 (UNCURLING) AND RUNNING 走.

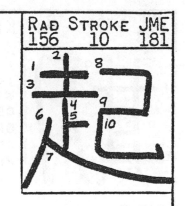

| Rad | Stroke | JME |
|-----|--------|-----|
| 156 | 10 | 181 |

土

EARTH, SOIL
JME 17

足

FOOT, LEG
JME 29

走

TO RUN
JME 105

起

TO GET UP, TO RAISE, TO RISE, SET UPRIGHT

己

TURN, CYCLE, AS COMPONENT I, MYSELF, ONESELF
JME 777

---

KI; KAERU, TO RETURN, TO COME BACK, TO LEAVE.

TO RETURN, TO COME BACK, TO LEAVE 帰 IS A COMPOSITE OF A DUSTING BRUSH 帚 COMPOSED OF A HAND 彐 HOLDING A COVERED 冖 CLOTH 巾 AS THE RIGHT COMPONENT; AND TWO VERTICAL STROKES 刂 AS AN ABBREVIATION OF THE EARLIER LEFT COMPONENT COMPOSED OF EARTH LAYERS 𠂤 (NOTE THE TWO STORY EFFECT) AND TO STOP 止 JME 220. THE DUSTING BRUSH OR FEATHER DUSTER REPRESENTS THE WIFE FOR WHOM IT IS TRADITIONAL TO MAKE STOPS 止 OR VISITS AT HER PARENTAL HOME 𠂤 TO WHICH SHE 帚 (THE DUSTING BRUSH) RETURNS, COMES BACK 帰.

| Rad | Stroke | JME |
|-----|--------|-----|
| 58 | 10 | 182 |

止

TO STOP

𣥂

BLDG. & STOP

帰

TO RETURN, COME BACK, LEAVE

帚

HAND & DUSTER

HAND GRIPS DUSTER

183-184

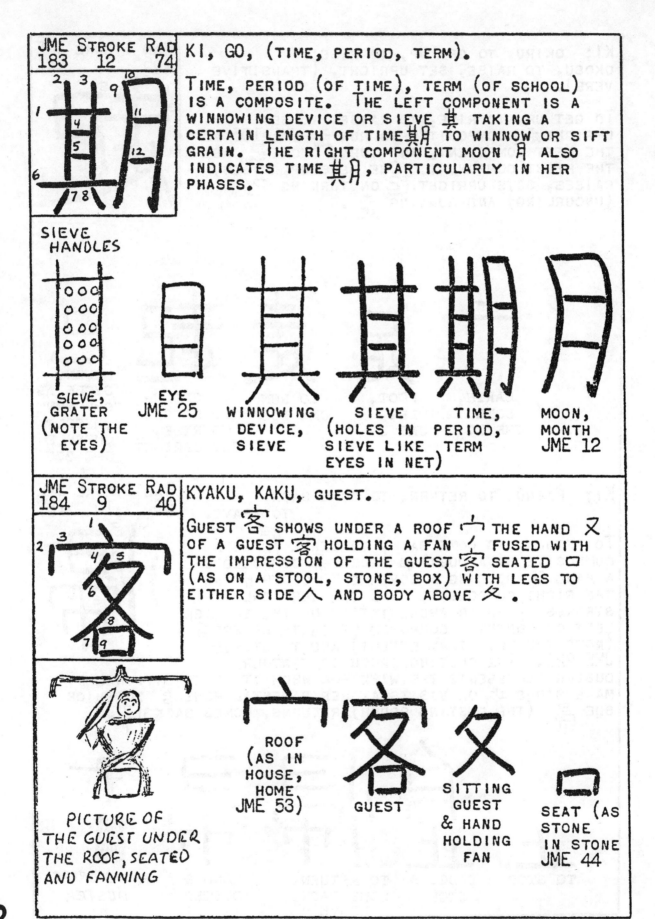

| JME | Stroke | Rad |
|-----|--------|-----|
| 183 | 12 | 74 |

KI, GO, (TIME, PERIOD, TERM).

TIME, PERIOD (OF TIME), TERM (OF SCHOOL) IS A COMPOSITE. THE LEFT COMPONENT IS A WINNOWING DEVICE OR SIEVE 其 TAKING A CERTAIN LENGTH OF TIME 期 TO WINNOW OR SIFT GRAIN. THE RIGHT COMPONENT MOON 月 ALSO INDICATES TIME 其月, PARTICULARLY IN HER PHASES.

SIEVE HANDLES

SIEVE, GRATER (NOTE THE EYES)

EYE JME 25

WINNOWING DEVICE, SIEVE

SIEVE (HOLES IN SIEVE LIKE EYES IN NET)

TIME, PERIOD, TERM

MOON, MONTH JME 12

| JME | Stroke | Rad |
|-----|--------|-----|
| 184 | 9 | 40 |

KYAKU, KAKU, GUEST.

GUEST 客 SHOWS UNDER A ROOF 宀 THE HAND 又 OF A GUEST 客 HOLDING A FAN 𠂉 FUSED WITH THE IMPRESSION OF THE GUEST 客 SEATED 口 (AS ON A STOOL, STONE, BOX) WITH LEGS TO EITHER SIDE 𠆢 AND BODY ABOVE 夂.

PICTURE OF THE GUEST UNDER THE ROOF, SEATED AND FANNING

ROOF (AS IN HOUSE, HOME JME 53)

GUEST

SITTING GUEST & HAND HOLDING FAN

SEAT (AS STONE IN STONE JME 44

KYŪ, (STUDY).

STUDY 究 GIVES THE IMPRESSION OF SOMETHING "TUMBLED" OR POLISHED IN A HOLE 穴 UNTIL IT IS NINE- 九 SIDED (NINE 九 JME 9) OR NEARLY ROUND. IN THE KANJI AS IN ENGLISH THERE IS THE ANALOGY OF STUDY 究 POLISHING A PERSON AND ROUNDING OFF HIS ROUGH CORNERS JUST AS STONES ARE TUMBLED IN A HOLE (UNDER WATER).

| RAD | STROKE | JME |
|-----|--------|-----|
| 116 | 7 | 185 |

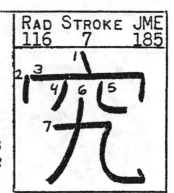

POLISHED EGGHEAD STUDYING IN HIS DEN OR HOLE

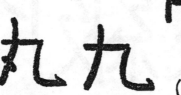

ROUND, SPHERICAL (DOTTED EXTENSION OF NINE)

NINE (NINE-SIDED IS NEARLY ROUND)

究 (STUDY)

HOLE (AS IN SKY JME 65

ROOF (AS IN HOUSE, HOME JME 53

---

KYŪ; ISOGU, TO HURRY.

TO HURRY 急 IS A BRUSH OR HAND ヨ SWEEPING ACROSS OR CLUTCHING THE HEART, MIND 心 OF A MAN BENDING OVER ク TO CATCH SOMETHING. THE MAN BENDING OVER ク AS TO CATCH SOMETHING IS A COMPONENT IN FISH 魚 JME 190 AND HORN, ANGLE 角 JME 173 AND THE SNAKE COMPONENT IN COLOR 色 JME 94. A MAN BENDING OVER ク TO CATCH SOMETHING IS IN A HURRY 急 AND IT IS AS THOUGH A BRUSH OR HAND ヨ SWEPT ACROSS HIS HEART, MIND 心.

| RAD | STROKE | JME |
|-----|--------|-----|
| 61 | 9 | 186 |

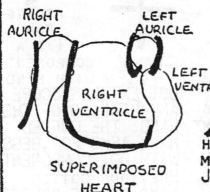

RIGHT AURICLE

LEFT AURICLE

LEFT VENTRICLE

RIGHT VENTRICLE

SUPERIMPOSED HEART

心 HEART, MIND JME 95

急 TO HURRY

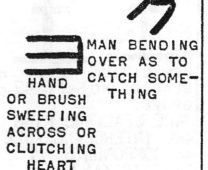

ヨ HAND OR BRUSH SWEEPING ACROSS OR CLUTCHING HEART

ク MAN BENDING OVER AS TO CATCH SOMETHING

| JME 187 | Stroke 9 | Rad 120 |
|---|---|---|

KYŪ, CLASS, GRADE, RANK.

CLASS, GRADE, RANK 級 IS A COMPOSITE OF THREAD 糸 JME 83 ON THE LEFT AND A HAND 又 GRASPING A BODY ア ON THE RIGHT. THE COMPOSITE REFERS TO GRASPING 又 THE BODY ア OF THE THREAD 糸, STRANDS OF THREAD BEING TWISTED FOR DIFFERENT CLASS, GRADE, RANK 級. THE HAND 又 PUTS SILK THREADS 糸 (CLOTHES) ON THE BODY, CORPSES ア OF CERTAIN RANK, CLASS, GRADE 級.

CORPSE IN A COFFIN (SUPER-IMPOSITION)

STORE-KEEPER BODY (SUPER-IMPOSI-TION) JME 161

THREAD JME 83

CLASS, GRADE, RANK

BODY GRADES OF THREAD AS ANALOGOUS TO HUMAN BODY SHOWN

HAND

| JME 188 | Stroke 11 | Rad 96 |
|---|---|---|

KYŪ, GLOBE, SPHERE, BALL, BULB.

GLOBE, SPHERE, BULB, BALL 球 IS A COMPOSITE OF JEWEL, ROUND OBJECT 玉 JME 64 (WITHOUT THE DOT) ON THE LEFT AND A HAND 十 (ONCE ) ASKING FOR 丬 (DOT) WATER 氺 ON THE RIGHT, JUST AS ONE ASKS FOR A BALL 球 ETC. IN PRIMITIVE SURROUNDINGS, IT IS WATER 氺 THAT IS ASKED FOR 丬 WITH THE OUTSTRETCHED HAND 十. IN ANCIENT TIMES, THE KINGS 王 WHO CONTROLED IRRIGATION AND WATER- 氺 ING RIGHTS WERE ASKED FOR 丬 WATER 氺.

JEWEL, JADE SEAL, ROUND OBJECT
JADE SEAL AND KING ARE INTERCHANGEABLE AS COMPONENTS IN CERTAIN KANJI

KING JME 49

GLOBE, BALL, SPHERE, BULB

WATER AS COMPONENT
WATER JME 14 RESEMBLES COMPONENT FORM ABOVE

丬 HAND ASKING FOR (AS A COMPONENT WITH HAND)
DOT EXTENDS SCOPE AND MEANING OF THE HAND: THE CUPPED HAND ASKS FOR, BEGS WITH DOT COMPONENT. PREVIOUS DOTTED HAND BECAME PULSE 丬 IN VILLAGE 村 JME 107

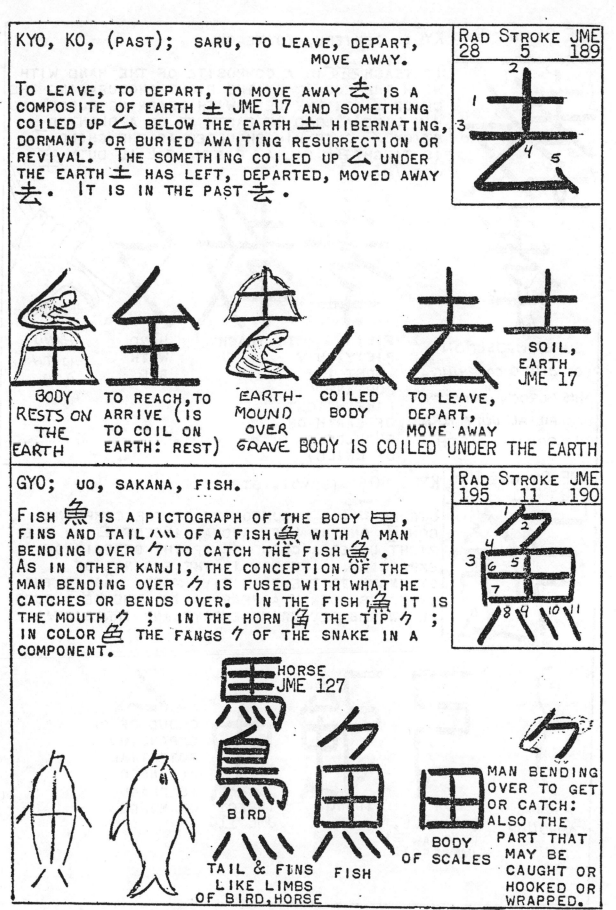

KYO, KO, (PAST);  SARU, TO LEAVE, DEPART, MOVE AWAY.

TO LEAVE, TO DEPART, TO MOVE AWAY 去 IS A COMPOSITE OF EARTH 土 JME 17 AND SOMETHING COILED UP ム BELOW THE EARTH 土 HIBERNATING, DORMANT, OR BURIED AWAITING RESURRECTION OR REVIVAL. THE SOMETHING COILED UP ム UNDER THE EARTH 土 HAS LEFT, DEPARTED, MOVED AWAY 去. IT IS IN THE PAST 去.

| Rad | Stroke | JME |
|---|---|---|
| 28 | 5 | 189 |

BODY RESTS ON THE EARTH

TO REACH, TO ARRIVE (IS TO COIL ON EARTH: REST)

EARTH-MOUND OVER GRAVE

COILED BODY

TO LEAVE, DEPART, MOVE AWAY BODY IS COILED UNDER THE EARTH

SOIL, EARTH JME 17

GYO;  UO, SAKANA, FISH.

FISH 魚 IS A PICTOGRAPH OF THE BODY 田, FINS AND TAIL 灬 OF A FISH 魚 WITH A MAN BENDING OVER ク TO CATCH THE FISH 魚. AS IN OTHER KANJI, THE CONCEPTION OF THE MAN BENDING OVER ク IS FUSED WITH WHAT HE CATCHES OR BENDS OVER.  IN THE FISH 魚 IT IS THE MOUTH ク ;  IN THE HORN 角 THE TIP ク ; IN COLOR 色 THE FANGS ク OF THE SNAKE IN A COMPONENT.

| Rad | Stroke | JME |
|---|---|---|
| 195 | 11 | 190 |

HORSE JME 127

BIRD

TAIL & FINS LIKE LIMBS OF BIRD, HORSE

FISH

BODY OF SCALES

MAN BENDING OVER TO GET OR CATCH: ALSO THE PART THAT MAY BE CAUGHT OR HOOKED OR WRAPPED.

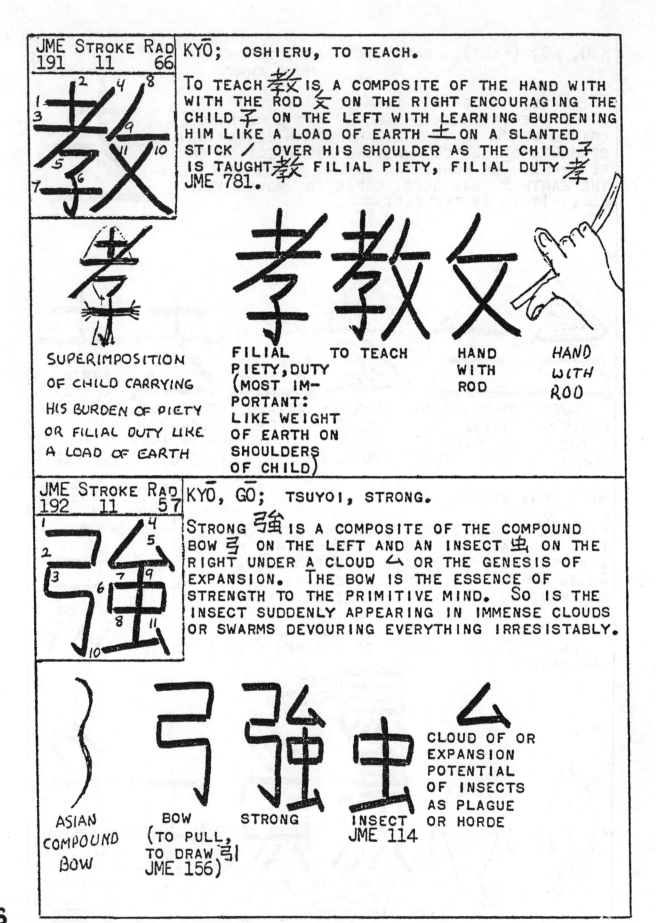

| JME 191 | Stroke 11 | Rad 66 |
|---|---|---|

KYŌ; OSHIERU, TO TEACH.

TO TEACH 教 IS A COMPOSITE OF THE HAND WITH WITH THE ROD 攵 ON THE RIGHT ENCOURAGING THE CHILD 子 ON THE LEFT WITH LEARNING BURDENING HIM LIKE A LOAD OF EARTH 土 ON A SLANTED STICK ノ OVER HIS SHOULDER AS THE CHILD 子 IS TAUGHT 教 FILIAL PIETY, FILIAL DUTY 孝 JME 781.

SUPERIMPOSITION OF CHILD CARRYING HIS BURDEN OF PIETY OR FILIAL DUTY LIKE A LOAD OF EARTH

FILIAL PIETY, DUTY (MOST IMPORTANT: LIKE WEIGHT OF EARTH ON SHOULDERS OF CHILD)

TO TEACH

HAND WITH ROD

HAND WITH ROD

| JME 192 | Stroke 11 | Rad 57 |
|---|---|---|

KYŌ, GŌ; TSUYOI, STRONG.

STRONG 強 IS A COMPOSITE OF THE COMPOUND BOW 弓 ON THE LEFT AND AN INSECT 虫 ON THE RIGHT UNDER A CLOUD ム OR THE GENESIS OF EXPANSION. THE BOW IS THE ESSENCE OF STRENGTH TO THE PRIMITIVE MIND. SO IS THE INSECT SUDDENLY APPEARING IN IMMENSE CLOUDS OR SWARMS DEVOURING EVERYTHING IRRESISTABLY.

ASIAN COMPOUND BOW

BOW (TO PULL, TO DRAW 引 JME 156)

STRONG

INSECT JME 114

CLOUD OF OR EXPANSION POTENTIAL OF INSECTS AS PLAGUE OR HORDE

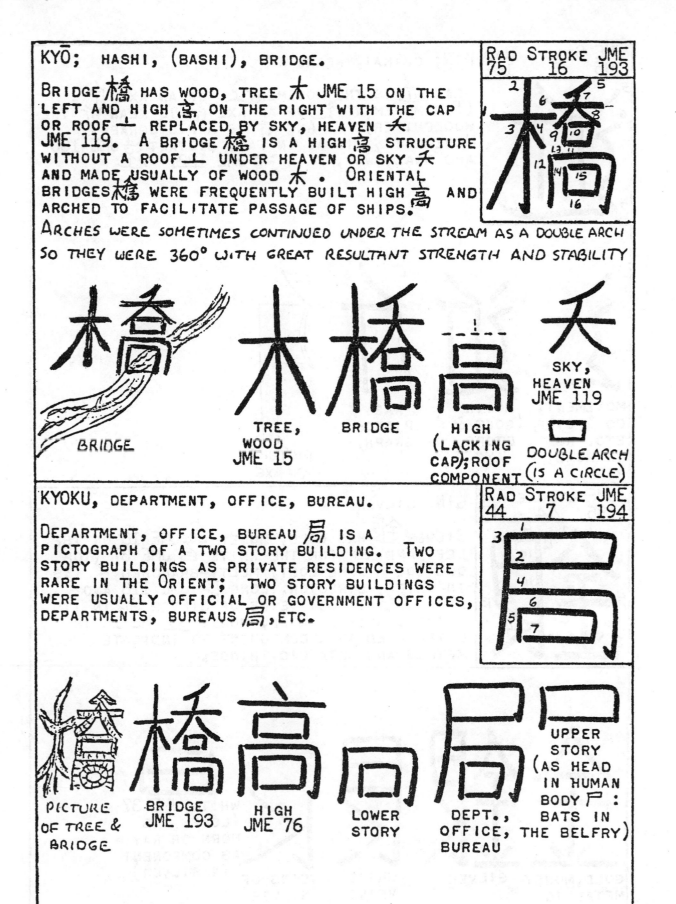

KYŌ; HASHI, (BASHI), BRIDGE.

| RAD | STROKE | JME |
|-----|--------|-----|
| 75  | 16     | 193 |

BRIDGE 橋 HAS WOOD, TREE 木 JME 15 ON THE LEFT AND HIGH 高 ON THE RIGHT WITH THE CAP OR ROOF 亠 REPLACED BY SKY, HEAVEN 夭 JME 119. A BRIDGE 橋 IS A HIGH 高 STRUCTURE WITHOUT A ROOF 亠 UNDER HEAVEN OR SKY 夭 AND MADE USUALLY OF WOOD 木. ORIENTAL BRIDGES 橋 WERE FREQUENTLY BUILT HIGH 高 AND ARCHED TO FACILITATE PASSAGE OF SHIPS.

ARCHES WERE SOMETIMES CONTINUED UNDER THE STREAM AS A DOUBLE ARCH SO THEY WERE 360° WITH GREAT RESULTANT STRENGTH AND STABILITY

BRIDGE

TREE, WOOD JME 15

BRIDGE

HIGH (LACKING CAP; ROOF COMPONENT

SKY, HEAVEN JME 119

DOUBLE ARCH (IS A CIRCLE)

KYOKU, DEPARTMENT, OFFICE, BUREAU.

| RAD | STROKE | JME |
|-----|--------|-----|
| 44  | 7      | 194 |

DEPARTMENT, OFFICE, BUREAU 局 IS A PICTOGRAPH OF A TWO STORY BUILDING. TWO STORY BUILDINGS AS PRIVATE RESIDENCES WERE RARE IN THE ORIENT; TWO STORY BUILDINGS WERE USUALLY OFFICIAL OR GOVERNMENT OFFICES, DEPARTMENTS, BUREAUS 局, ETC.

PICTURE OF TREE & BRIDGE

BRIDGE JME 193

HIGH JME 76

LOWER STORY

DEPT., OFFICE, BUREAU

UPPER STORY (AS HEAD IN HUMAN BODY 尸: BATS IN THE BELFRY)

| JME 195 | Stroke 7 | Rad 162 |
|---------|----------|---------|

KIN; CHIKAI, NEAR.

NEAR 近 IS THE MOVEMENT 辶 OF AN AXE 斤.
(THE MOVEMENT 辶 OF AN AXE 斤 IS NEAR 近 THE
WOODCUTTER).    AXE 斤 IS A PICTOGRAPH.
MOVEMENT 辶 IS AS IN FAR, DISTANT 達 JME 160
AND ROAD, WAY, PATH 道 JME 122.   達

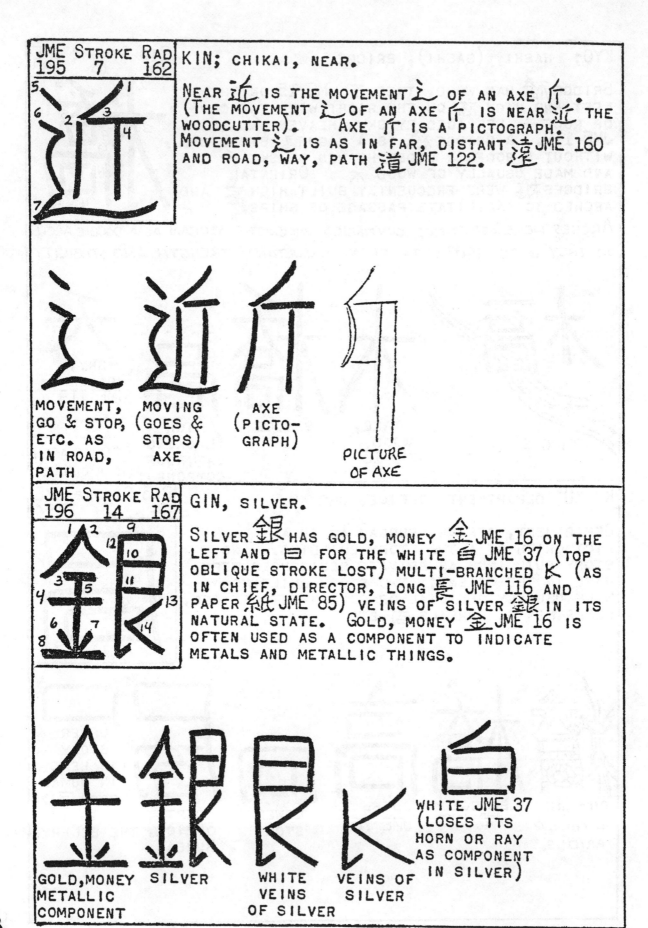

MOVEMENT,
GO & STOP,
ETC. AS
IN ROAD,
PATH

MOVING
(GOES &
STOPS)
AXE

AXE
(PICTO-
GRAPH)

PICTURE
OF AXE

| JME 196 | Stroke 14 | Rad 167 |
|---------|-----------|---------|

GIN, SILVER.

SILVER 銀 HAS GOLD, MONEY 金 JME 16 ON THE
LEFT AND 日 FOR THE WHITE 白 JME 37 (TOP
OBLIQUE STROKE LOST) MULTI-BRANCHED 𠄌 (AS
IN CHIEF, DIRECTOR, LONG 長 JME 116 AND
PAPER 紙 JME 85) VEINS OF SILVER 銀 IN ITS
NATURAL STATE.   GOLD, MONEY 金 JME 16 IS
OFTEN USED AS A COMPONENT TO INDICATE
METALS AND METALLIC THINGS.

GOLD, MONEY
METALLIC
COMPONENT

SILVER

WHITE
VEINS
OF SILVER

VEINS OF
SILVER

WHITE JME 37
(LOSES ITS
HORN OR RAY
AS COMPONENT
IN SILVER)

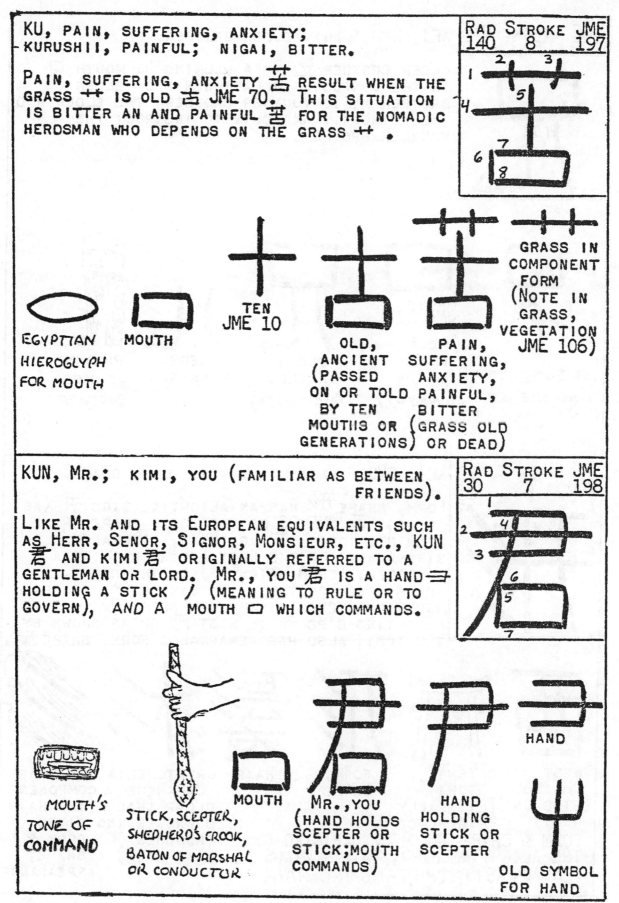

KU, PAIN, SUFFERING, ANXIETY;
KURUSHII, PAINFUL; NIGAI, BITTER.

PAIN, SUFFERING, ANXIETY 苦 RESULT WHEN THE
GRASS ⺿ IS OLD 古 JME 70. THIS SITUATION
IS BITTER AN AND PAINFUL 苦 FOR THE NOMADIC
HERDSMAN WHO DEPENDS ON THE GRASS ⺿ .

| RAD | STROKE | JME |
|-----|--------|-----|
| 140 | 8 | 197 |

EGYPTIAN
HIEROGLYPH
FOR MOUTH

MOUTH

TEN
JME 10

OLD,
ANCIENT
(PASSED
ON OR TOLD
BY TEN
MOUTHS OR
GENERATIONS)

PAIN,
SUFFERING,
ANXIETY,
PAINFUL,
BITTER
(GRASS OLD
OR DEAD)

GRASS IN
COMPONENT
FORM
(NOTE IN
GRASS,
VEGETATION
JME 106)

KUN, MR.; KIMI, YOU (FAMILIAR AS BETWEEN
FRIENDS).

LIKE MR. AND ITS EUROPEAN EQUIVALENTS SUCH
AS HERR, SENOR, SIGNOR, MONSIEUR, ETC., KUN
君 AND KIMI 君 ORIGINALLY REFERRED TO A
GENTLEMAN OR LORD. MR., YOU 君 IS A HAND ⺕
HOLDING A STICK ノ (MEANING TO RULE OR TO
GOVERN), AND A MOUTH ロ WHICH COMMANDS.

| RAD | STROKE | JME |
|-----|--------|-----|
| 30 | 7 | 198 |

MOUTH'S
TONE OF
COMMAND

STICK, SCEPTER,
SHEPHERD'S CROOK,
BATON OF MARSHAL
OR CONDUCTOR

MOUTH

MR., YOU
(HAND HOLDS
SCEPTER OR
STICK; MOUTH
COMMANDS)

HAND
HOLDING
STICK OR
SCEPTER

HAND

OLD SYMBOL
FOR HAND

| JME | Stroke | Rad |
|-----|--------|-----|
| 199 | 5 | 10 |

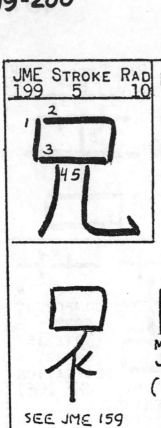

KEI, KYŌ; ANI, ELDER BROTHER.

ELDER BROTHER 兄 IS A WALKING 儿 MOUTH 口.
IN THE CONFUCIAN RELATIONSHIP OF ELDER
BROTHER 兄 TO YOUNGER BROTHER, THE ELDER HAD
THE AUTHORITY AND DUTY TO INSTRUCT THE
YOUNGER BROTHER.

SEE JME 159
AND JME 160

MOUTH
JME 27

(MOUTH-
HEAD-
PELVIS
CONCEPT)

ELDER
BROTHER
(BIG-MOUTH)

LEGS,
WALKING

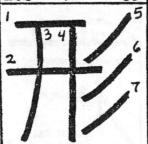
PICTURE
OF OLDER
BROTHER

| JME | Stroke | Rad |
|-----|--------|-----|
| 200 | 7 | 59 |

KEI, GYŌ; KATACHI, -GATA, FORM, SHAPE.

FORM, SHAPE 形 HAS AN ALIGHTING BIRD 开 (AS
IN WEST 西 JME 96 OR THE FORM, SHAPE 形 OF
A SHINTO TORII 开 GATEWAY, LITERALLY
BIRD-PLACE) ON THE LEFT AND HAIR 彡 AS A
COMPONENT (FROM HAIR 髪) ON THE RIGHT.
THE HAIR 彡 OF THE HEAD, SIDEBURNS, BEARD,
MOUSTACHE, ETC. GIVES FORM_SHAPE 形. THE
ALIGHTING BIRD 开 IN WEST 西 OR AS SHOWN BY
THE TORII ALSO HAS REMARKABLE FORM, SHAPE 形.

WEST
JME 96
(BIRD ON
NEST)

GATEWAY,
TORII
(LITERALLY
"BIRDPLACE")

FORM,
SHAPE

HAIR

CRYPTOMERIA,
JAPANESE
CEDAR (HAS
DOWNSWEEPING
BRANCHES
LIKE HAIR)

HAIR AS
COMPONENT
(THE HAIR
GIVES
FORM &
SHAPE,
APPEARANCE)

FORM & SHAPE ARE BEST DEPICTED BY
THE ALIGHTING BIRD, TAIL & WINGS
SPREAD, AS IN TORII; AND THE HAIR

# VOLUME THREE: KANJI 201-300

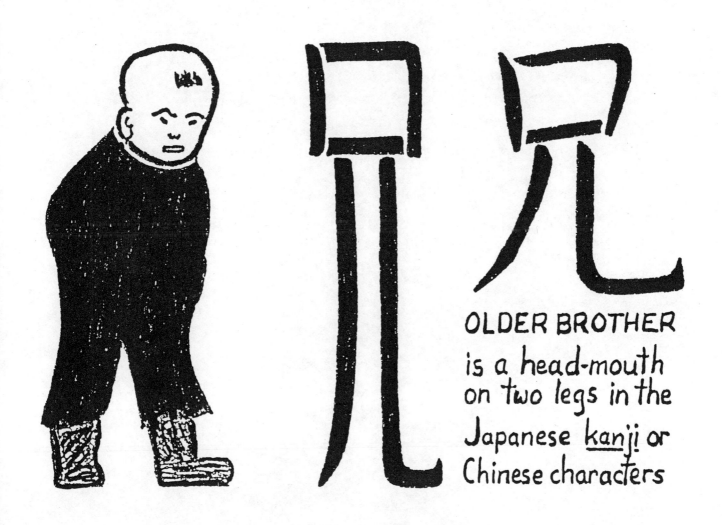

OLDER BROTHER

is a head-mouth on two legs in the Japanese <u>kanji</u> or Chinese characters

**KEI; HAKARU, TO MEASURE.**

| RAD | STROKE | JME |
|-----|--------|-----|
| 149 | 9 | 201 |

ONE MEASURES 計 BY SPEECH 言 JME 392 IN TENTHS AND TENS 十 JME 10 WHICH ARE THE BASIS OF MEASURING 計 . THE TEN 十 JME 10 ALSO REPRESENTS THE FIVE DIRECTIONS: NORTH, EAST, SOUTH, WEST, CENTER AND IS PART OF THE DIPPER 斗 (AS IN GREAT DIPPER ⌇ )USED TO MEASURE 計 .

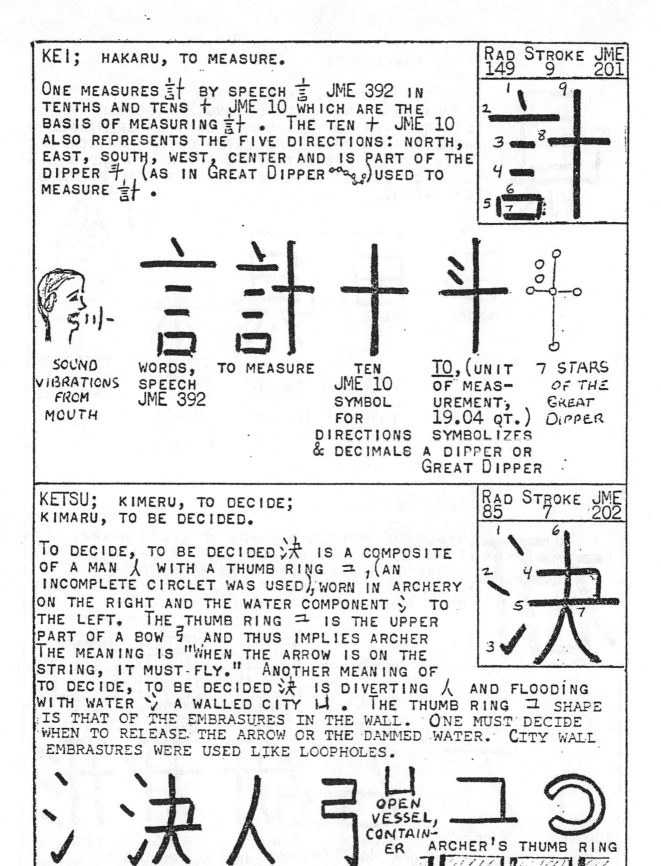

SOUND VIBRATIONS FROM MOUTH

WORDS, SPEECH JME 392

TO MEASURE

TEN JME 10 SYMBOL FOR DIRECTIONS & DECIMALS

TO, (UNIT OF MEAS- UREMENT; 19.04 QT.) SYMBOLIZES A DIPPER OR GREAT DIPPER

7 STARS OF THE GREAT DIPPER

---

**KETSU; KIMERU, TO DECIDE; KIMARU, TO BE DECIDED.**

| RAD | STROKE | JME |
|-----|--------|-----|
| 85 | 7 | 202 |

TO DECIDE, TO BE DECIDED 決 IS A COMPOSITE OF A MAN 人 WITH A THUMB RING ユ ,(AN INCOMPLETE CIRCLET WAS USED),WORN IN ARCHERY ON THE RIGHT AND THE WATER COMPONENT 氵 TO THE LEFT. THE THUMB RING ユ IS THE UPPER PART OF A BOW 弓 AND THUS IMPLIES ARCHER THE MEANING IS "WHEN THE ARROW IS ON THE STRING, IT MUST FLY." ANOTHER MEANING OF TO DECIDE, TO BE DECIDED 決 IS DIVERTING 人 AND FLOODING WITH WATER 氵 A WALLED CITY 凵 . THE THUMB RING ユ SHAPE IS THAT OF THE EMBRASURES IN THE WALL. ONE MUST DECIDE WHEN TO RELEASE THE ARROW OR THE DAMMED WATER. CITY WALL EMBRASURES WERE USED LIKE LOOPHOLES.

WATER AS COM- PONENT

TO DECIDE, TO BE DECIDED

MAN, PERSON DIVERSION

BOW

OPEN VESSEL, CONTAIN- ER

ARCHER'S THUMB RING

CITY WALL EMBRASURES

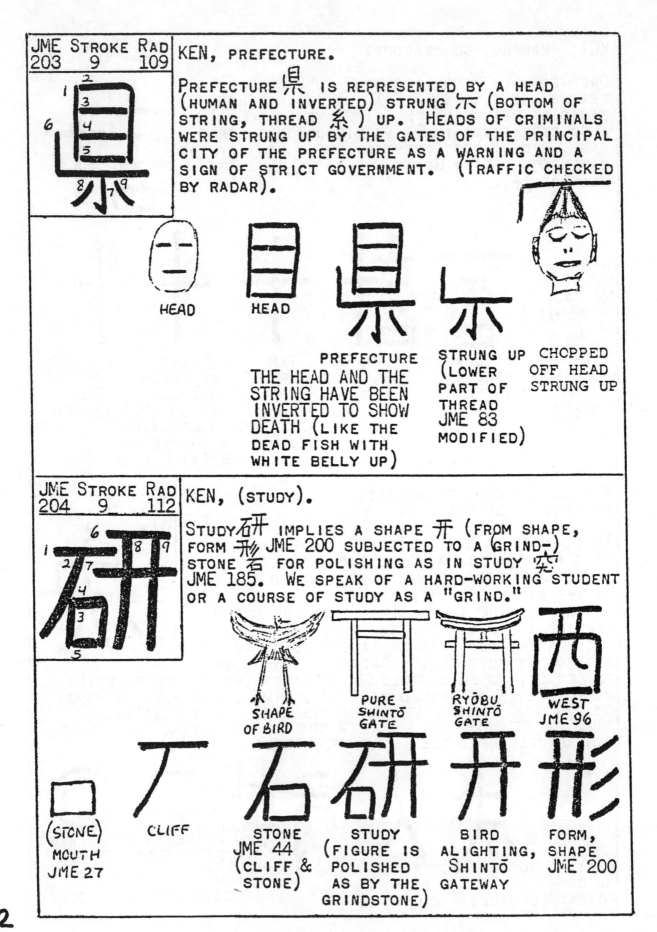

| JME | STROKE | RAD |
|-----|--------|-----|
| 203 | 9 | 109 |

KEN, PREFECTURE.

PREFECTURE 県 IS REPRESENTED BY A HEAD (HUMAN AND INVERTED) STRUNG 示 (BOTTOM OF STRING, THREAD 糸) UP. HEADS OF CRIMINALS WERE STRUNG UP BY THE GATES OF THE PRINCIPAL CITY OF THE PREFECTURE AS A WARNING AND A SIGN OF STRICT GOVERNMENT. (TRAFFIC CHECKED BY RADAR).

HEAD

HEAD

PREFECTURE
THE HEAD AND THE STRING HAVE BEEN INVERTED TO SHOW DEATH (LIKE THE DEAD FISH WITH WHITE BELLY UP)

STRUNG UP (LOWER PART OF THREAD JME 83 MODIFIED)

CHOPPED OFF HEAD STRUNG UP

| JME | STROKE | RAD |
|-----|--------|-----|
| 204 | 9 | 112 |

KEN, (STUDY).

STUDY 研 IMPLIES A SHAPE 开 (FROM SHAPE, FORM 形 JME 200 SUBJECTED TO A GRIND-) STONE 石 FOR POLISHING AS IN STUDY 究 JME 185. WE SPEAK OF A HARD-WORKING STUDENT OR A COURSE OF STUDY AS A "GRIND."

SHAPE OF BIRD

PURE SHINTŌ GATE

RYŌBU SHINTŌ GATE

WEST JME 96

(STONE) MOUTH JME 27

CLIFF

STONE JME 44 (CLIFF & STONE)

STUDY (FIGURE IS POLISHED AS BY THE GRINDSTONE)

BIRD ALIGHTING, SHINTŌ GATEWAY

FORM, SHAPE JME 200

GEN, ORIGIN;  HARA, (WARA), FIELD, MEADOW.

FIELD, MEADOW 原 IS REPRESENTED BY A WHITE 白 JME 37 LITTLE 小 JME 24 (ORIGINALLY WATER 水 JME 14) STREAM FROM A CLIFF 厂 TO SUPPLY A FIELD, MEADOW 原. SUCH A FIELD, MEADOW 原 IS THE ORIGIN 原 OF A HOMESTEAD OR FAMILY.

| Rad | Stroke | JME |
|-----|--------|-----|
| 27  | 10     | 205 |

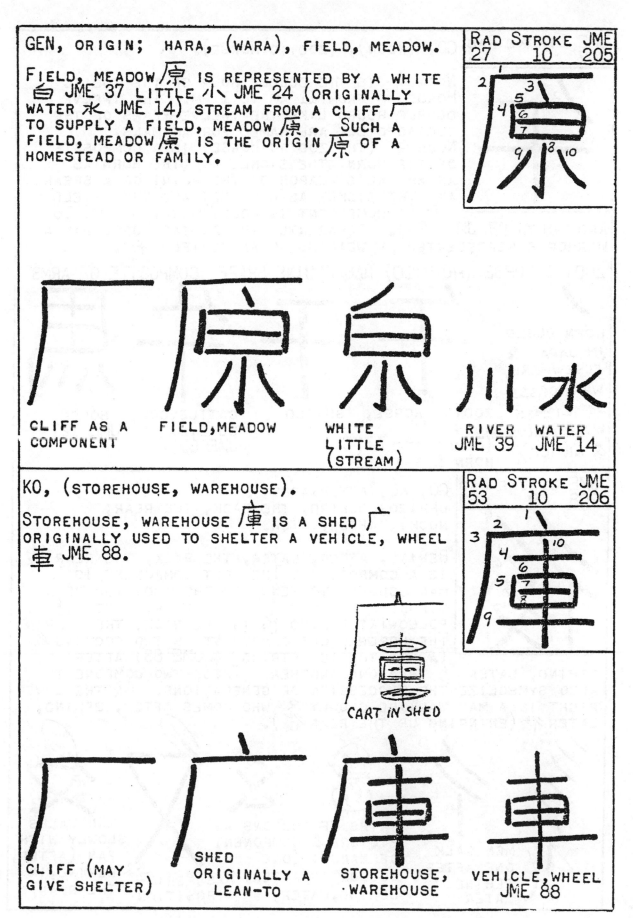

厂
CLIFF AS A COMPONENT

原
FIELD, MEADOW

泉
WHITE
LITTLE
(STREAM)

川
RIVER
JME 39

水
WATER
JME 14

---

KO, (STOREHOUSE, WAREHOUSE).

STOREHOUSE, WAREHOUSE 庫 IS A SHED 广 ORIGINALLY USED TO SHELTER A VEHICLE, WHEEL 車 JME 88.

| Rad | Stroke | JME |
|-----|--------|-----|
| 53  | 10     | 206 |

CART IN SHED

厂
CLIFF (MAY GIVE SHELTER)

广
SHED
ORIGINALLY A LEAN-TO

庫
STOREHOUSE, WAREHOUSE

車
VEHICLE, WHEEL
JME 88

| JME 207 | Stroke 4 | Rad 24 |
|---|---|---|

GO, (NOON), (ZODIAC HORSE).

NOON 午 IS THE DOUBLE HOUR OF THE ZODIAC HORSE 午 FROM 11 AM TO 1 PM. THE TWELVE DOUBLE HOURS LIKE THE TWELVE YEARS OF THE ZODIAC CYCLE ARE NAMED FOR ANIMALS. NOON 午 (THE ZODIAC HORSE) IS A COMPOSITE OF THE HORN, THE SICKLE ノ (THE HORN AS AN ANIMAL'S WEAPON OR THE POINT OF A SPEAR, AND THE SICKLE AS A KNIFE) AND THE SHIELD 干 (A COMPONENT IN GOLD, MONEY 金 JME 16 AND SOUTH 南 JME 124). APPARENTLY THE ZODIAC HORSE WAS A WARHORSE REPRESENTED BY WEAPONS ノ AND SHIELD 干.

ZODIAC HORSE (HORNED) HAS EQUINE SHAPE: COMPOSITE OF ARMS

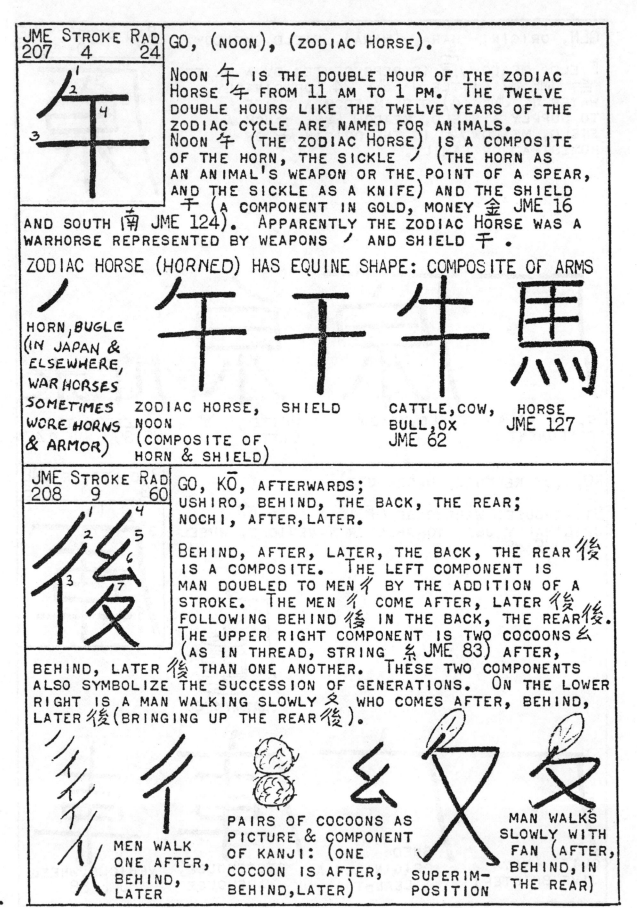

HORN, BUGLE (IN JAPAN & ELSEWHERE, WAR HORSES SOMETIMES WORE HORNS & ARMOR)

ZODIAC HORSE, NOON (COMPOSITE OF HORN & SHIELD)

SHIELD

CATTLE, COW, BULL, OX JME 62

HORSE JME 127

| JME 208 | Stroke 9 | Rad 60 |
|---|---|---|

GO, KŌ, AFTERWARDS; USHIRO, BEHIND, THE BACK, THE REAR; NOCHI, AFTER, LATER.

BEHIND, AFTER, LATER, THE BACK, THE REAR 後 IS A COMPOSITE. THE LEFT COMPONENT IS MAN DOUBLED TO MEN 彳 BY THE ADDITION OF A STROKE. THE MEN 彳 COME AFTER, LATER 後 FOLLOWING BEHIND 後 IN THE BACK, THE REAR 後. THE UPPER RIGHT COMPONENT IS TWO COCOONS 幺 (AS IN THREAD, STRING 糸 JME 83) AFTER, BEHIND, LATER 後 THAN ONE ANOTHER. THESE TWO COMPONENTS ALSO SYMBOLIZE THE SUCCESSION OF GENERATIONS. ON THE LOWER RIGHT IS A MAN WALKING SLOWLY 夂 WHO COMES AFTER, BEHIND, LATER 後 (BRINGING UP THE REAR 後).

MEN WALK ONE AFTER, BEHIND, LATER

PAIRS OF COCOONS AS PICTURE & COMPONENT OF KANJI: (ONE COCOON IS AFTER, BEHIND, LATER)

SUPERIMPOSITION

MAN WALKS SLOWLY WITH FAN (AFTER, BEHIND, IN THE REAR)

GO, WORD, SPEECH; KATARI, NARRATIVE;
KATARU, SPEAK, TALK, NARRATE.

WORD, SPEECH, NARRATIVE, SPEAK, TALK,
NARRATE 語 IS A COMPOSITE OF WORD, SPEECH 言
JME 392 ON THE LEFT (MOUTH 口 AND SOUND
VIBRATIONS 亠) AND THE MOUTH 口 SPEAKING IN
FIVE 五 (ALL) DIRECTIONS ON THE RIGHT. THE
MEANING 吾 IS FROM COMMANDING BY MOUTH
A SQUAD OF FIVE 五 MEN.

| Rad | Stroke | JME |
|-----|--------|-----|
| 149 | 14 | 209 |

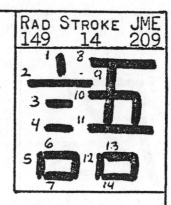

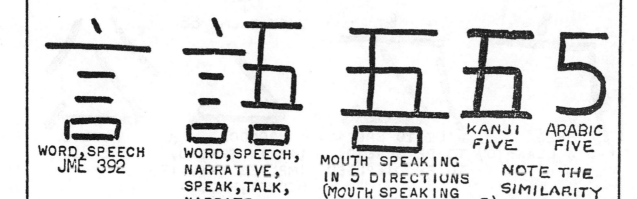

WORD, SPEECH
JME 392

WORD, SPEECH,
NARRATIVE,
SPEAK, TALK,
NARRATE

MOUTH SPEAKING
IN 5 DIRECTIONS
(MOUTH SPEAKING
SQUAD LEADER OF 5)

KANJI
FIVE

ARABIC
FIVE

NOTE THE
SIMILARITY
ABOVE

---

KŌ; OYAKE, PUBLIC.

| Rad | Stroke | JME |
|-----|--------|-----|
| 12 | 4 | 210 |

PUBLIC 公 IS A DIVISION 八 OF WHAT WAS
PRIVATE, SECRET, HIDDEN 厶 (AS IN A COCOON
厶) SO THAT IT EXPANDS 厶 IN PUBLIC, USE.
THE SYMBOL 厶 AS IN A CLOUD 雲 OR THE CONE
厶 OF A PINE TREE IS CAPABLE OF IMMENSE
EXPANSION. YET AS A COCOON 厶 (HALF OF
THE TWO COCOONS 幺 IN THREAD, STRING 糸 ),
IT SUGGESTS PRIVATE, SECRET, HIDDEN 厶 WITH
A FUTURE IN TRANSFORMATION. WHAT IS PUBLIC
SUCH AS A PARK OR PUBLIC BUILDING IS USUALLY SPREAD OUT.
THE COCOON 厶 UNWOUND EXPANDS INTO THREAD AND BECOMES
PUBLIC 公.

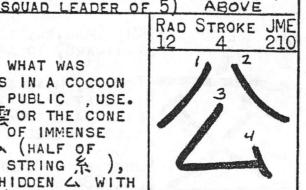

EIGHT JME 8
(IMPLIES TO
DIVIDE,
DIVISION)

PUBLIC

PRIVATE, HIDDEN,
SECRET AS IN A
COCOON, BUT READY
TO BECOME PUBLIC

THREAD JME 83
(EARLY MEANING
SILK: THREAD
FROM COCOON)

| JME | STROKE | RAD |
|-----|--------|-----|
| 211 | 5 | 53 |

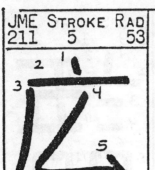

KŌ; HIROI, WIDE; HIROGARU, TO SPREAD,(I.V.);
HIROGERU, TO SPREAD, (T.V.);
HIROMARU, TO BE SPREAD, TO BE DIFFUSED.

WIDE, TO SPREAD, TO BE SPREAD, TO BE
DIFFUSED 広 IS REPRESENTED BY THE COCOON ム
IN THE SHED 广 WHICH IS UNWOUND AND SPREADS,
IS SPREAD, IS DIFFUSED 広 AS THREAD 糸 AND
EVENTUALLY AS SILK CLOTH FOR CLOTHING, ETC.

THE COCOON UNDER THE SHED IS SPREAD WIDE AS IT IS UNWOUND

THREAD JME 83

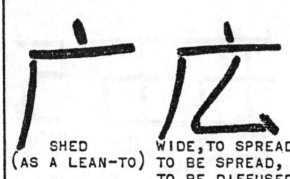
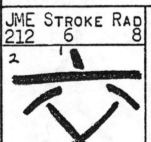

SHED
(AS A LEAN-TO)

WIDE,TO SPREAD,
TO BE SPREAD,
TO BE DIFFUSED

COCOON
(AS IN THREAD)
IMPLIES PRIVATE,
SECRET,HIDDEN

PUBLIC
JME 210

| JME | STROKE | RAD |
|-----|--------|-----|
| 212 | 6 | 8 |

KŌ; MAJIRU, TO MIX, MINGLE, TO BE MIXED;
MAJIWARU, TO ASSOCIATE, KEEP COMPANY.

TO MIX, MINGLE, ASSOCIATE, KEEP COMPANY 交
IS WHAT THE FATHERS 父 JME 131 WEARING THE
BIRETTA OR SCHOLARS' CAP ⊥ DO. THERE IS
ALSO IMPLIED A MIXING, MINGLING 交 BY THE
CROSSING OF LINES ✕ (AS WITH THE LETTER ✕)
JUST AS IN COMPOSITION, ESSAY, SENTENCE 文
JME 134 WITH THE MIXED, MINGLED, ASSOCIATED,
COMPANY KEEPING 交 LINES OF THE KANJI.

THE FATHERS WHO ARE SCHOLARS MIX, MINGLE, ASSOCIATE, KEEP
COMPANY (AS THEY ENJOY) COMPOSITIONS, ESSAYS, SENTENCES

SUPER-
IMPOSITION

FATHER
JME 131

MIX,MINGLE,
TO BE MIXED,
TO ASSOCIATE,
KEEP COMPANY

COMPOSITION,
ESSAY,
SENTENCE
JME 134

SCHOLARS'
CAP OR
BIRETTA
(SUGGESTS
DIRECTION,
CONTROL,
THE CIVIL
SERVICE)

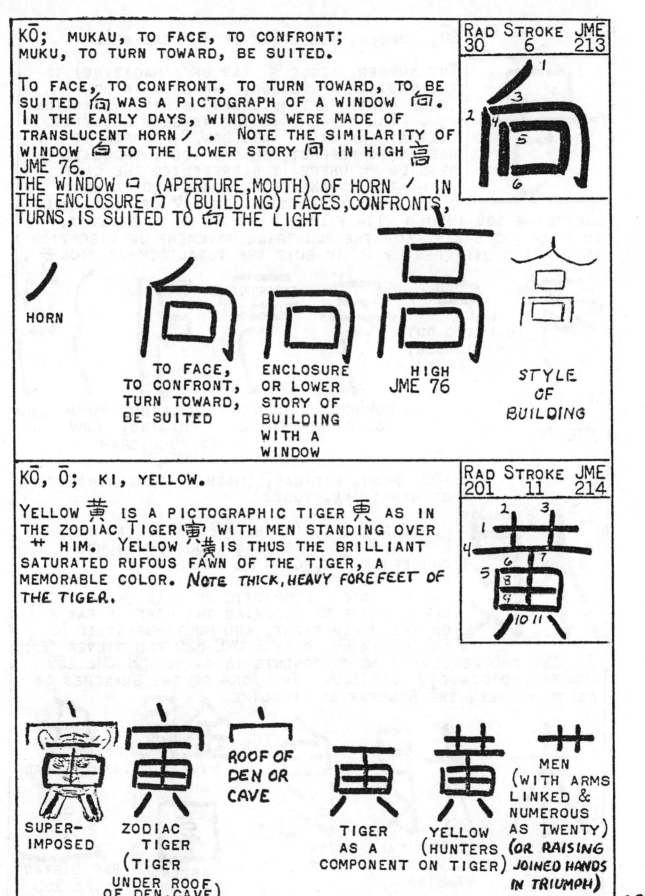

KŌ; MUKAU, TO FACE, TO CONFRONT;
MUKU, TO TURN TOWARD, BE SUITED.

| RAD | STROKE | JME |
|---|---|---|
| 30 | 6 | 213 |

TO FACE, TO CONFRONT, TO TURN TOWARD, TO BE
SUITED 向 WAS A PICTOGRAPH OF A WINDOW 向.
IN THE EARLY DAYS, WINDOWS WERE MADE OF
TRANSLUCENT HORN ╱ . NOTE THE SIMILARITY OF
WINDOW 向 TO THE LOWER STORY 回 IN HIGH 高
JME 76.
THE WINDOW ▢ (APERTURE, MOUTH) OF HORN ╱ IN
THE ENCLOSURE 冂 (BUILDING) FACES, CONFRONTS,
TURNS, IS SUITED TO 向 THE LIGHT

HORN

TO FACE,
TO CONFRONT,
TURN TOWARD,
BE SUITED

ENCLOSURE
OR LOWER
STORY OF
BUILDING
WITH A
WINDOW

HIGH
JME 76

STYLE
OF
BUILDING

KŌ, Ō; KI, YELLOW.

| RAD | STROKE | JME |
|---|---|---|
| 201 | 11 | 214 |

YELLOW 黄 IS A PICTOGRAPHIC TIGER 寅 AS IN
THE ZODIAC TIGER 寅 WITH MEN STANDING OVER
⧻ HIM. YELLOW 黄 IS THUS THE BRILLIANT
SATURATED RUFOUS FAWN OF THE TIGER, A
MEMORABLE COLOR. NOTE THICK, HEAVY FOREFEET OF
THE TIGER.

SUPER-
IMPOSED

ZODIAC
TIGER
(TIGER
UNDER ROOF
OF DEN, CAVE)

ROOF OF
DEN OR
CAVE

TIGER
AS A
COMPONENT

YELLOW
(HUNTERS
ON TIGER)

MEN
(WITH ARMS
LINKED &
NUMEROUS
AS TWENTY)
(OR RAISING
JOINED HANDS
IN TRIUMPH)

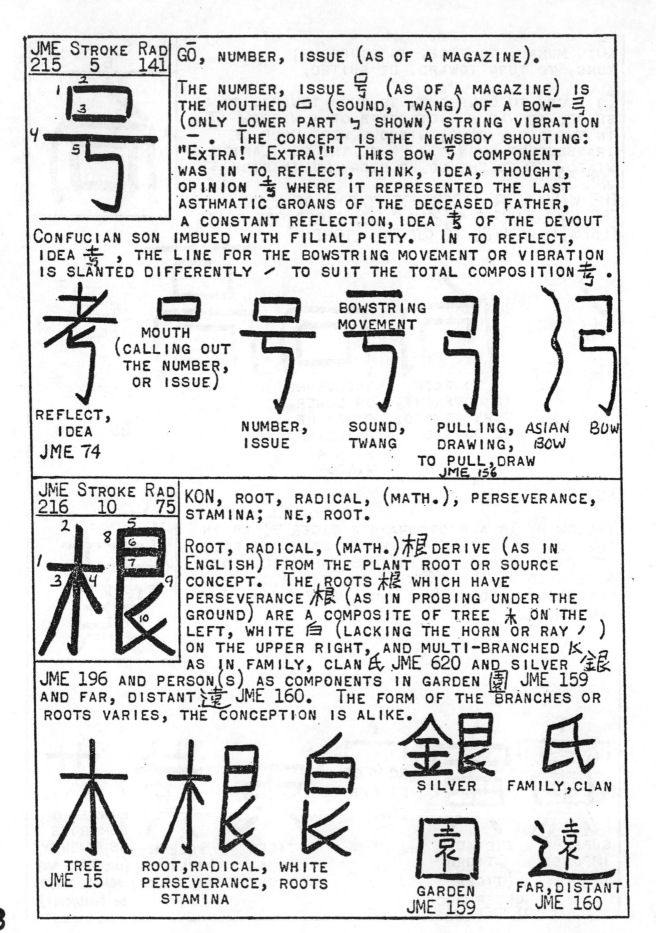

| JME | Stroke | Rad |
|-----|--------|-----|
| 215 | 5 | 141 |

GŌ, NUMBER, ISSUE (AS OF A MAGAZINE).

THE NUMBER, ISSUE 号 (AS OF A MAGAZINE) IS THE MOUTHED 口 (SOUND, TWANG) OF A BOW 弓 (ONLY LOWER PART 丂 SHOWN) STRING VIBRATION 一. THE CONCEPT IS THE NEWSBOY SHOUTING: "EXTRA! EXTRA!" THIS BOW 丂 COMPONENT WAS IN TO REFLECT, THINK, IDEA, THOUGHT, OPINION 考 WHERE IT REPRESENTED THE LAST ASTHMATIC GROANS OF THE DECEASED FATHER, A CONSTANT REFLECTION, IDEA 考 OF THE DEVOUT CONFUCIAN SON IMBUED WITH FILIAL PIETY. IN TO REFLECT, IDEA 考, THE LINE FOR THE BOWSTRING MOVEMENT OR VIBRATION IS SLANTED DIFFERENTLY ╱ TO SUIT THE TOTAL COMPOSITION 考.

REFLECT, IDEA
JME 74

MOUTH (CALLING OUT THE NUMBER, OR ISSUE)

NUMBER, ISSUE

SOUND, TWANG

BOWSTRING MOVEMENT

PULLING, DRAWING, TO PULL, DRAW
JME 156

ASIAN BOW

BOW

| JME | Stroke | Rad |
|-----|--------|-----|
| 216 | 10 | 75 |

KON, ROOT, RADICAL, (MATH.), PERSEVERANCE, STAMINA; NE, ROOT.

ROOT, RADICAL, (MATH.) 根 DERIVE (AS IN ENGLISH) FROM THE PLANT ROOT OR SOURCE CONCEPT. THE ROOTS 根 WHICH HAVE PERSEVERANCE 根 (AS IN PROBING UNDER THE GROUND) ARE A COMPOSITE OF TREE 木 ON THE LEFT, WHITE 白 (LACKING THE HORN OR RAY ╱) ON THE UPPER RIGHT, AND MULTI-BRANCHED 氏 AS IN FAMILY, CLAN 氏 JME 620 AND SILVER 銀 JME 196 AND PERSON(S) AS COMPONENTS IN GARDEN 園 JME 159 AND FAR, DISTANT 遠 JME 160. THE FORM OF THE BRANCHES OR ROOTS VARIES, THE CONCEPTION IS ALIKE.

TREE
JME 15

ROOT, RADICAL, PERSEVERANCE, STAMINA

WHITE ROOTS

SILVER

FAMILY, CLAN

GARDEN
JME 159

FAR, DISTANT
JME 160

SAI, TALENT, SUFFIX AS YEARS OF AGE.

TALENT, "YEARS OLD" 才 IS A PICTOGRAPH OF
A TREE 木 PRUNED AND THINNED 才 SO THAT
THE "DEADWOOD," AND EXCESS GROWTH IS
REMOVED AS WITH FRUIT TREES. THIS IS DONE
AT CERTAIN STAGES IN TIME OR "YEARS OLD" 才.
THE PROCESS WITH TREES IS REGARDED AS
ANALOGOUS TO THAT IN EDUCATING OR DEVELOPING
PEOPLE TO THEIR TALENT(S) 才.

| Rad | Stroke | JME |
|-----|--------|-----|
| 64 | 3 | 217 |

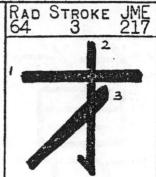

TREE, WOOD
JME 15
(COMMON WOOD)

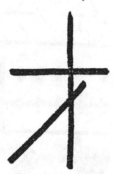

TALENT,
YEARS OF AGE
(TREE ANNUALLY
PRUNED & THINNED
LEAVING BEST GROWTH)

HAND
(COMPONENT)

ACTION OF THE
PRUNING KNIFE
WHICH TRIMS &
PRUNES TREES

SAI; HOSOI, SLENDER, NARROW;
KOMAKAI, FINE, DETAILED, MINUTE.

SLENDER, NARROW, FINE, DETAILED, MINUTE 細
IS THE APPEARANCE OF A RICE FIELD OR PADDY 田
WHICH IS LIKE THREADS, STRANDS 糸. SUCH
FIELDS ARE PARTICULARLY SEEN ON THE TERRACED
MOUNTAIN SIDES WHERE THE RETAINING WALLS IN
THE DISTANCE CURVE LIKE WINDING THREADS 糸.

| Rad | Stroke | JME |
|-----|--------|-----|
| 120 | 11 | 218 |

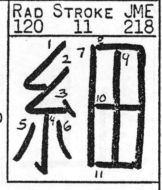

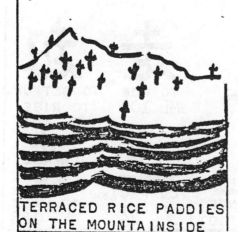

TERRACED RICE PADDIES
ON THE MOUNTAINSIDE

THREAD,
STRING
JME 83

SLENDER,
NARROW,
FINE,
DETAILED,
MINUTE

RICE FIELD
OR PADDY
JME 40

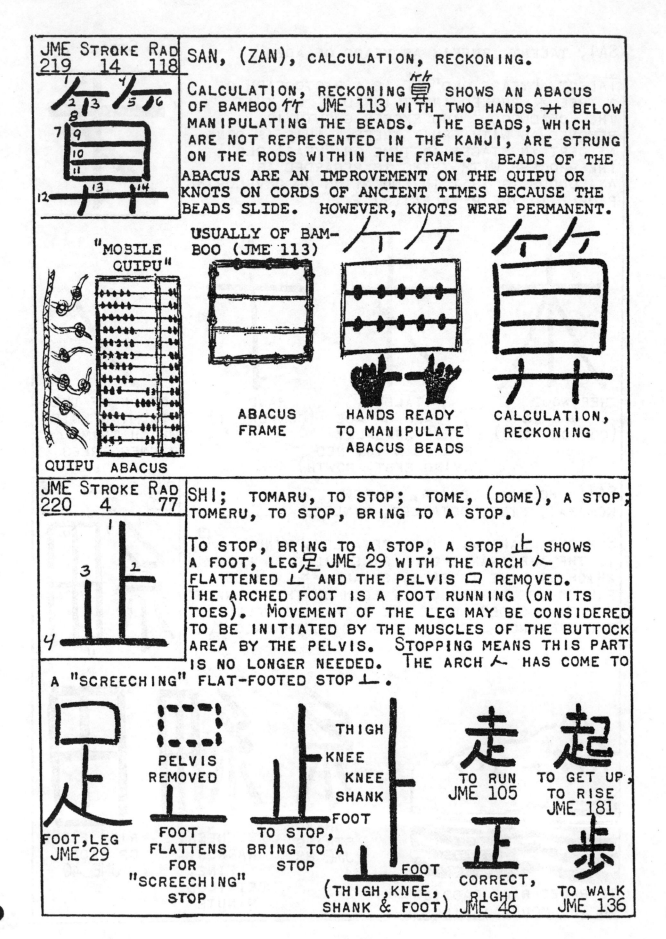

| JME | Stroke | Rad |
|---|---|---|
| 219 | 14 | 118 |

SAN, (ZAN), CALCULATION, RECKONING.

CALCULATION, RECKONING 算 SHOWS AN ABACUS OF BAMBOO 竹 JME 113 WITH TWO HANDS 廾 BELOW MANIPULATING THE BEADS. THE BEADS, WHICH ARE NOT REPRESENTED IN THE KANJI, ARE STRUNG ON THE RODS WITHIN THE FRAME. BEADS OF THE ABACUS ARE AN IMPROVEMENT ON THE QUIPU OR KNOTS ON CORDS OF ANCIENT TIMES BECAUSE THE BEADS SLIDE. HOWEVER, KNOTS WERE PERMANENT.

"MOBILE QUIPU"

USUALLY OF BAMBOO (JME 113)

QUIPU   ABACUS

ABACUS FRAME

HANDS READY TO MANIPULATE ABACUS BEADS

CALCULATION, RECKONING

| JME | Stroke | Rad |
|---|---|---|
| 220 | 4 | 77 |

SHI; TOMARU, TO STOP; TOME, (DOME), A STOP; TOMERU, TO STOP, BRING TO A STOP.

TO STOP, BRING TO A STOP, A STOP 止 SHOWS A FOOT, LEG 足 JME 29 WITH THE ARCH 人 FLATTENED ⊥ AND THE PELVIS 口 REMOVED. THE ARCHED FOOT IS A FOOT RUNNING (ON ITS TOES). MOVEMENT OF THE LEG MAY BE CONSIDERED TO BE INITIATED BY THE MUSCLES OF THE BUTTOCK AREA BY THE PELVIS. STOPPING MEANS THIS PART IS NO LONGER NEEDED. THE ARCH 人 HAS COME TO A "SCREECHING" FLAT-FOOTED STOP ⊥.

FOOT, LEG JME 29

PELVIS REMOVED

FOOT FLATTENS FOR "SCREECHING" STOP

TO STOP, BRING TO A STOP

THIGH
KNEE
KNEE
SHANK
FOOT

FOOT (THIGH, KNEE, SHANK & FOOT)

TO RUN JME 105

CORRECT, RIGHT JME 46

TO GET UP, TO RISE JME 181

TO WALK JME 136

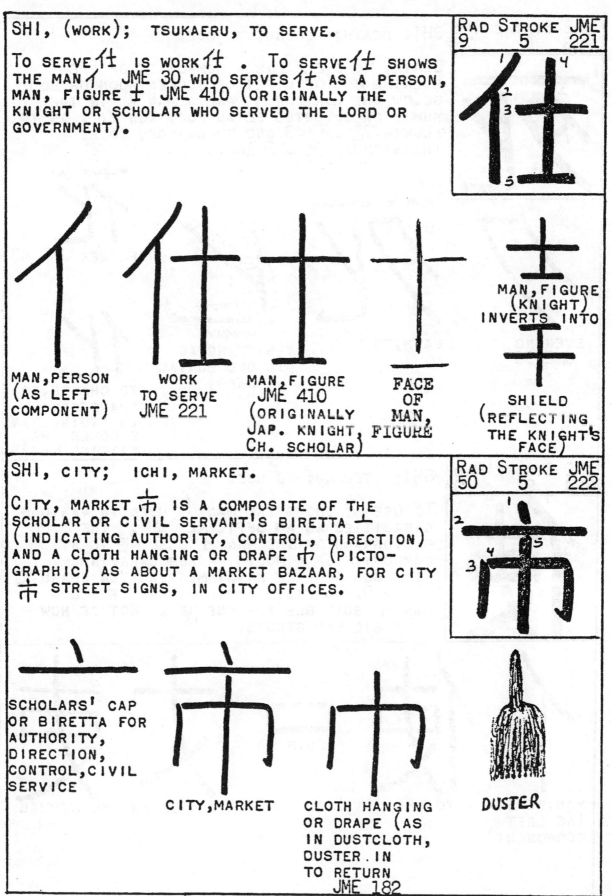

SHI, (WORK); TSUKAERU, TO SERVE.

TO SERVE 仕 IS WORK 仕 . TO SERVE 仕 SHOWS THE MAN 亻 JME 30 WHO SERVES 仕 AS A PERSON, MAN, FIGURE 士 JME 410 (ORIGINALLY THE KNIGHT OR SCHOLAR WHO SERVED THE LORD OR GOVERNMENT).

RAD 9 STROKE 5 JME 221

MAN, PERSON (AS LEFT COMPONENT)

WORK TO SERVE JME 221

MAN, FIGURE JME 410 (ORIGINALLY JAP. KNIGHT, CH. SCHOLAR)

FACE OF MAN, FIGURE

MAN, FIGURE (KNIGHT) INVERTS INTO

SHIELD (REFLECTING THE KNIGHT'S FACE)

SHI, CITY; ICHI, MARKET.

CITY, MARKET 市 IS A COMPOSITE OF THE SCHOLAR OR CIVIL SERVANT'S BIRETTA 亠 (INDICATING AUTHORITY, CONTROL, DIRECTION) AND A CLOTH HANGING OR DRAPE 巾 (PICTO-GRAPHIC) AS ABOUT A MARKET BAZAAR, FOR CITY 市 STREET SIGNS, IN CITY OFFICES.

RAD 50 STROKE 5 JME 222

SCHOLARS' CAP OR BIRETTA FOR AUTHORITY, DIRECTION, CONTROL, CIVIL SERVICE

CITY, MARKET

CLOTH HANGING OR DRAPE (AS IN DUSTCLOTH, DUSTER. IN TO RETURN JME 182

DUSTER

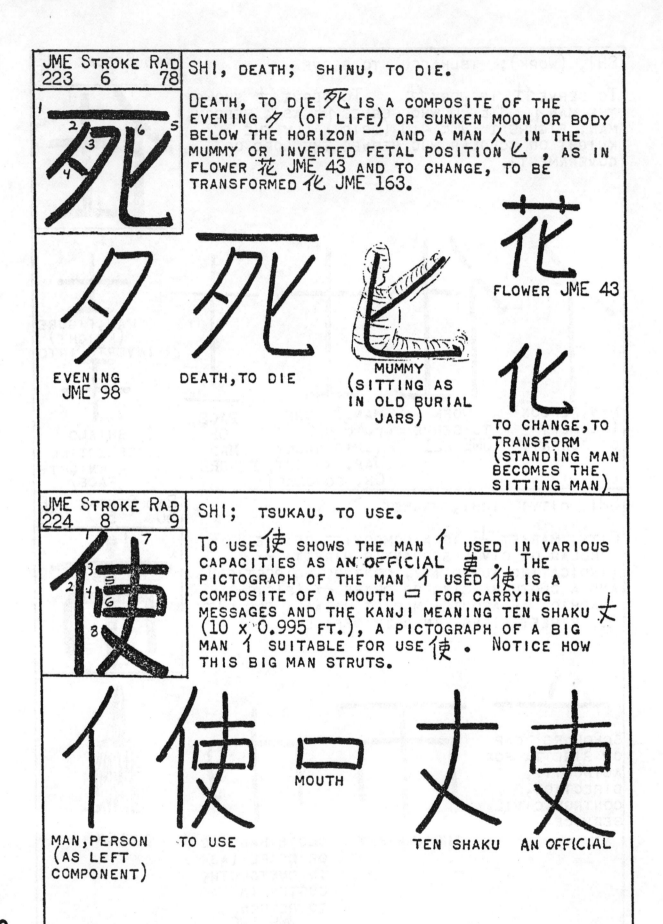

| JME 223 | Stroke 6 | Rad 78 |
|---|---|---|

SHI, DEATH; SHINU, TO DIE.

DEATH, TO DIE 死 IS A COMPOSITE OF THE EVENING 夕 (OF LIFE) OR SUNKEN MOON OR BODY BELOW THE HORIZON 一 AND A MAN 人 IN THE MUMMY OR INVERTED FETAL POSITION 匕, AS IN FLOWER 花 JME 43 AND TO CHANGE, TO BE TRANSFORMED 化 JME 163.

夕
EVENING
JME 98

死
DEATH, TO DIE

匕
MUMMY
(SITTING AS
IN OLD BURIAL
JARS)

花
FLOWER JME 43

化
TO CHANGE, TO
TRANSFORM
(STANDING MAN
BECOMES THE
SITTING MAN)

| JME 224 | Stroke 8 | Rad 9 |
|---|---|---|

SHI; TSUKAU, TO USE.

TO USE 使 SHOWS THE MAN イ USED IN VARIOUS CAPACITIES AS AN OFFICIAL 吏. THE PICTOGRAPH OF THE MAN イ USED 使 IS A COMPOSITE OF A MOUTH 口 FOR CARRYING MESSAGES AND THE KANJI MEANING TEN SHAKU 丈 (10 x 0.995 FT.), A PICTOGRAPH OF A BIG MAN イ SUITABLE FOR USE 使. NOTICE HOW THIS BIG MAN STRUTS.

イ
MAN, PERSON
(AS LEFT
COMPONENT)

使
TO USE

口
MOUTH

丈
TEN SHAKU

吏
AN OFFICIAL

SHI; HAJIMARU, TO BEGIN, (I.V.); HAJIMERU, TO BEGIN, (T.V.).

| Rad 38 | Stroke 8 | JME 225 |
|---|---|---|

TO BEGIN 始 IS THE PURSED UP, COILED MOUTH 厶 OF A WOMAN 女 READY TO BEGIN HER TIRADE, ETC., COMFORTABLY SEATED ON A STOOL, STONE OR BOX 口 .

WOMAN, GIRL, FEMALE
JME 32

TO BEGIN

THE "PURSED-UP" MOUTH (SEATED ON A STOOL, ETC. READY TO BEGIN)

PICTURE OF THE WOMAN'S MOUTH ABOUT TO BEGIN

SHI; YUBI, FINGER.

| Rad 64 | Stroke 9 | JME 226 |
|---|---|---|

FINGER 指 IS A COMPOSITE OF HAND 扌 (THE ABBREVIATED COMPONENT FORM OF HAND 手 JME 28) TO POINT OR INDICATE 匕 (VISUALIZE AS A SITTING PERSON 匕 IN PROFILE WITH HAND / EXTENDED TO INDICATE, AND A MOUTH SPEAKING 日 TO SUPPLEMENT THE POINTING 匕 (COMMANDS 旨). IT IS THE FINGER 指 THAT IS SIGNIFICANT WHEN THE SITTING MAN'S 匕 HAND 扌 IS EXTENDED AS HE SPEAKS 日 .

MAN SITS: ARM INDICATES, FINGER POINTS

YEARS OF AGE, TALENT
JME 217

COMPONENT HAND, ARM (INDICATES DIRECTIONALLY LIKE PRUNE TREE)

FINGER

MOUTH SPEAKS (SUPPLEMENTS ARM & FINGER)

COMMANDS (COMPOSITE OF SPEAKING & POINTING WHILE SITTING)

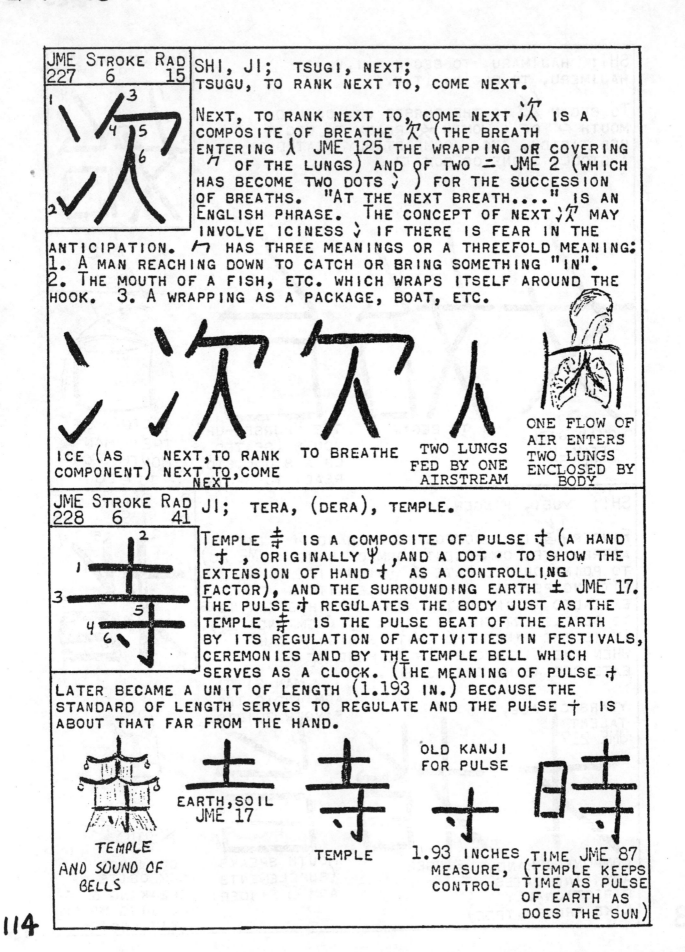

| JME 227 | Stroke 6 | Rad 15 |
|---|---|---|

SHI, JI; TSUGI, NEXT; TSUGU, TO RANK NEXT TO, COME NEXT.

NEXT, TO RANK NEXT TO, COME NEXT 次 IS A COMPOSITE OF BREATHE 欠 (THE BREATH ENTERING 人 JME 125 THE WRAPPING OR COVERING 勹 OF THE LUNGS) AND OF TWO 二 JME 2 (WHICH HAS BECOME TWO DOTS ⟩ ) FOR THE SUCCESSION OF BREATHS. "AT THE NEXT BREATH...." IS AN ENGLISH PHRASE. THE CONCEPT OF NEXT 次 MAY INVOLVE ICINESS ⟩ IF THERE IS FEAR IN THE ANTICIPATION. 勹 HAS THREE MEANINGS OR A THREEFOLD MEANING:
1. A MAN REACHING DOWN TO CATCH OR BRING SOMETHING "IN".
2. THE MOUTH OF A FISH, ETC. WHICH WRAPS ITSELF AROUND THE HOOK. 3. A WRAPPING AS A PACKAGE, BOAT, ETC.

ICE (AS COMPONENT)

NEXT, TO RANK NEXT TO, COME NEXT

TO BREATHE

TWO LUNGS FED BY ONE AIRSTREAM

ONE FLOW OF AIR ENTERS TWO LUNGS ENCLOSED BY BODY

| JME 228 | Stroke 6 | Rad 41 |
|---|---|---|

JI; TERA, (DERA), TEMPLE.

TEMPLE 寺 IS A COMPOSITE OF PULSE 寸 (A HAND 寸, ORIGINALLY Ψ, AND A DOT • TO SHOW THE EXTENSION OF HAND 寸 AS A CONTROLLING FACTOR), AND THE SURROUNDING EARTH 土 JME 17. THE PULSE 寸 REGULATES THE BODY JUST AS THE TEMPLE 寺 IS THE PULSE BEAT OF THE EARTH BY ITS REGULATION OF ACTIVITIES IN FESTIVALS, CEREMONIES AND BY THE TEMPLE BELL WHICH SERVES AS A CLOCK. (THE MEANING OF PULSE 寸 LATER BECAME A UNIT OF LENGTH (1.193 IN.) BECAUSE THE STANDARD OF LENGTH SERVES TO REGULATE AND THE PULSE 寸 IS ABOUT THAT FAR FROM THE HAND.

TEMPLE AND SOUND OF BELLS

EARTH, SOIL JME 17

TEMPLE

OLD KANJI FOR PULSE

1.93 INCHES MEASURE, CONTROL

TIME JME 87 (TEMPLE KEEPS TIME AS PULSE OF EARTH AS DOES THE SUN)

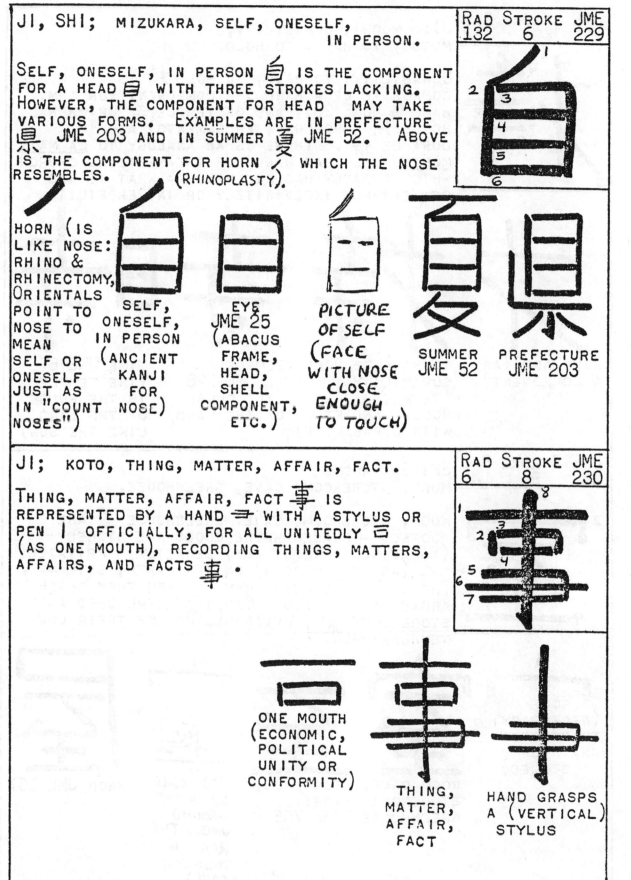

JI, SHI; MIZUKARA, SELF, ONESELF, IN PERSON.

| RAD 132 | STROKE 6 | JME 229 |
|---|---|---|

SELF, ONESELF, IN PERSON 自 IS THE COMPONENT FOR A HEAD 首 WITH THREE STROKES LACKING. HOWEVER, THE COMPONENT FOR HEAD MAY TAKE VARIOUS FORMS. EXAMPLES ARE IN PREFECTURE 県 JME 203 AND IN SUMMER 夏 JME 52. ABOVE IS THE COMPONENT FOR HORN ノ WHICH THE NOSE RESEMBLES. (RHINOPLASTY).

HORN (IS LIKE NOSE: RHINO & RHINECTOMY, ORIENTALS POINT TO NOSE TO MEAN SELF OR ONESELF JUST AS IN "COUNT NOSES")

SELF, ONESELF, IN PERSON (ANCIENT KANJI FOR NOSE)

EYE JME 25 (ABACUS FRAME, HEAD, SHELL COMPONENT, ETC.)

PICTURE OF SELF (FACE WITH NOSE CLOSE ENOUGH TO TOUCH)

SUMMER JME 52

PREFECTURE JME 203

JI; KOTO, THING, MATTER, AFFAIR, FACT.

| RAD 6 | STROKE 8 | JME 230 |
|---|---|---|

THING, MATTER, AFFAIR, FACT 事 IS REPRESENTED BY A HAND ⺕ WITH A STYLUS OR PEN | OFFICIALLY, FOR ALL UNITEDLY 口 (AS ONE MOUTH), RECORDING THINGS, MATTERS, AFFAIRS, AND FACTS 事.

ONE MOUTH (ECONOMIC, POLITICAL UNITY OR CONFORMITY)

THING, MATTER, AFFAIR, FACT

HAND GRASPS A (VERTICAL) STYLUS

| JME | Stroke | Rad |
|---|---|---|
| 231 | 9 | 64 |

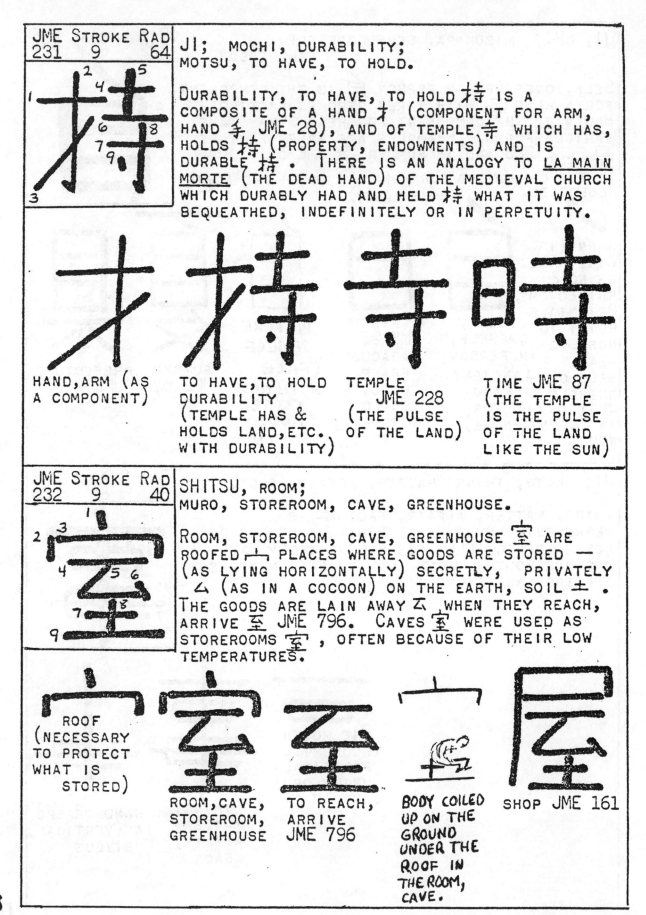

JI; MOCHI, DURABILITY;
MOTSU, TO HAVE, TO HOLD.

DURABILITY, TO HAVE, TO HOLD 持 IS A
COMPOSITE OF A HAND 扌 (COMPONENT FOR ARM,
HAND 手 JME 28), AND OF TEMPLE 寺 WHICH HAS,
HOLDS 持 (PROPERTY, ENDOWMENTS) AND IS
DURABLE 持. THERE IS AN ANALOGY TO <u>LA MAIN
MORTE</u> (THE DEAD HAND) OF THE MEDIEVAL CHURCH
WHICH DURABLY HAD AND HELD 持 WHAT IT WAS
BEQUEATHED, INDEFINITELY OR IN PERPETUITY.

HAND, ARM (AS
A COMPONENT)

TO HAVE, TO HOLD
DURABILITY
(TEMPLE HAS &
HOLDS LAND, ETC.
WITH DURABILITY)

TEMPLE
        JME 228
(THE PULSE
OF THE LAND)

TIME JME 87
(THE TEMPLE
IS THE PULSE
OF THE LAND
LIKE THE SUN)

| JME | Stroke | Rad |
|---|---|---|
| 232 | 9 | 40 |

SHITSU, ROOM;
MURO, STOREROOM, CAVE, GREENHOUSE.

ROOM, STOREROOM, CAVE, GREENHOUSE 室 ARE
ROOFED 宀 PLACES WHERE GOODS ARE STORED —
(AS LYING HORIZONTALLY) SECRETLY, PRIVATELY
厶 (AS IN A COCOON) ON THE EARTH, SOIL 土.
THE GOODS ARE LAIN AWAY 至 WHEN THEY REACH,
ARRIVE 至 JME 796. CAVES 室 WERE USED AS
STOREROOMS 室, OFTEN BECAUSE OF THEIR LOW
TEMPERATURES.

ROOF
(NECESSARY
TO PROTECT
WHAT IS
STORED)

ROOM, CAVE,
STOREROOM,
GREENHOUSE

TO REACH,
ARRIVE
JME 796

BODY COILED
UP ON THE
GROUND
UNDER THE
ROOF IN
THE ROOM,
CAVE.

SHOP JME 161

| RAD | STROKE | JME |
|-----|--------|-----|
| 40 | 8 | 233 |

JITSU, TRUTH, REALITY;  MI, FRUIT, NUT;
MINORU, TO BEAR FRUIT.

TRUTH, REALITY, FRUIT, NUT, TO BEAR FRUIT 実
IS A PICTOGRAPH OF A MAN 人 LADEN WITH NUTS,
FRUIT 㞮 UNDER HIS ROOF 宀 . THE ENGLISH
CONCEPT OF A PROJECT OR ENTERPRISE BEARING
FRUIT (ABSTRACT) IS ALSO JAPANESE.
NOTE THE SIMILARITY OF TRUTH, REALITY,
FRUIT, NUT, TO BEAR FRUIT 実 JME 233 TO
SPRING 春 JME 91. ABSTRACTLY, FRUIT PRODUCED IS
ALSO TRUTH OR REALITY 実 . "BY THEIR FRUITS YE SHALL KNOW
THEM."

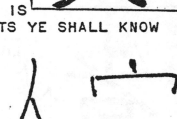

| 春 | 青 | 生 | 実 | 人 | 宀 |
|---|---|---|---|---|---|
| SPRING JME 91 | BLUE, GREEN JME 36 | EXISTENCE, LIFE, BORN JME 34 | FRUIT, NUT, BEAR FRUIT | PERSON, MAN JME 30 | ROOF |
| SUN THROUGH THICK FOLIAGE | MOON LIGHT THRU PLANTS | PLANTS & YIELD | | | |

| RAD | STROKE | JME |
|-----|--------|-----|
| 113 | 7 | 234 |

SHA, (JA), COMPANY, CORPORATION, FIRM;
YASHIRO, A SHINTO SHRINE.

COMPANY, CORPORATION, FIRM, SHINTO SHRINE 社
IS A COMPOSITE OF THE COMPONENT FORM ネ OF
TO SHOW, TO POINT OUT 示 JME 622 AND OF SOIL
EARTH 土 REFERRING TO THE LOCAL DEITIES OF
THE PHYSICAL TERRAIN (LIKE THE ROMAN MANES).
TO SHOW, POINT OUT 示 JME 622 REPRESENTS
HEAVEN'S 二 (OR SUN, MOON AND STARS' 二 )
ILLUMINATION 小 (THREE SPREADING RAYS) WHICH
SHOW, POINT OUT 示 TO MAN ON EARTH. THE PRIESTS OF THE
SHINTO SHRINE 社 WERE A COMPANY 社 (IN THE SENSE OF A
GROUP) AND THIS MEANING WAS EXTENDED TO COMPANY, FIRM,
CORPORATION 社 .

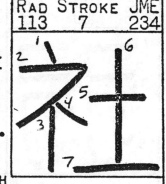

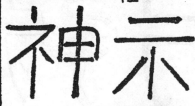

| 神 | 示 | 未 | ネ | 社 | 土 |
|---|---|---|---|---|---|
| GOD JME 257 | TO SHOW, POINT OUT JME 622 | KANJI BECOMES COMPONENT | COMPONENT FORM OF COMPONENT JME 622 | COMPANY, CORPORATION, FIRM, SHINTO SHRINE | EARTH, SOIL JME 17 |

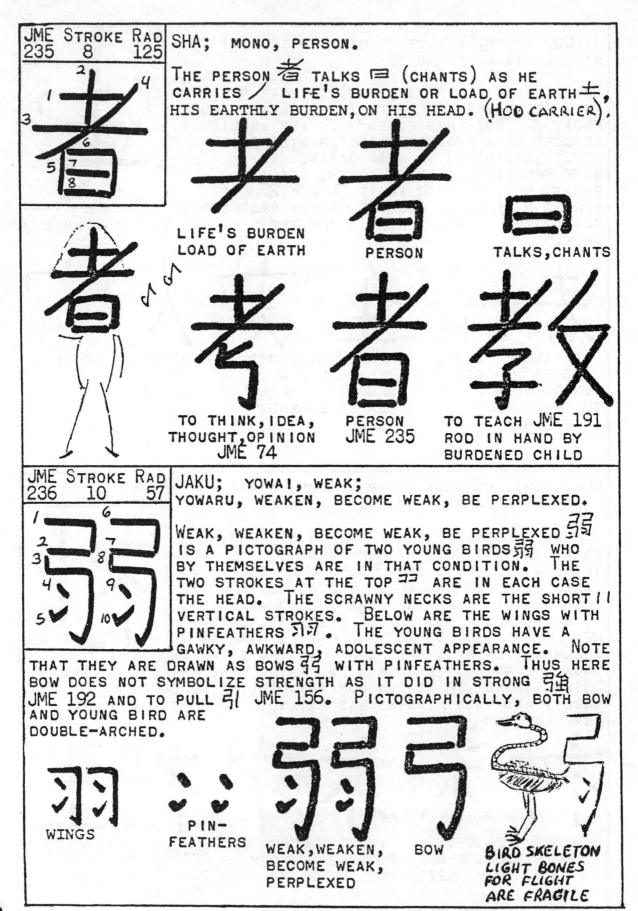

**JME 235 Stroke 8 Rad 125**

SHA; MONO, PERSON.

THE PERSON 者 TALKS 曰 (CHANTS) AS HE
CARRIES ノ LIFE'S BURDEN OR LOAD OF EARTH 土,
HIS EARTHLY BURDEN, ON HIS HEAD. (HOD CARRIER).

LIFE'S BURDEN
LOAD OF EARTH

PERSON

TALKS, CHANTS

TO THINK, IDEA,
THOUGHT, OPINION
JME 74

PERSON
JME 235

TO TEACH JME 191
ROD IN HAND BY
BURDENED CHILD

**JME 236 Stroke 10 Rad 57**

JAKU; YOWAI, WEAK;
YOWARU, WEAKEN, BECOME WEAK, BE PERPLEXED.

WEAK, WEAKEN, BECOME WEAK, BE PERPLEXED 弱
IS A PICTOGRAPH OF TWO YOUNG BIRDS 弱 WHO
BY THEMSELVES ARE IN THAT CONDITION. THE
TWO STROKES AT THE TOP ㄫ ARE IN EACH CASE
THE HEAD. THE SCRAWNY NECKS ARE THE SHORT ||
VERTICAL STROKES. BELOW ARE THE WINGS WITH
PINFEATHERS 冫冫. THE YOUNG BIRDS HAVE A
GAWKY, AWKWARD, ADOLESCENT APPEARANCE. NOTE
THAT THEY ARE DRAWN AS BOWS 弱 WITH PINFEATHERS. THUS HERE
BOW DOES NOT SYMBOLIZE STRENGTH AS IT DID IN STRONG 強
JME 192 AND TO PULL 引 JME 156. PICTOGRAPHICALLY, BOTH BOW
AND YOUNG BIRD ARE
DOUBLE-ARCHED.

WINGS

PIN-
FEATHERS

WEAK, WEAKEN,
BECOME WEAK,
PERPLEXED

BOW

BIRD SKELETON
LIGHT BONES
FOR FLIGHT
ARE FRAGILE

SHU, SU; NUSHI, OWNER, MASTER.

| Rad | Stroke | JME |
|---|---|---|
| 8 | 5 | 237 |

OWNER, MASTER 主 IS AN EXTENSION ` OF
KINGSHIP 王 JME 49 TO THE OWNER, MASTER 主
(OF THE HOUSEHOLD, PATRIARCHAL FAMILY, ETC.)
NOTE THE ANALOGY IN THE USE OF THE DOT TO
SHOW EXTENSION OF SCOPE OR POWER IN OWNER,
MASTER 主 AND OTHER DOTTED KANJI.

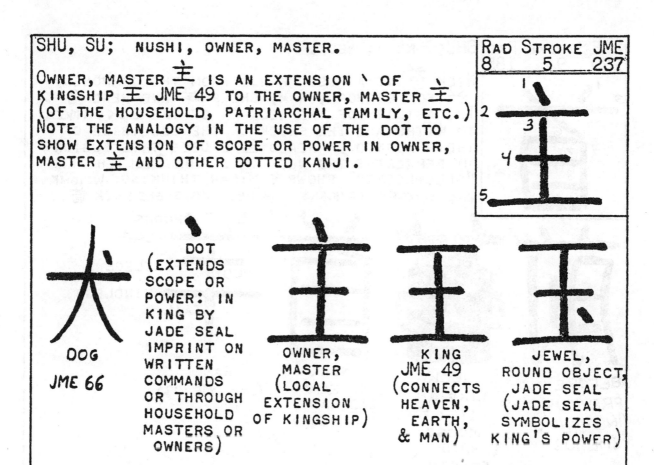

DOG
JME 66

DOT (EXTENDS SCOPE OR POWER: IN KING BY JADE SEAL IMPRINT ON WRITTEN COMMANDS OR THROUGH HOUSEHOLD MASTERS OR OWNERS)

OWNER, MASTER (LOCAL EXTENSION OF KINGSHIP)

KING JME 49 (CONNECTS HEAVEN, EARTH, & MAN)

JEWEL, ROUND OBJECT, JADE SEAL (JADE SEAL SYMBOLIZES KING'S POWER)

SHU; TORU, TO TAKE.

| Rad | Stroke | JME |
|---|---|---|
| 128 | 8 | 238 |

TO TAKE 取 IS A COMPOSITE OF EAR 耳 JME 26
AND HAND 又 ORIGINALLY ⴲ . TO TAKE 取 IS
ASSOCIATED WITH THE HAND 又 WHICH TAKES, AND
THE HANDLES AS OF A BOWL WHICH ARE TAKEN.
THE EARS 耳 CLOSELY RESEMBLE THE HANDLES OF
A BOWL OR URN. A SMALL BOY CAN BE TAKEN
BY THE EAR 耳 (WITH THE HAND 又). IN WAR,
WHEN THE ENEMY WAS TAKEN 取 (KILLED), HIS
EAR 耳 WAS TAKEN 取 (BY THE HAND 又 ) AS
EVIDENCE. HIDEYOSHI'S CONQUEST OF KOREA HAS AS MEMENTOS
EAR-MOUNDS MADE FROM THE EARS 耳 TAKEN 取 IN BATTLE. THE
VIETNAM WAR IS RUMORED TO HAVE CONTINUED THE PRACTICE.

BOWL WITH
HANDLES AS
EARS
(JUG EARED)

EAR      TO TAKE      HAND
(COMPONENT)

TO TAKE
(HAND TAKES
THE EAR)

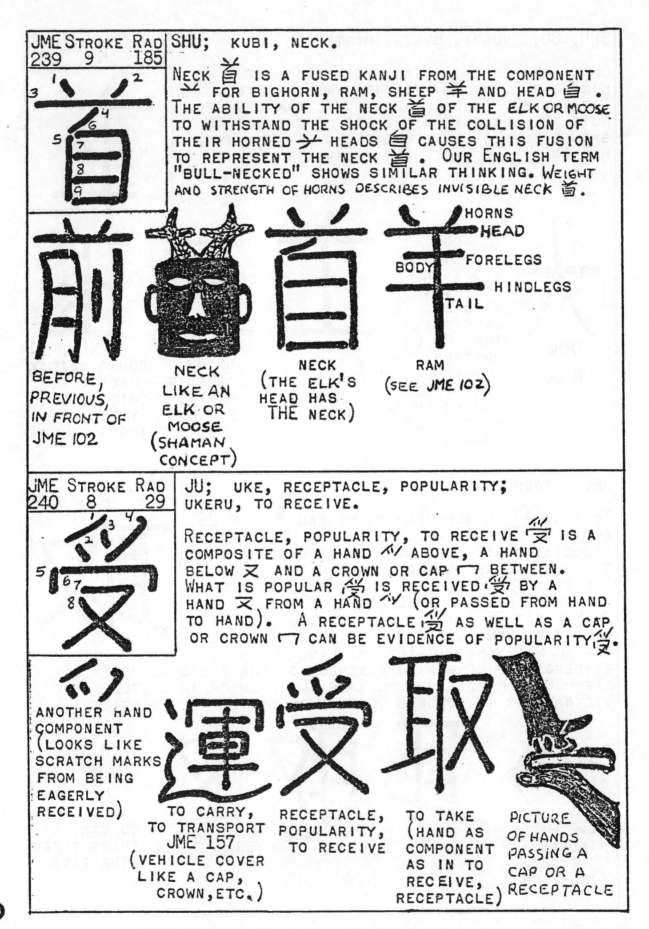

| JME | Stroke | Rad |
|-----|--------|-----|
| 239 | 9 | 185 |

SHU; KUBI, NECK.

NECK 首 IS A FUSED KANJI FROM THE COMPONENT ⸜ FOR BIGHORN, RAM, SHEEP 羊 AND HEAD 自. THE ABILITY OF THE NECK 首 OF THE ELK OR MOOSE TO WITHSTAND THE SHOCK OF THE COLLISION OF THEIR HORNED ⸜ HEADS 自 CAUSES THIS FUSION TO REPRESENT THE NECK 首. OUR ENGLISH TERM "BULL-NECKED" SHOWS SIMILAR THINKING. WEIGHT AND STRENGTH OF HORNS DESCRIBES INVISIBLE NECK 首.

HORNS
HEAD
BODY    FORELEGS
HINDLEGS
TAIL

BEFORE, PREVIOUS, IN FRONT OF JME 102

NECK LIKE AN ELK OR MOOSE (SHAMAN CONCEPT)

NECK (THE ELK'S HEAD HAS THE NECK)

RAM (SEE JME 102)

| JME | Stroke | Rad |
|-----|--------|-----|
| 240 | 8 | 29 |

JU; UKE, RECEPTACLE, POPULARITY; UKERU, TO RECEIVE.

RECEPTACLE, POPULARITY, TO RECEIVE 受 IS A COMPOSITE OF A HAND 𚅢 ABOVE, A HAND BELOW 又 AND A CROWN OR CAP ⼍ BETWEEN. WHAT IS POPULAR 受 IS RECEIVED 受 BY A HAND 又 FROM A HAND 𚅢 (OR PASSED FROM HAND TO HAND). A RECEPTACLE 受 AS WELL AS A CAP OR CROWN ⼍ CAN BE EVIDENCE OF POPULARITY 受.

ANOTHER HAND COMPONENT (LOOKS LIKE SCRATCH MARKS FROM BEING EAGERLY RECEIVED)

TO CARRY, TO TRANSPORT JME 157 (VEHICLE COVER LIKE A CAP, CROWN, ETC.)

RECEPTACLE, POPULARITY, TO RECEIVE

TO TAKE (HAND AS COMPONENT AS IN TO RECEIVE, RECEPTACLE)

PICTURE OF HANDS PASSING A CAP OR A RECEPTACLE

| RAD | STROKE | JME |
| 120 | 11 | 241 |

SHŪ; OWARI, END; OWARU, TO COME TO AN END, TO END; OERU, TO END, TO FINISH, COMPLETE.

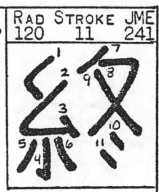

END, TO COME TO AN END, TO END, TO FINISH, TO COMPLETE 終 IS A COMPOSITE OF WINTER 冬 JME 120 AND THREAD, STRING 糸 JME 83. WITH WINTER 冬 THE THREAD 糸 (OF TIME, OF THE SEASONS) ENDS, FINISHES, IS COMPLETE 終. WINTER SYMBOLIZES DEATH OR THE END; SPRING SYMBOLIZES BIRTH, LIFE. WE SPEAK OF THE THREAD OF LIFE, THE THREAD OF TIME.

TWO COCOONS OF THE SILKWORM, THREADS DANGLING

THREAD, STRING JME 83

END, TO END, TO FINISH, TO COMPLETE, TO COME TO AN END

WINTER JME 120 (MAN WITH STICK WALKS ON ICE)

| RAD | STROKE | JME |
| 162 | 11 | 242 |

SHŪ, WEEK.

WEEK 週 HAS THREE COMPONENTS: EARTH, SOIL 土 JME 17; MOVEMENT OR GO AND STOP 辶 ; AND TURN, ROTATE, ROLL 回 JME 168. THE LAST COMPONENT 回 IS WRITTEN IN AN OLDER FORM 冋 WITHOUT THE BOTTOM STROKE ─ . THE WEEKS 週 MOVE OR GO AND STOP 辶 AS THE EARTH 土 TURNS, ROTATES, ROLLS 回 IN ITS ENCLOSURE 冂 OF ATMOSPHERE.

MOVEMENT, TO GO AND STOP

WEEK

TURN, ROTATE, ROLL, A TURN, A ROUND, A TIME

EARTH JME 17 (IN ITS ATMOSPHERIC ENCLOSURE OR WRAPPER)

243-24

| JME | Stroke | Rad |
|-----|--------|-----|
| 243 | 12 | 172 |

SHŪ; ATSUMERU, TO GATHER, COLLECT, (T.V.); ATSUMARU, TO GATHER, ASSEMBLE, TO FLOCK, TO SWARM, (I.V.).

TO GATHER, COLLECT, ASSEMBLE, FLOCK, SWARM 集 IS A COMPOSITE OF A SHORT-TAILED BIRD 隹 (ORIGINALLY 𠁥 ) REPRESENTING MANY SHORT-TAILED BIRDS ON A TREE 木 JME 15. NOTE TO ADVANCE, TO PROGRESS 進 JME 259. SHORT-TAILED BIRDS 隹 COLLECT, GATHER, FLOCK, OR ASSEMBLE 集 IN TREES.

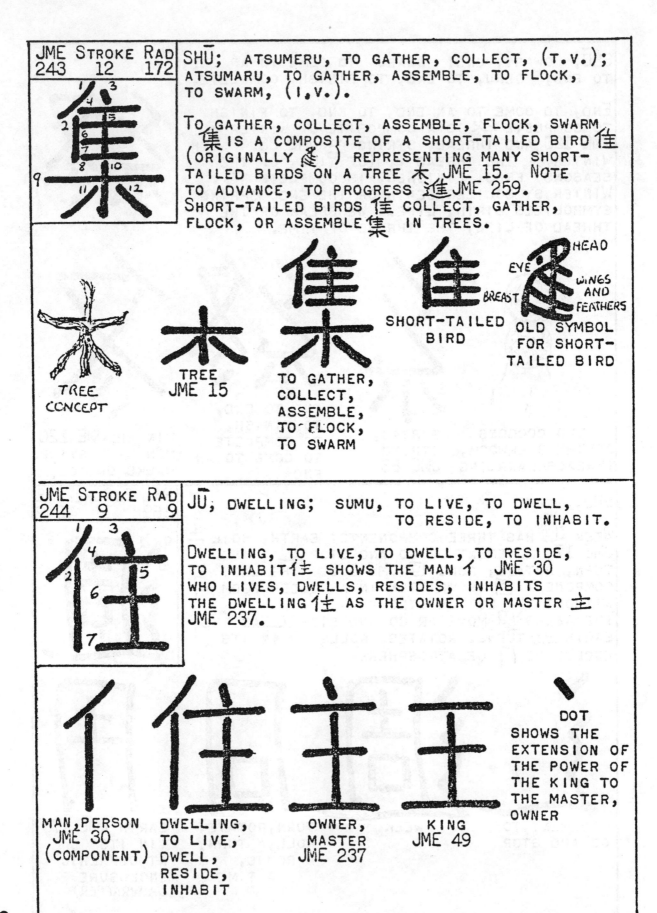

TREE CONCEPT

TREE JME 15

TO GATHER, COLLECT, ASSEMBLE, TO FLOCK, TO SWARM

SHORT-TAILED BIRD

OLD SYMBOL FOR SHORT-TAILED BIRD

HEAD · EYE · BREAST · WINGS AND FEATHERS

| JME | Stroke | Rad |
|-----|--------|-----|
| 244 | 9 | 9 |

JŪ, DWELLING; SUMU, TO LIVE, TO DWELL, TO RESIDE, TO INHABIT.

DWELLING, TO LIVE, TO DWELL, TO RESIDE, TO INHABIT 住 SHOWS THE MAN 亻 JME 30 WHO LIVES, DWELLS, RESIDES, INHABITS THE DWELLING 住 AS THE OWNER OR MASTER 主 JME 237.

MAN, PERSON JME 30 (COMPONENT)

DWELLING, TO LIVE, DWELL, RESIDE, INHABIT

OWNER, MASTER JME 237

KING JME 49

DOT SHOWS THE EXTENSION OF THE POWER OF THE KING TO THE MASTER, OWNER

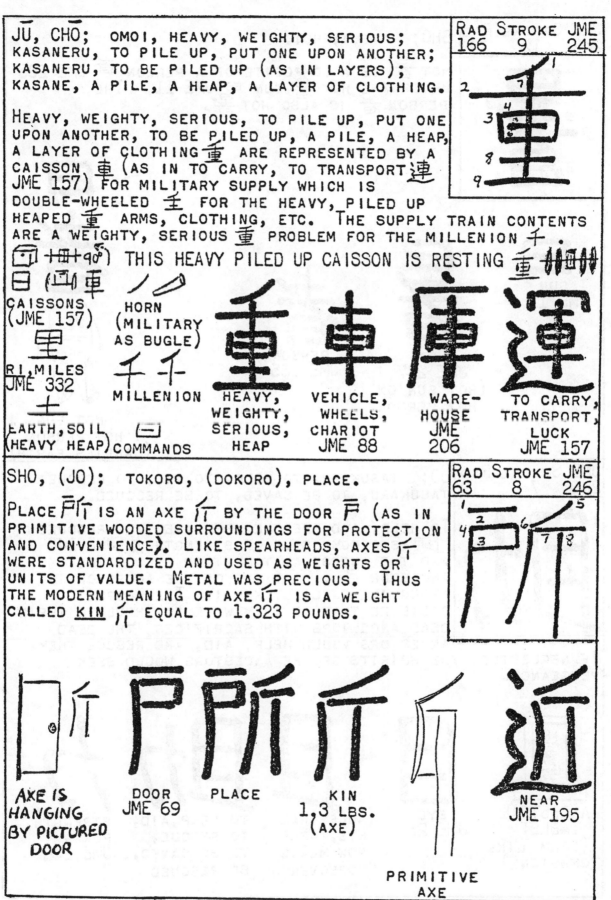

JŪ, CHŌ;  OMOI, HEAVY, WEIGHTY, SERIOUS;
KASANERU, TO PILE UP, PUT ONE UPON ANOTHER;
KASANERU, TO BE PILED UP (AS IN LAYERS);
KASANE, A PILE, A HEAP, A LAYER OF CLOTHING.

| RAD | STROKE | JME |
|-----|--------|-----|
| 166 | 9 | 245 |

HEAVY, WEIGHTY, SERIOUS, TO PILE UP, PUT ONE
UPON ANOTHER, TO BE PILED UP, A PILE, A HEAP,
A LAYER OF CLOTHING 重 ARE REPRESENTED BY A
CAISSON 車 (AS IN TO CARRY, TO TRANSPORT 運
JME 157) FOR MILITARY SUPPLY WHICH IS
DOUBLE-WHEELED 壬 FOR THE HEAVY, PILED UP
HEAPED 重 ARMS, CLOTHING, ETC.  THE SUPPLY TRAIN CONTENTS
ARE A WEIGHTY, SERIOUS 重 PROBLEM FOR THE MILLENION 千.
THIS HEAVY PILED UP CAISSON IS RESTING

CAISSONS
(JME 157)

RI, MILES
JME 332

EARTH, SOIL
(HEAVY HEAP)

HORN
(MILITARY
AS BUGLE)

MILLENION

COMMANDS

HEAVY,
WEIGHTY,
SERIOUS,
HEAP

VEHICLE,
WHEELS,
CHARIOT
JME 88

WARE-
HOUSE
JME
206

TO CARRY,
TRANSPORT,
LUCK
JME 157

---

SHO, (JO);  TOKORO, (DOKORO), PLACE.

| RAD | STROKE | JME |
|-----|--------|-----|
| 63 | 8 | 246 |

PLACE 所 IS AN AXE 斤 BY THE DOOR 戸 (AS IN
PRIMITIVE WOODED SURROUNDINGS FOR PROTECTION
AND CONVENIENCE).  LIKE SPEARHEADS, AXES 斤
WERE STANDARDIZED AND USED AS WEIGHTS OR
UNITS OF VALUE.  METAL WAS PRECIOUS.  THUS
THE MODERN MEANING OF AXE 斤 IS A WEIGHT
CALLED KIN 斤 EQUAL TO 1.323 POUNDS.

AXE IS
HANGING
BY PICTURED
DOOR

DOOR
JME 69

PLACE

KIN
1,3 LBS.
(AXE)

NEAR
JME 195

PRIMITIVE
AXE

247-248

| JME 247 | Stroke 12 | Rad 72 |
|---------|-----------|--------|

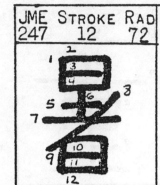

SHO; ATSUI, HOT.

HOT 暑 IS A COMPOSITE OF A PERSON 者 JME 235 UNDER THE HOT 暑 SUN 日 JME 11. THE PERSON 者 IS ALSO HOT 暑.

HOT SUN
HOT PERSON
(CARRIES EARTH)

SUN
JME 11

HOT
JME 247
(HOT SUN ON
HOT PERSON)

PERSON
JME 235

| JME 248 | Stroke 7 | Rad 19 |
|---------|----------|--------|

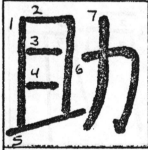

JO; TASUKERU, TO HELP, TO AID, TO RESCUE; TASUKARU, TO BE SAVED, TO BE RESCUED.

TO HELP, AID, RESCUE, BE SAVED, BE RESCUED 助 IS A COMPOSITE OF STRENGTH 力 JME 148 AND THE ANCESTRAL TABLET OR EYE OF THE ANCESTOR 且. THE EYE OF THE ANCESTOR IS AMONG THE EARLIEST KANJI. THE PEOPLE BELIEVED THAT IF THEY WERE FAITHFUL TO THEIR DEAD ANCESTORS WITH SACRIFICES, THE DEAD ANCESTORS WOULD HELP, AID, AND RESCUE THEM. IF NEGLECTED, THE SPIRITS OF THE ANCESTORS WOULD SEEK VENGEANCE.

ANCESTRAL
TABLET
(FORM LIKE
TOMBSTONE)

EYE
JME 25

(ANCESTRAL
EYE, TABLET)
NOW MEANS
"MOREOVER"

TO HELP, AID,
TO RESCUE,
TO BE SAVED,
BE RESCUED

STRENGTH,
POWER
JME 148

SHŌ, (BRIGHT).

BRIGHT 昭 IS A COMPOSITE OF SUN 日 AND CALL, SUMMON 召 . CALL, SUMMON 召 IS A COMPOSITE OF KNIFE 刀 (CUTTING UP A KILLED ANIMAL FOR FOOD) AND THE MOUTH 口 CALLING OR SUMMONING 召 (TO EAT). THE SUN 日 CALLS OR SUMMONS 召 TO ITS BRIGHTNESS 昭 . THE CONCEPT INVOLVES HELIOTROPISM.

| RAD | STROKE | JME |
|-----|--------|-----|
| 72  | 9      | 249 |

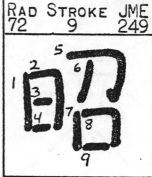

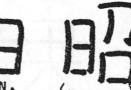 

PUEBLO PETROGLYPH SUN SYMBOL

EGYPTIAN HIEROGLYPH SUN SYMBOL

SUN, DAY JME 11

昭 (BRIGHT)

召 TO CALL, SUMMON

召

---

SHŌ; KATSU, TO WIN, TO CONQUER, TO DEFEAT.

TO WIN, TO CONQUER, TO DEFEAT 勝 IS A COMPOSITE OF THE MOON 月 JME 12 WHICH WAXES AND WANES LIKE EMPIRES (ACCORDING TO THE Three Kingdoms OR San Kuo), AND THE STRENGTH 力 JME 148 OF FIRE 火 JME 13 (THE RAVAGER OR DESTROYER) SHOWN FUSED WITH TWO LINES 二 LIKE FOUR LEGS OF THE COW 牛 OR GOAT 羊 TO INDICATE THE RAPID RUNNING MOVEMENT OF THE WINNING, CONQUERING, DEFEATING FIRE.

| RAD | STROKE | JME |
|-----|--------|-----|
| 130 | 12     | 250 |

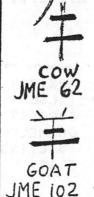

COW JME 62

GOAT JME 102

月 MOON JME 12 WAXES & WANES AS EMPIRES

勝 TO WIN, CONQUER, TO DEFEAT

火 FIRE JME 13 (RAVAGES & DESTROYS)

二 TWO LINES. AS FOR FOUR LEGS OF THE COW OR GOAT

力 STRENGTH, POWER JME 148

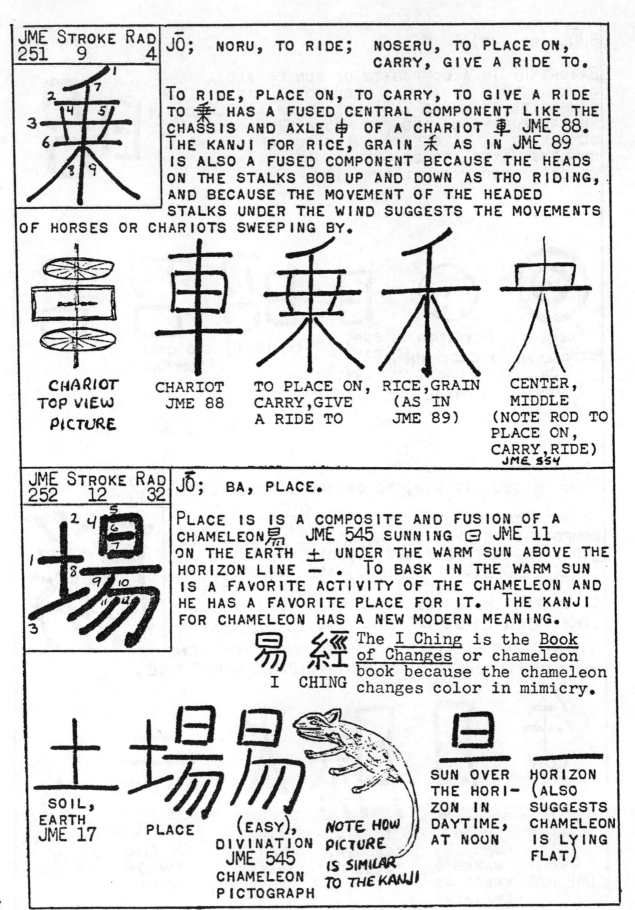

| JME 251 | Stroke 9 | Rad 4 |
|---|---|---|

JŌ; NORU, TO RIDE; NOSERU, TO PLACE ON, CARRY, GIVE A RIDE TO.

TO RIDE, PLACE ON, TO CARRY, TO GIVE A RIDE TO 乗 HAS A FUSED CENTRAL COMPONENT LIKE THE CHASSIS AND AXLE 東 OF A CHARIOT 車 JME 88. THE KANJI FOR RICE, GRAIN 禾 AS IN JME 89 IS ALSO A FUSED COMPONENT BECAUSE THE HEADS ON THE STALKS BOB UP AND DOWN AS THO RIDING, AND BECAUSE THE MOVEMENT OF THE HEADED STALKS UNDER THE WIND SUGGESTS THE MOVEMENTS OF HORSES OR CHARIOTS SWEEPING BY.

CHARIOT TOP VIEW PICTURE

CHARIOT JME 88

TO PLACE ON, CARRY, GIVE A RIDE TO

RICE, GRAIN (AS IN JME 89)

CENTER, MIDDLE (NOTE ROD TO PLACE ON, CARRY, RIDE) JME 554

| JME 252 | Stroke 12 | Rad 32 |
|---|---|---|

JŌ; BA, PLACE.

PLACE IS IS A COMPOSITE AND FUSION OF A CHAMELEON 昜 JME 545 SUNNING ⊟ JME 11 ON THE EARTH 土 UNDER THE WARM SUN ABOVE THE HORIZON LINE 一 . TO BASK IN THE WARM SUN IS A FAVORITE ACTIVITY OF THE CHAMELEON AND HE HAS A FAVORITE PLACE FOR IT. THE KANJI FOR CHAMELEON HAS A NEW MODERN MEANING.

易經

I CHING

The I Ching is the Book of Changes or chameleon book because the chameleon changes color in mimicry.

SOIL, EARTH JME 17

PLACE

(EASY), DIVINATION JME 545 CHAMELEON PICTOGRAPH

NOTE HOW PICTURE IS SIMILAR TO THE KANJI

SUN OVER THE HORIZON IN DAYTIME, AT NOON

HORIZON (ALSO SUGGESTS CHAMELEON IS LYING FLAT)

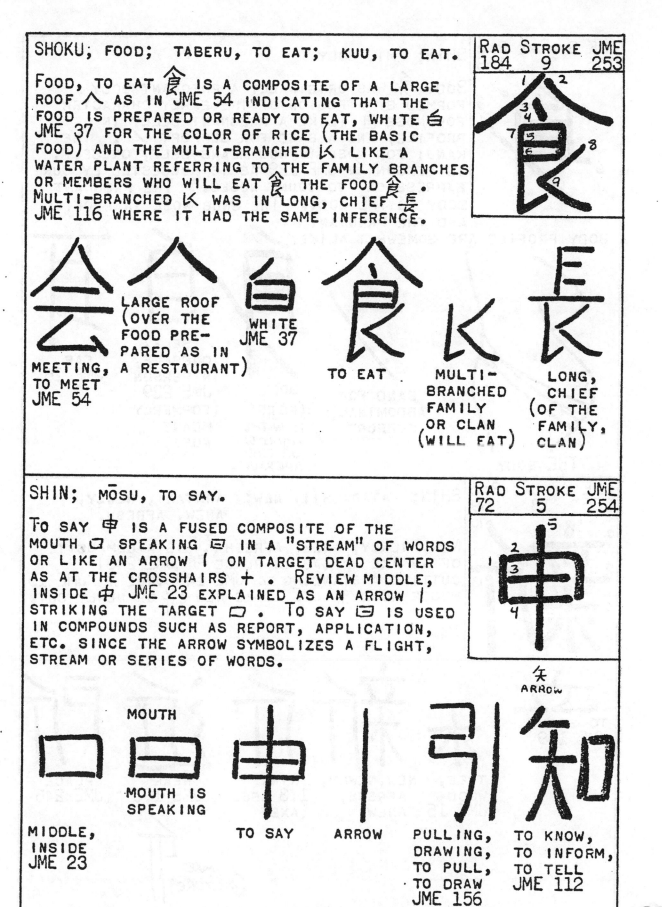

SHOKU; FOOD; TABERU, TO EAT; KUU, TO EAT.

| RAD 184 | STROKE 9 | JME 253 |
|---|---|---|

FOOD, TO EAT 食 IS A COMPOSITE OF A LARGE ROOF 人 AS IN JME 54 INDICATING THAT THE FOOD IS PREPARED OR READY TO EAT, WHITE 白 JME 37 FOR THE COLOR OF RICE (THE BASIC FOOD) AND THE MULTI-BRANCHED 以 LIKE A WATER PLANT REFERRING TO THE FAMILY BRANCHES OR MEMBERS WHO WILL EAT 食 THE FOOD 食. MULTI-BRANCHED 以 WAS IN LONG, CHIEF 長 JME 116 WHERE IT HAD THE SAME INFERENCE.

会 MEETING, TO MEET JME 54

人 LARGE ROOF (OVER THE FOOD PREPARED AS IN A RESTAURANT)

白 WHITE JME 37

食 TO EAT

以 MULTI-BRANCHED FAMILY OR CLAN (WILL EAT)

長 LONG, CHIEF (OF THE FAMILY, CLAN)

SHIN; MŌSU, TO SAY.

| RAD 72 | STROKE 5 | JME 254 |
|---|---|---|

TO SAY 申 IS A FUSED COMPOSITE OF THE MOUTH 口 SPEAKING 曰 IN A "STREAM" OF WORDS OR LIKE AN ARROW | ON TARGET DEAD CENTER AS AT THE CROSSHAIRS +. REVIEW MIDDLE, INSIDE 中 JME 23 EXPLAINED AS AN ARROW | STRIKING THE TARGET 口. TO SAY 曰 IS USED IN COMPOUNDS SUCH AS REPORT, APPLICATION, ETC. SINCE THE ARROW SYMBOLIZES A FLIGHT, STREAM OR SERIES OF WORDS.

矢 ARROW

口 MOUTH

曰 MOUTH IS SPEAKING

中 MIDDLE, INSIDE JME 23

申 TO SAY

| ARROW

引 PULLING, DRAWING, TO PULL, TO DRAW JME 156

知 TO KNOW, TO INFORM, TO TELL JME 112

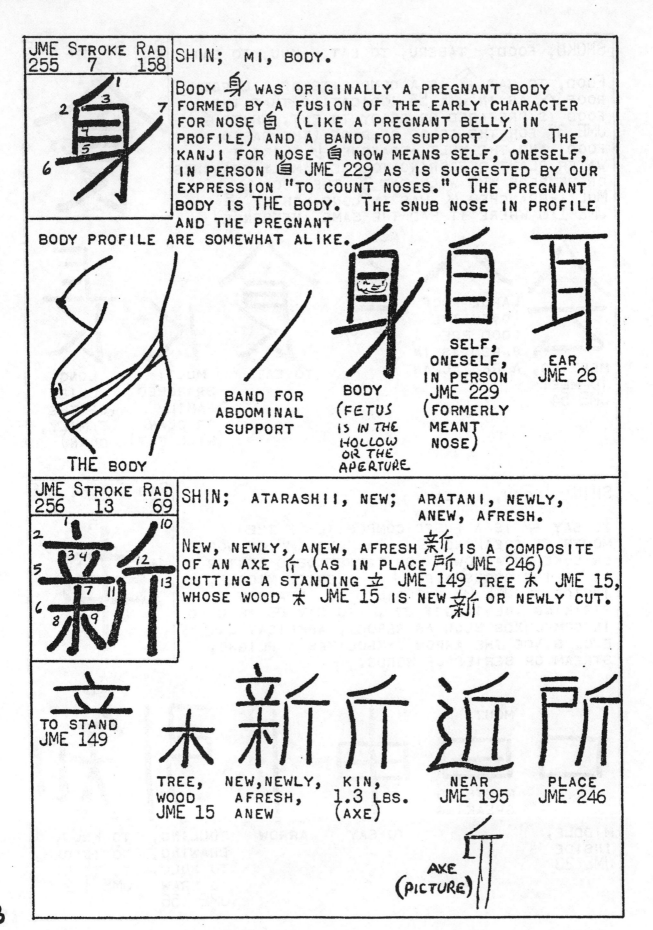

| JME 255 | Stroke 7 | Rad 158 |
| --- | --- | --- |

SHIN; MI, BODY.

BODY 身 WAS ORIGINALLY A PREGNANT BODY FORMED BY A FUSION OF THE EARLY CHARACTER FOR NOSE 自 (LIKE A PREGNANT BELLY IN PROFILE) AND A BAND FOR SUPPORT ノ. THE KANJI FOR NOSE 自 NOW MEANS SELF, ONESELF, IN PERSON 自 JME 229 AS IS SUGGESTED BY OUR EXPRESSION "TO COUNT NOSES." THE PREGNANT BODY IS THE BODY. THE SNUB NOSE IN PROFILE AND THE PREGNANT BODY PROFILE ARE SOMEWHAT ALIKE.

THE BODY

BAND FOR ABDOMINAL SUPPORT

BODY (FETUS IS IN THE HOLLOW OR THE APERTURE

SELF, ONESELF, IN PERSON JME 229 (FORMERLY MEANT NOSE)

EAR JME 26

| JME 256 | Stroke 13 | Rad 69 |
| --- | --- | --- |

SHIN; ATARASHII, NEW; ARATANI, NEWLY, ANEW, AFRESH.

NEW, NEWLY, ANEW, AFRESH 新 IS A COMPOSITE OF AN AXE 斤 (AS IN PLACE 所 JME 246) CUTTING A STANDING 立 JME 149 TREE 木 JME 15, WHOSE WOOD 木 JME 15 IS NEW 新 OR NEWLY CUT.

TO STAND JME 149

TREE, WOOD JME 15

NEW, NEWLY, AFRESH, ANEW

KIN, 1.3 LBS. (AXE)

NEAR JME 195

PLACE JME 246

AXE (PICTURE)

| RAD | STROKE | JME |
|-----|--------|-----|
| 113 | 9 | 257 |

SHIN, JIN; KAMI, (GAMI), GOD, DEITY, SPIRIT.

DIETY, GOD, SPIRIT 神 IS A COMPOSITE OF
TO SHOW, POINT OUT, INDICATE 示 IN ITS
COMPONENT FORM 礻 AND TO SAY 申 JME 254.
TO SHOW, POINT OUT, INDICATE 示 JME 622
IS A COMPOSITE OF WHAT IS ABOVE 二 (AS IN
THE LAYERS 二 OF CLOUD 雲 JME 47) AND THREE
RAYS SPREADING RADIANCE 小 AS FROM THE SUN,
MOON, AND STARS WHICH SHOW, POINT OUT, AND
INDICATE 示 IN ASTROLOGY AND NAVIGATION.
THE COMPONENT FORM DEVELOPED FOR CONVENIENCE IN WRITING 礻.

社

COMPANY, FIRM,
CORPORATION,
SHINTO SHRINE
JME 234

示

TO SHOW,
POINT OUT,
INDICATE
JME 622

礻

TO SHOW,
POINT OUT,
INDICATE
(COMPONENT)

神

GOD,
DEITY,
SPIRIT

申

TO SAY,
IS CALLED
JME 254

| RAD | STROKE | JME |
|-----|--------|-----|
| 85 | 11 | 258 |

SHIN; FUKAI, DEEP, PROFOUND, DENSE;
FUKASA, DEPTH, PROFUNDITY.

DEEP, PROFOUND, DENSE, DEPTH, PROFUNDITY
IS A COMPOSITE OF A STICK 木 (AS IN TREE
JME 15) IN THE WATERY 氵 JME 14 DEEP,
PROFOUND DEPTHS 深 OF A HOLE 冗 (AS IN
SKY 空 JME 65). 深 NOTE THAT THE SKY HAS
DEPTHS AND A HOLE.

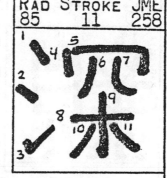

De blind horse stick'n in a big mud hole,
    Doodah! doodah!
Can't touch de bottom wid a ten-foot pole,
    Oh! doodah day! (Foster, Camptown Races).

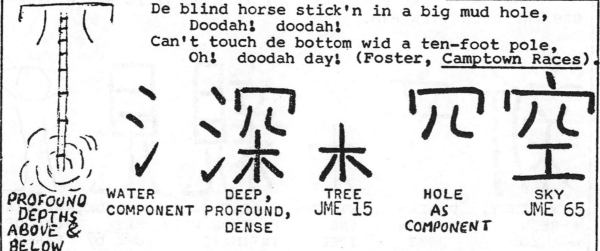

PROFOUND
DEPTHS
ABOVE &
BELOW

氵

WATER
COMPONENT

深

DEEP,
PROFOUND,
DENSE

木

TREE
JME 15

冗

HOLE
AS
COMPONENT

空

SKY
JME 65

| JME 259 | STROKE 11 | RAD 162 |
|---|---|---|

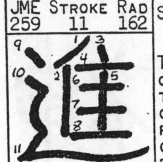

SHIN; SUSUMU, TO ADVANCE, TO PROGRESS, TO PROCEED.

TO ADVANCE, TO PROGRESS, TO PROCEED 進 IS A COMPOSITE OF A SHORT-TAILED BIRD 隹 (AS IN TO GATHER, TO COLLECT 集 JME 243) AND TO GO FAST AND STOP SUDDENLY 辶 (AS IN ROAD, PATH 道 JME 122). THE SHORT-TAILED BIRDS 隹 GO FAST AND STOP SUDDENLY AS THEY ADVANCE, PROGRESS, PROCEED 進. THE SHORT-TAILED BIRDS 隹 SUGGEST THE MILITARY SINCE THEY HAVE LEADERS, POST SENTINELS, ADVANCE IN FLOCKS, AND DESPOIL THE COUNTRYSIDE OF CROPS LIKE A MARAUDING ARMY.

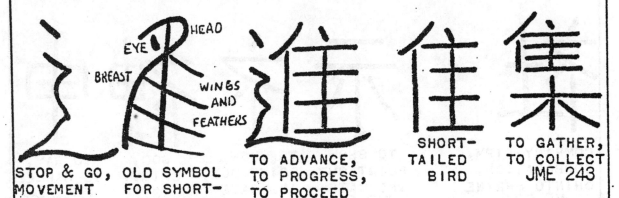

STOP & GO, MOVEMENT

OLD SYMBOL FOR SHORT-TAILED BIRD

TO ADVANCE, TO PROGRESS, TO PROCEED

SHORT-TAILED BIRD

TO GATHER, TO COLLECT JME 243

| JME 260 | STROKE 16 | RAD 147 |
|---|---|---|

SHIN; OYA, PARENT; SHITASHIMU, MAKE FRIENDS WITH, BECOME INTIMATE WITH; SHITASHII, INTIMATE, FRIENDLY.

PARENT, MAKE FRIENDS WITH, BECOME INTIMATE WITH, INTIMATE, FRIENDLY 親 SEES OR LOOKS AFTER 見 JME 67 (THE CHILD OR FRIEND) AS THO FROM A STANDING 立 JME 149 TREE 木 JME 15. OBSERVATION POSTS WERE IN TREES FOR A SUPERIOR VIEW. TO THE SMALL CHILD, ADULTS ARE SOMEWHAT LIKE WALKING TREES WHICH OVERSEE AND OVER VIEW HIM.

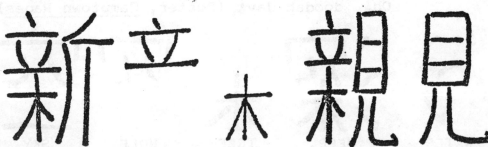

NEW, NEWLY, AFRESH JME 256

OBSERVATION POST

STANDING TREE

PARENT, MAKE FRIENDS WITH, INTIMATE

TO LOOK, SEE JME 67

WALKING EYE OF PARENT

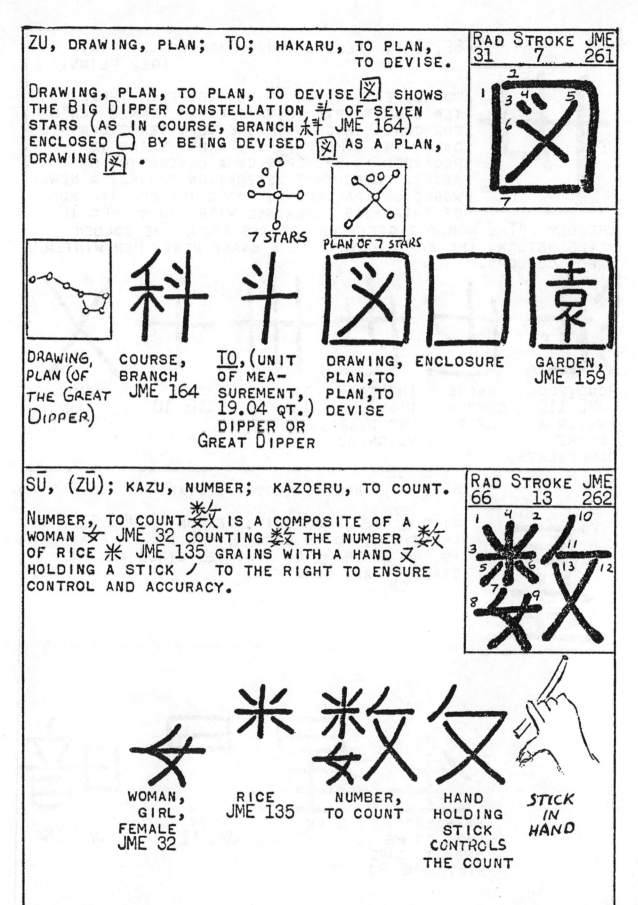

ZU, DRAWING, PLAN; TO; HAKARU, TO PLAN, TO DEVISE.

| RAD | STROKE | JME |
|-----|--------|-----|
| 31  | 7      | 261 |

DRAWING, PLAN, TO PLAN, TO DEVISE 図 SHOWS THE BIG DIPPER CONSTELLATION 斗 OF SEVEN STARS (AS IN COURSE, BRANCH 科 JME 164) ENCLOSED ☐ BY BEING DEVISED 図 AS A PLAN, DRAWING 図.

7 STARS

PLAN OF 7 STARS

DRAWING, PLAN (OF THE GREAT DIPPER)

COURSE, BRANCH JME 164

TO, (UNIT OF MEA-SUREMENT, 19.04 QT.) DIPPER OR GREAT DIPPER

DRAWING, PLAN, TO PLAN, TO DEVISE

ENCLOSURE

GARDEN, JME 159

---

SŪ, (ZŪ); KAZU, NUMBER; KAZOERU, TO COUNT.

| RAD | STROKE | JME |
|-----|--------|-----|
| 66  | 13     | 262 |

NUMBER, TO COUNT 数 IS A COMPOSITE OF A WOMAN 女 JME 32 COUNTING 数 THE NUMBER 数 OF RICE 米 JME 135 GRAINS WITH A HAND 又 HOLDING A STICK ノ TO THE RIGHT TO ENSURE CONTROL AND ACCURACY.

WOMAN, GIRL, FEMALE JME 32

RICE JME 135

NUMBER, TO COUNT

HAND HOLDING STICK CONTROLS THE COUNT

STICK IN HAND

| JME 263 | Stroke 5 | Rad 1 |
|---|---|---|

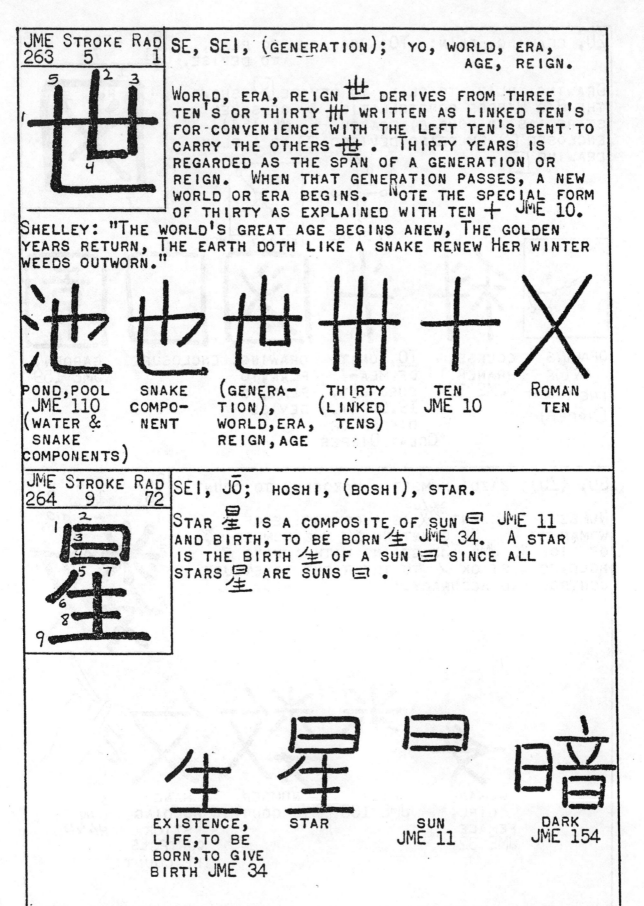

SE, SEI, (GENERATION); YO, WORLD, ERA, AGE, REIGN.

WORLD, ERA, REIGN 世 DERIVES FROM THREE TEN'S OR THIRTY 卅 WRITTEN AS LINKED TEN'S FOR CONVENIENCE WITH THE LEFT TEN'S BENT TO CARRY THE OTHERS 世. THIRTY YEARS IS REGARDED AS THE SPAN OF A GENERATION OR REIGN. WHEN THAT GENERATION PASSES, A NEW WORLD OR ERA BEGINS. NOTE THE SPECIAL FORM OF THIRTY AS EXPLAINED WITH TEN 十 JME 10.

SHELLEY: "THE WORLD'S GREAT AGE BEGINS ANEW, THE GOLDEN YEARS RETURN, THE EARTH DOTH LIKE A SNAKE RENEW HER WINTER WEEDS OUTWORN."

POND, POOL
JME 110
(WATER &
SNAKE
COMPONENTS)

SNAKE
COMPO-
NENT

(GENERA-
TION),
WORLD, ERA,
REIGN, AGE

THIRTY
(LINKED
TENS)

TEN
JME 10

ROMAN
TEN

| JME 264 | Stroke 9 | Rad 72 |
|---|---|---|

SEI, JŌ; HOSHI, (BOSHI), STAR.

STAR 星 IS A COMPOSITE OF SUN 日 JME 11 AND BIRTH, TO BE BORN 生 JME 34. A STAR IS THE BIRTH 生 OF A SUN 日 SINCE ALL STARS 星 ARE SUNS 日.

EXISTENCE,
LIFE, TO BE
BORN, TO GIVE
BIRTH JME 34

STAR

SUN
JME 11

DARK
JME 154

SEI; HARE, FINE WEATHER.
HARERU, TO CLEAR, BECOME CLEAR (WEATHER),
TO BE DISPELLED.

| RAD | STROKE | JME |
|-----|--------|-----|
| 72  | 12     | 265 |

CLEAR WEATHER, FINE WEATHER, TO CLEAR,
TO BECOME CLEAR, TO BE DISPELLED 晴 IS A
COMPOSITE OF BLUE 青 JME 36 (OR GREEN) FOR
THE SKY, AND THE SUN 日 JME 11 TO EMPHASIZE
THE FINE CLEAR WEATHER 晴 . THE FINE CLEAR
WEATHER 日青 IS SUCH AS WHEN THE MOON IS ABLE
TO PENETRATE THE THICK FOLIAGE 三 CASTING
BLUE SHADOWS LIKE THE BLUE 青 OF A SUNNY 日 CLEAR WEATHER 晴

| 日 | 晴 | 青 | 明 |
|----|----|----|----|
| SUN, DAY JME 11 | FINE WEATHER, TO CLEAR, BECOME CLEAR, BE DISPELLED | BLUE JME 36 | LIGHT, CLEAR, BRIGHT, TO DAWN JME 141 |

SEN; FUNA, FUNE, (BUNE), SHIP, BOAT, LINER.

| RAD | STROKE | JME |
|-----|--------|-----|
| 137 | 11     | 266 |

SHIP, BOAT, LINER 船 IS A COMPOSITE OF A
PICTOGRAPH OF A BOAT 舟 AND EIGHT 八 JME 8
MOUTHS 口 JME 27 FOR THE FAMILY OR CREW
ON BOARD. THE IDEAL FAMILY CONSISTS OF
EIGHT MEMBERS. THE CATHOLIC FATHERS
SUGGESTED THAT THE EIGHT MEMBERS WERE NOAH
AND HIS FAMILY ON THE ARK. THE PICTOGRAPH
OF A BOAT SHOWS THE RUDDER, SAIL, TWO
OCCUPANTS, AND A HULL OPEN-ENDED TOWARDS THE
BOW ABOVE THE WATER LINE AS ORIENTAL SKIFFS OFTEN ARE.

RUDDER - - - -
SAILOR - - - -
SAIL - - - -
SAILOR - - - -
OPEN BOW - -

| TOP VIEW OF BOAT | 舟 BOAT | 船 SHIP, BOAT, LINER | 八 EIGHT JME 8 | 口 MOUTH JME 27 (PERSON) |
|---|---|---|---|---|

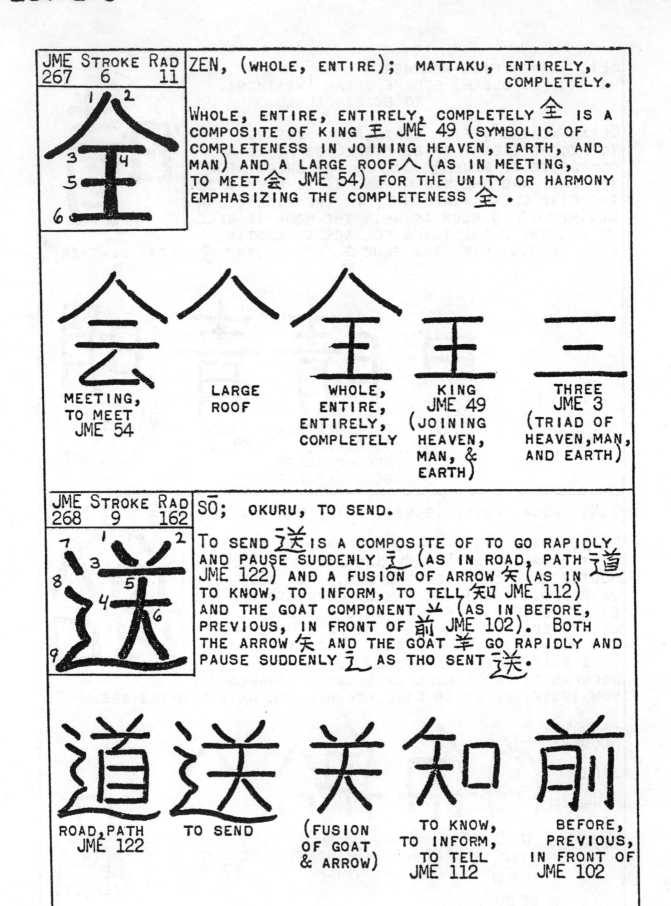

| JME 267 | Stroke 6 | Rad 11 |
| --- | --- | --- |

ZEN, (WHOLE, ENTIRE); MATTAKU, ENTIRELY, COMPLETELY.

WHOLE, ENTIRE, ENTIRELY, COMPLETELY 全 IS A COMPOSITE OF KING 王 JME 49 (SYMBOLIC OF COMPLETENESS IN JOINING HEAVEN, EARTH, AND MAN) AND A LARGE ROOF 入 (AS IN MEETING, TO MEET 会 JME 54) FOR THE UNITY OR HARMONY EMPHASIZING THE COMPLETENESS 全.

会
MEETING, TO MEET JME 54

入
LARGE ROOF

全
WHOLE, ENTIRE, ENTIRELY, COMPLETELY

王
KING JME 49 (JOINING HEAVEN, MAN, & EARTH)

三
THREE JME 3 (TRIAD OF HEAVEN, MAN, AND EARTH)

| JME 268 | Stroke 9 | Rad 162 |
| --- | --- | --- |

SŌ; OKURU, TO SEND.

TO SEND 送 IS A COMPOSITE OF TO GO RAPIDLY AND PAUSE SUDDENLY ⻌ (AS IN ROAD, PATH 道 JME 122) AND A FUSION OF ARROW 矢 (AS IN TO KNOW, TO INFORM, TO TELL 知 JME 112) AND THE GOAT COMPONENT 丷 (AS IN BEFORE, PREVIOUS, IN FRONT OF 前 JME 102). BOTH THE ARROW 矢 AND THE GOAT 羊 GO RAPIDLY AND PAUSE SUDDENLY ⻌ AS THO SENT 送.

道
ROAD, PATH JME 122

送
TO SEND

关
(FUSION OF GOAT & ARROW)

知
TO KNOW, TO INFORM, TO TELL JME 112

前
BEFORE, PREVIOUS, IN FRONT OF JME 102

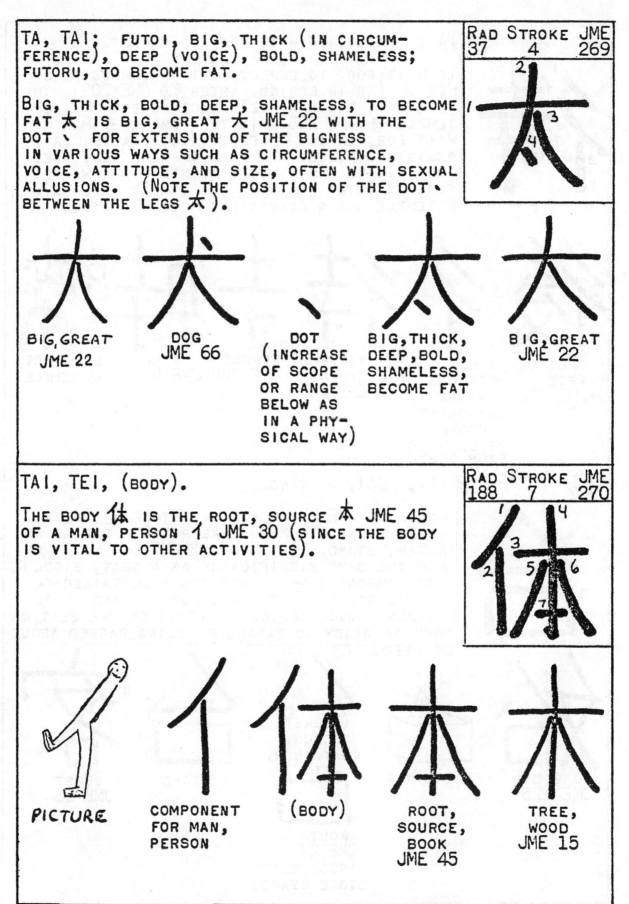

TA, TAI; FUTOI, BIG, THICK (IN CIRCUM-
FERENCE), DEEP (VOICE), BOLD, SHAMELESS;
FUTORU, TO BECOME FAT.

BIG, THICK, BOLD, DEEP, SHAMELESS, TO BECOME
FAT 太 IS BIG, GREAT 大 JME 22 WITH THE
DOT 、 FOR EXTENSION OF THE BIGNESS
IN VARIOUS WAYS SUCH AS CIRCUMFERENCE,
VOICE, ATTITUDE, AND SIZE, OFTEN WITH SEXUAL
ALLUSIONS. (NOTE THE POSITION OF THE DOT 、
BETWEEN THE LEGS 太).

| RAD | STROKE | JME |
|-----|--------|-----|
| 37 | 4 | 269 |

BIG, GREAT
JME 22

DOG
JME 66

DOT
(INCREASE
OF SCOPE
OR RANGE
BELOW AS
IN A PHY-
SICAL WAY)

BIG, THICK,
DEEP, BOLD,
SHAMELESS,
BECOME FAT

BIG, GREAT
JME 22

TAI, TEI, (BODY).

THE BODY 体 IS THE ROOT, SOURCE 本 JME 45
OF A MAN, PERSON イ JME 30 (SINCE THE BODY
IS VITAL TO OTHER ACTIVITIES).

| RAD | STROKE | JME |
|-----|--------|-----|
| 188 | 7 | 270 |

PICTURE

COMPONENT
FOR MAN,
PERSON

(BODY)

ROOT,
SOURCE,
BOOK
JME 45

TREE,
WOOD
JME 15

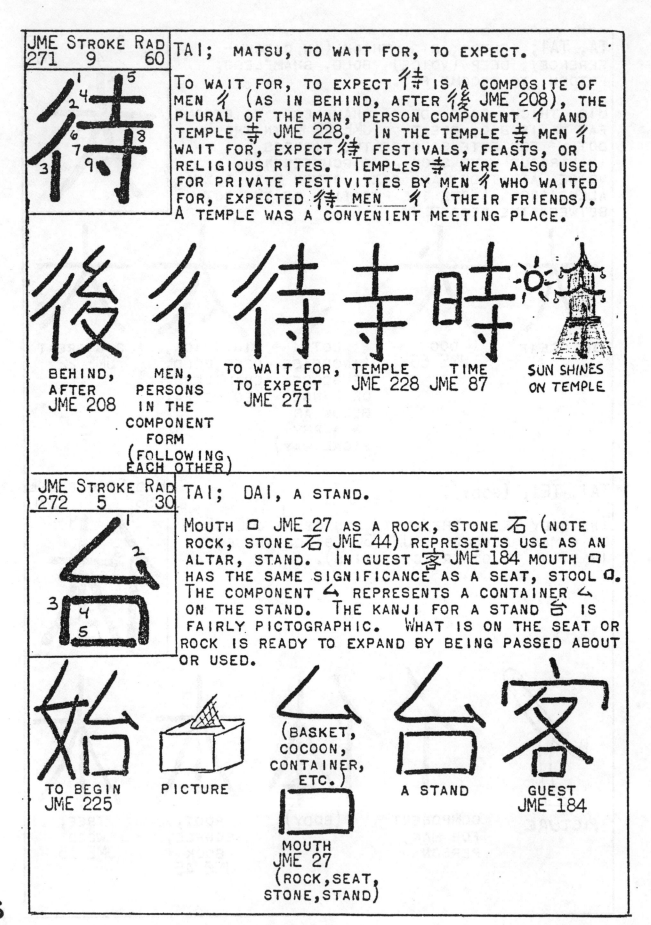

| JME 271 | Stroke 9 | Rad 60 |
|---|---|---|

TAI; MATSU, TO WAIT FOR, TO EXPECT.

TO WAIT FOR, TO EXPECT 待 IS A COMPOSITE OF MEN 彳 (AS IN BEHIND, AFTER 後 JME 208), THE PLURAL OF THE MAN, PERSON COMPONENT 亻 AND TEMPLE 寺 JME 228. IN THE TEMPLE 寺 MEN 彳 WAIT FOR, EXPECT 待 FESTIVALS, FEASTS, OR RELIGIOUS RITES. TEMPLES 寺 WERE ALSO USED FOR PRIVATE FESTIVITIES BY MEN 彳 WHO WAITED FOR, EXPECTED 待 MEN 彳 (THEIR FRIENDS). A TEMPLE WAS A CONVENIENT MEETING PLACE.

BEHIND, AFTER
JME 208

MEN, PERSONS IN THE COMPONENT FORM (FOLLOWING EACH OTHER)

TO WAIT FOR, TO EXPECT
JME 271

TEMPLE
JME 228

TIME
JME 87

SUN SHINES ON TEMPLE

| JME 272 | Stroke 5 | Rad 30 |
|---|---|---|

TAI; DAI, A STAND.

MOUTH 口 JME 27 AS A ROCK, STONE 石 (NOTE ROCK, STONE 石 JME 44) REPRESENTS USE AS AN ALTAR, STAND. IN GUEST 客 JME 184 MOUTH 口 HAS THE SAME SIGNIFICANCE AS A SEAT, STOOL ロ. THE COMPONENT ム REPRESENTS A CONTAINER ム ON THE STAND. THE KANJI FOR A STAND 台 IS FAIRLY PICTOGRAPHIC. WHAT IS ON THE SEAT OR ROCK IS READY TO EXPAND BY BEING PASSED ABOUT OR USED.

TO BEGIN
JME 225

PICTURE

(BASKET, COCOON, CONTAINER, ETC.)

MOUTH
JME 27
(ROCK, SEAT, STONE, STAND)

A STAND

GUEST
JME 184

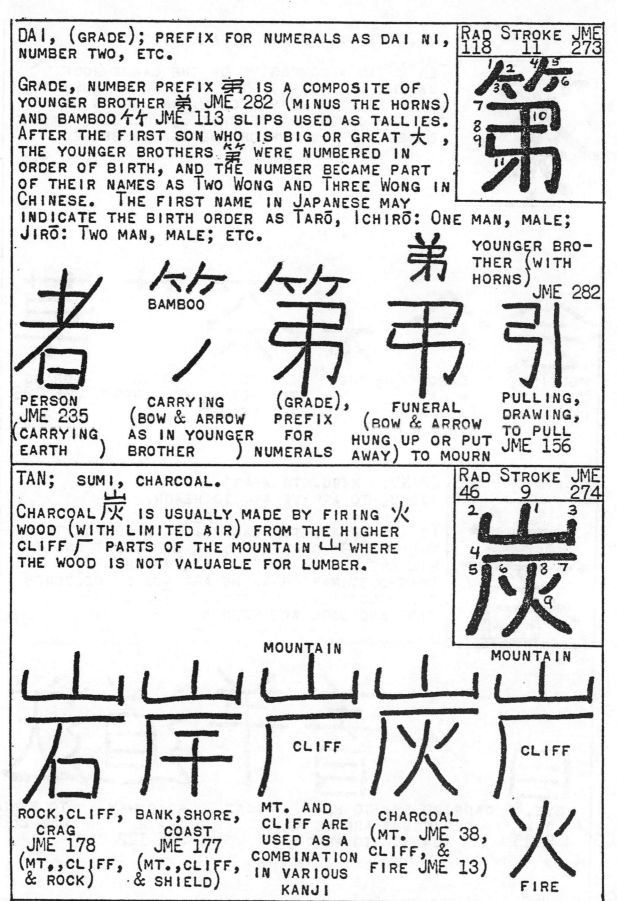

DAI, (GRADE); PREFIX FOR NUMERALS AS DAI NI, NUMBER TWO, ETC.

GRADE, NUMBER PREFIX 第 IS A COMPOSITE OF YOUNGER BROTHER 弟 JME 282 (MINUS THE HORNS) AND BAMBOO 竹 JME 113 SLIPS USED AS TALLIES. AFTER THE FIRST SON WHO IS BIG OR GREAT 大 , THE YOUNGER BROTHERS 第 WERE NUMBERED IN ORDER OF BIRTH, AND THE NUMBER BECAME PART OF THEIR NAMES AS TWO WONG AND THREE WONG IN CHINESE. THE FIRST NAME IN JAPANESE MAY INDICATE THE BIRTH ORDER AS TARŌ, ICHIRŌ: ONE MAN, MALE; JIRŌ: TWO MAN, MALE; ETC.

| RAD | STROKE | JME |
|-----|--------|-----|
| 118 | 11 | 273 |

PERSON
JME 235
(CARRYING
EARTH )

BAMBOO

CARRYING
(BOW & ARROW
AS IN YOUNGER
BROTHER )

(GRADE),
PREFIX
FOR
NUMERALS

FUNERAL
(BOW & ARROW
HUNG UP OR PUT
AWAY) TO MOURN

YOUNGER BRO-
THER (WITH
HORNS)
JME 282

PULLING,
DRAWING,
TO PULL
JME 156

TAN; SUMI, CHARCOAL.

CHARCOAL 炭 IS USUALLY MADE BY FIRING 火 WOOD (WITH LIMITED AIR) FROM THE HIGHER CLIFF 厂 PARTS OF THE MOUNTAIN 山 WHERE THE WOOD IS NOT VALUABLE FOR LUMBER.

| RAD | STROKE | JME |
|-----|--------|-----|
| 46 | 9 | 274 |

MOUNTAIN

MOUNTAIN

ROCK,CLIFF,
CRAG
JME 178
(MT.,CLIFF,
& ROCK)

BANK,SHORE,
COAST
JME 177
(MT.,CLIFF,
& SHIELD)

CLIFF

MT. AND
CLIFF ARE
USED AS A
COMBINATION
IN VARIOUS
KANJI

CHARCOAL
(MT. JME 38,
CLIFF, &
FIRE JME 13)

CLIFF

FIRE

| JME 275 | Stroke 9 | Rad 140 |
|---------|----------|---------|

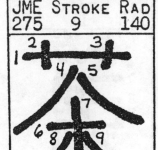

CHA, TEA, TEA PLANT, TEA LEAVES.

TEA 茶 IS A COMPOSITE OF THE LARGE ROOF 𠆢 (OF THE TEA HOUSE), THE TREE 木 OR BUSH ON WHICH THE TEA LEAVES GROW, AND GRASS 艹 THE TOP COMPONENT OF LEAF 葉 JME 327 FOR THE LEAVES 葉 FROM WHICH THE TEA IS BREWED.

会
MEETING,
TO MEET
JME 54

𠆢
LARGE
ROOF
(AS OF
TEAHOUSE)

木
TREE

茶
TEA,
TEA PLANT,
TEA LEAVES

艹
GRASS
COMPONENT

草
GRASS
JME 106

| JME 276 | Stroke 12 | Rad 123 |
|---------|-----------|---------|

CHAKU; KIRU, TO WEAR; TSUKU, TO ARRIVE AT, TO REACH.

TO ARRIVE AT, TO REACH 着 IS A COMPOSITE OF THE GOAT 羊 CARRIED BY OR DEPENDENT ON 丿 HIS EYE 目 WHO ARRIVES AT, REACHES 着 (HIS DESTINATION AS HE ASCENDS OR DESCENDS THE PRECIPITOUS HEIGHTS). THE GOAT'S HIDE AND WOOL ARE WORN 着.

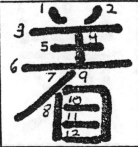

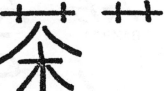

目
EYE,
A LOOK
JME 25

丿
CARRIED BY,
DEPENDENT
ON

着
TO WEAR,
ARRIVE AT,
TO REACH

羊
GOAT

道
ROAD, WAY,
PATH
JME 122

送
TO SEND
JME 268

CHŪ; SOSOGU, TO POUR, CONCENTRATE ON.

TO POUR, TO CONCENTRATE ON 注 IS WHAT THE MASTER, OWNER 主 JME 237 DOES WITH THE LIQUID 氵 JME 14 (TEA OR WINE) FOR GUESTS. THE MASTER, OWNER 主 CONCENTRATES ON 注 THE LIQUID 氵 HE POURS 注.

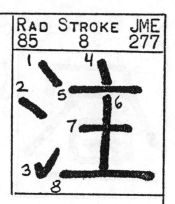

| Rad | Stroke | JME |
|-----|--------|-----|
| 85  | 8      | 277 |

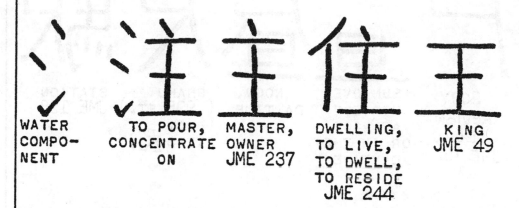

| WATER COMPONENT | TO POUR, CONCENTRATE ON | MASTER, OWNER JME 237 | DWELLING, TO LIVE, TO DWELL, TO RESIDE JME 244 | KING JME 49 |

CHŪ; HASHIRA, (BASHIRA), PILLAR, POST.

THE PILLAR, POST 柱 IS THE MASTER, OWNER 主 JME 237 AMONG THE TREES 木 JME 15 SINCE IT MUST BE SUPERIOR TIMBER FOR CONSTRUCTION PURPOSES ANALOGOUS TO THE MASTER AMONG THE HOUSEHOLD. IN OUR CARPENTRY, THERE IS THE KING POST WHICH VERTICALLY JOINS THE APEX OF A TRUSS TO THE BASE. QUEEN POSTS ALSO EXIST.

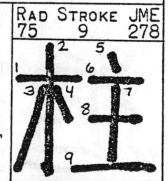

| Rad | Stroke | JME |
|-----|--------|-----|
| 75  | 9      | 278 |

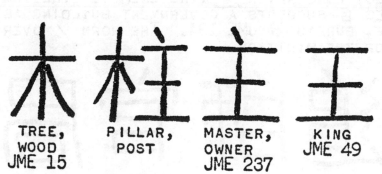

| TREE, WOOD JME 15 | PILLAR, POST | MASTER, OWNER JME 237 | KING JME 49 |

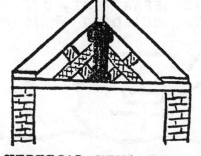

VERTICAL KING POST SHOWN IN BLACK

| JME 279 | STROKE 9 | RAD 1 |
|---|---|---|

CHŪ; HIRU, NOON, DAYTIME.

NOON, DAYTIME 昼 IS A COMPOSITE OF LENGTH (THE BODY'S 尸 FOOT 尺 AS IN STATION 駅 JME 158) FOR THE LENGTH 尺 OF THE SUN'S 日 SHADOW — AT NOON 昼 OR IN THE DAYTIME 昼.

BODY IN COFFIN

尸 BODY REVIEW SHOP JME 161

旦 SUN OVER HORIZON AT NOON OR IN THE DAYTIME

昼 NOON, DAYTIME

尺 SHAKU (.995 FT.) (BODY STEPS 尺)

駅 STATION JME 158

| JME 280 | STROKE 9 | RAD 162 |
|---|---|---|

TSUI; OU, TO DRIVE AWAY, TO PURSUE, TO RUN AFTER.

TO DRIVE AWAY, TO PURSUE, TO RUN AFTER IS A COMPOSITE OF TO GO FAR AND PAUSE SUDDENLY 辶 (AS IN ADVANCE 進 JME 259) AND THE LEFT COMPONENT 𠂤 OF TEACHER, ARMY 師 JME 624. THE ARMY 師 GOES FAR AND PAUSES SUDDENLY 辶 AS IT DRIVES AWAY, PURSUES, RUNS AFTER 追 (THE ENEMY). THE TWO STORIES 𠂤 SUGGESTS A GOVERNMENT BUILDING AS IN DEPARTMENT, OFFICE, BUREAU 局 JME 194. THE HORN ノ OVER THE BUILDING 𠂤 IS FOR THE MILITARY.

運 LUCK, TO CARRY, TO TRANSPORT JME 157

辶 MOVEMENT, STOP & GO

追 DRIVE AWAY, PURSUE, RUN AFTER

師 TEACHER, ARMY JME 624

官 GOV'T., GOV'T. SERVICE OR POSITION (NOTE ROOF) JME 364

局 DEPT., OFFICE, BUREAU JME 194

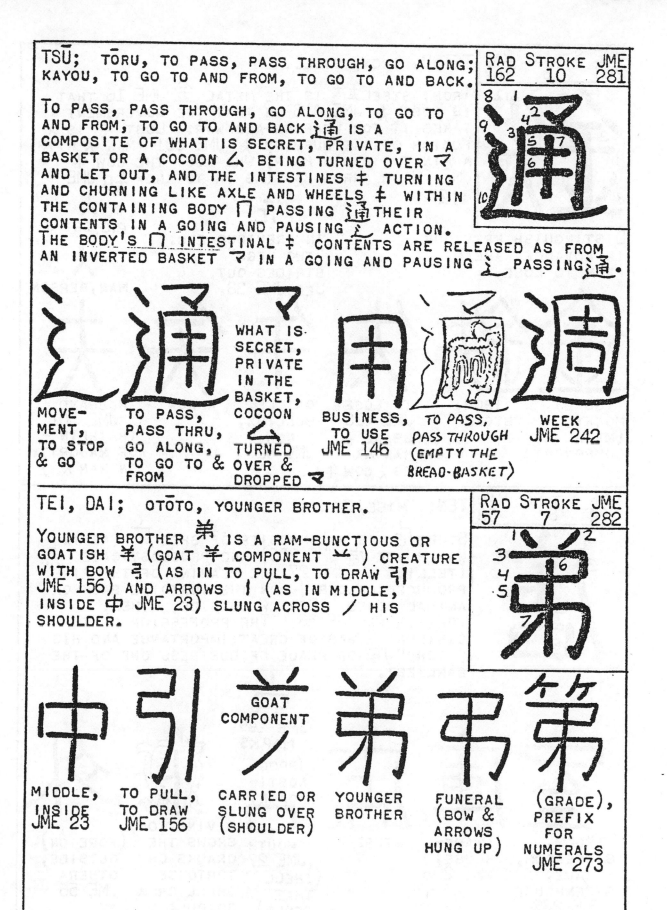

TSŪ; TŌRU, TO PASS, PASS THROUGH, GO ALONG; KAYOU, TO GO TO AND FROM, TO GO TO AND BACK.

| Rad | Stroke | JME |
|---|---|---|
| 162 | 10 | 281 |

TO PASS, PASS THROUGH, GO ALONG, TO GO TO AND FROM, TO GO TO AND BACK 通 IS A COMPOSITE OF WHAT IS SECRET, PRIVATE, IN A BASKET OR A COCOON ム BEING TURNED OVER マ AND LET OUT, AND THE INTESTINES ‡ TURNING AND CHURNING LIKE AXLE AND WHEELS ‡ WITHIN THE CONTAINING BODY 冂 PASSING 通 THEIR CONTENTS IN A GOING AND PAUSING ⻌ ACTION. THE BODY'S 冂 INTESTINAL ‡ CONTENTS ARE RELEASED AS FROM AN INVERTED BASKET マ IN A GOING AND PAUSING ⻌ PASSING 通.

MOVE-MENT, TO STOP & GO

TO PASS, PASS THRU, GO ALONG, TO GO TO & FROM

WHAT IS SECRET, PRIVATE IN THE BASKET, COCOON ム TURNED OVER & DROPPED マ

BUSINESS, TO USE JME 146

TO PASS, PASS THROUGH (EMPTY THE BREAD-BASKET)

WEEK JME 242

TEI, DAI; OTŌTO, YOUNGER BROTHER.

| Rad | Stroke | JME |
|---|---|---|
| 57 | 7 | 282 |

YOUNGER BROTHER 弟 IS A RAM-BUNCTIOUS OR GOATISH 羊 (GOAT 羊 COMPONENT ⺷ ) CREATURE WITH BOW 弓 (AS IN TO PULL, TO DRAW 引 JME 156) AND ARROWS 丨 (AS IN MIDDLE, INSIDE 中 JME 23) SLUNG ACROSS ノ HIS SHOULDER.

MIDDLE, INSIDE JME 23

TO PULL, TO DRAW JME 156

GOAT COMPONENT

CARRIED OR SLUNG OVER (SHOULDER)

YOUNGER BROTHER

FUNERAL (BOW & ARROWS HUNG UP)

(GRADE), PREFIX FOR NUMERALS JME 273

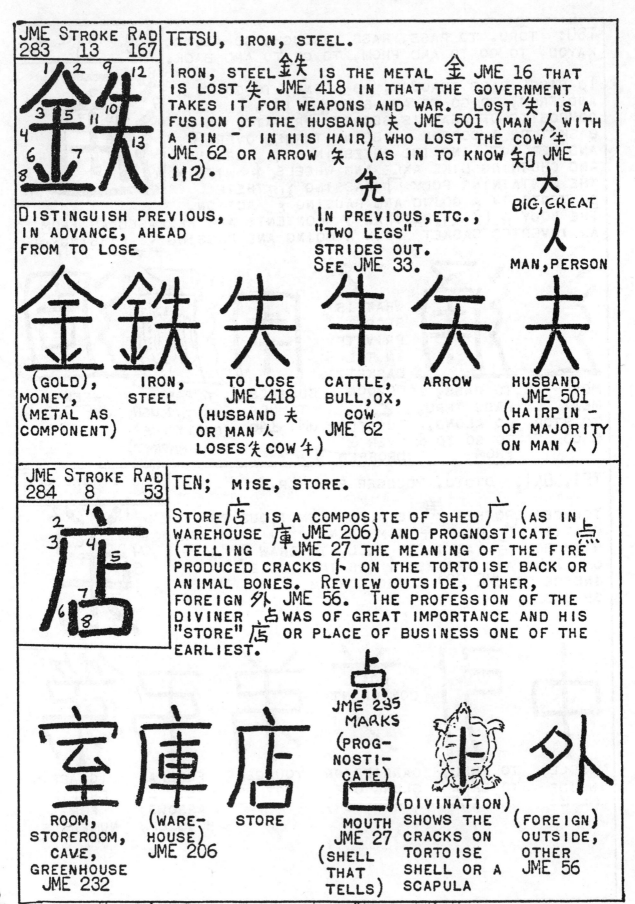

| JME 283 | Stroke 13 | Rad 167 |
|---|---|---|

TETSU, IRON, STEEL.

IRON, STEEL 鉄 IS THE METAL 金 JME 16 THAT IS LOST 失 JME 418 IN THAT THE GOVERNMENT TAKES IT FOR WEAPONS AND WAR. LOST 失 IS A FUSION OF THE HUSBAND 夫 JME 501 (MAN 人 WITH A PIN ｰ IN HIS HAIR) WHO LOST THE COW 牛 JME 62 OR ARROW 矢 (AS IN TO KNOW 知 JME 112).

先
IN PREVIOUS, ETC., "TWO LEGS" STRIDES OUT. SEE JME 33.

大 BIG, GREAT
人 MAN, PERSON

DISTINGUISH PREVIOUS, IN ADVANCE, AHEAD FROM TO LOSE

金 (GOLD), MONEY, (METAL AS COMPONENT)

鉄 IRON, STEEL

失 TO LOSE JME 418 (HUSBAND 夫 OR MAN 人 LOSES 失 COW 牛)

牛 CATTLE, BULL, OX, COW JME 62

矢 ARROW

夫 HUSBAND JME 501 (HAIRPIN ｰ OF MAJORITY ON MAN 人 )

| JME 284 | Stroke 8 | Rad 53 |
|---|---|---|

TEN; MISE, STORE.

STORE 店 IS A COMPOSITE OF SHED 广 (AS IN WAREHOUSE 庫 JME 206) AND PROGNOSTICATE 点 (TELLING JME 27 THE MEANING OF THE FIRE PRODUCED CRACKS ⼘ ON THE TORTOISE BACK OR ANIMAL BONES. REVIEW OUTSIDE, OTHER, FOREIGN 外 JME 56. THE PROFESSION OF THE DIVINER 占 WAS OF GREAT IMPORTANCE AND HIS "STORE" 店 OR PLACE OF BUSINESS ONE OF THE EARLIEST.

室 ROOM, STOREROOM, CAVE, GREENHOUSE JME 232

庫 (WAREHOUSE) JME 206

店 STORE

点 JME 285 MARKS (PROGNOSTICATE)
口 MOUTH JME 27 (SHELL THAT TELLS)

(DIVINATION) SHOWS THE CRACKS ON TORTOISE SHELL OR A SCAPULA

外 (FOREIGN) OUTSIDE, OTHER JME 56

TEN, MARKS, POINT, SPOT.

MARKS, POINT, SPOT 点 IS A COMPOSITE OF EXPLAINING 占 OR DIVINING BY THE CRACKS ┣ (AS IN OUTSIDE, OTHER, FOREIGN 外 JME 56) ON THE TORTOISE SHELL OR ANIMAL BONE WHEN HEATED BY FIRE 灬 WHICH PRODUCES THE MARKS, POINTS, SPOTS 点.

| Rad 203 | Stroke 9 | JME 285 |
|---|---|---|

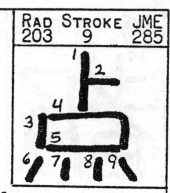

FIRE MAKES PATTERN OF CRACKS ON SHELL ○ OF TORTOISE

MOUTH ロ OF THE DIVINER INTERPRETS CRACKS ┣

MARKS, POINT, SPOT

STORE JME 284

(FOREIGN), OUTSIDE, OTHER JME 56

---

DEN, (LIGHTNING, ELECTRICITY).

LIGHTNING, ELECTRICITY 電 IS A COMPOSITE OF RAIN 雨 JME 42 (THE SIGNIFIER FOR KANJI MEANING SNOW, CLOUD, THUNDER, DEW, ETC.) AND THE FIELD 田 JME 40 THROUGH WHICH THE LIGHTNING BOLT ⌐ PASSES.

| Rad 173 | Stroke 13 | JME 286 |
|---|---|---|

RAIN JME 42

CLOUD JME 47

(LIGHTNING, ELECTRICITY)

RICE FIELD, PADDY JME 40

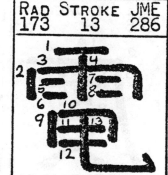

LIGHTNING BOLT

(STRIKES LIKE SNAKE'S TAIL).

| JME 287 | Stroke 11 | Rad 163 |
|---|---|---|

都

TO, TSU; MIYAKO, CAPITAL, METROPOLIS.

CAPITAL, METROPOLIS 都 IS A COMPOSITE OF PERSONS 者 JME 235 AND TOWN, CITY 阝 (AN ABBREVIATION OF 邑) WHICH IS A COMPOSITE OF MOUTH 口 JME 27 FOR THE WAY THE CITY CONTAINS ITS PEOPLE 者 AND SNAKE 巴 FOR THE SINUOUS APPEARANCE OF THE CITY WALL WHICH COILS ABOUT THE CAPITAL OR METROPOLIS 都.

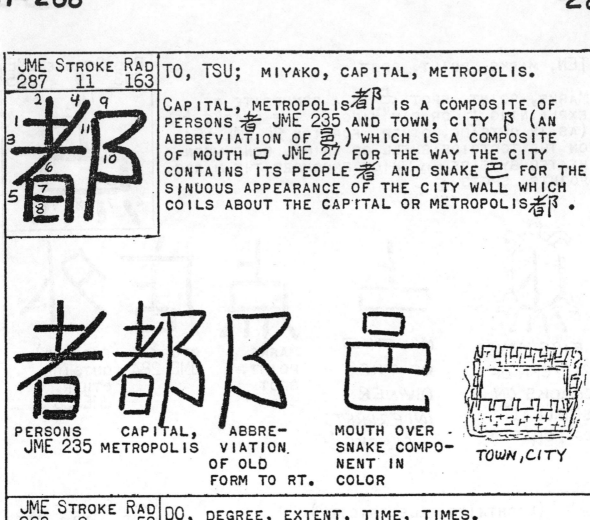

PERSONS JME 235

CAPITAL, METROPOLIS

ABBRE- VIATION. OF OLD FORM TO RT.

MOUTH OVER - SNAKE COMPO- NENT IN COLOR

TOWN, CITY

| JME 288 | Stroke 9 | Rad 53 |
|---|---|---|

度

DO, DEGREE, EXTENT, TIME, TIMES.

DEGREE, EXTENT, TIME, TIMES 度 IS A COMPOSITE OF A HAND 又 UNDER A SHED-TYPE ROOF 广 (AS IN STORE 店 JME 284) WITH NUMBERS OR LAYERS 廿 FOR THE DEGREE, EXTENT, TIME, TIMES 度. THE IMPLICATION IS THAT THE LAYERS ARE SEPARATED OR DIVIDED TO A CERTAIN DEGREE, EXTENT, OR NUMBER OF TIMES 度. THIS SAME COMPONENT 廿 IS USED TO REPRESENT AN INDEFINITE NUMBER OF "THINGS" IN THE BACKGROUND AND EVOLVED FROM HANDS IN COOPERATION.

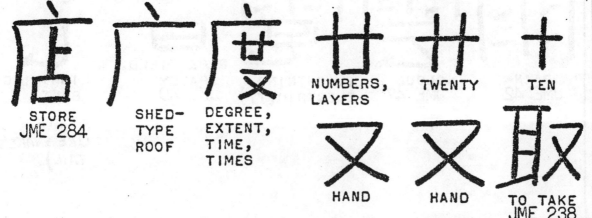

STORE JME 284

SHED- TYPE ROOF

DEGREE, EXTENT, TIME, TIMES

NUMBERS, LAYERS

TWENTY

TEN

HAND

HAND

TO TAKE JME 238

| Rad | Stroke | JME |
|-----|--------|-----|
| 18 | 2 | 289 |

TŌ; KATANA, (GATANA), SWORD, BLADE.

SWORD, BLADE 刀 IS A REPRESENTATION OF THE
SWEEP OF THE ARM ノ WITH THE SWORD OR
BLADE MOVING フ IN THE HAND. NOTE SWORD,
BLADE'S 刀 CORRESPONDENCE TO A QUADRANT 卐
OF THE SWASTIKA 卐 AND SIMILARITY TO SUCH
KANJI AS STRENGTH 力 JME 148. THE COMPONENT
FORM OF SWORD, BLADE 刂 IS MORE PICTOGRAPHIC.

| STRENGTH, POWER JME 148 | SUPER-IMPOSITION | SWASTIKA | SWEEP OR STROKE OF ARM | SWORD, BLADE | ARC OR MOVEMENT OF BLADE |
|---|---|---|---|---|---|

| Rad | Stroke | JME |
|-----|--------|-----|
| 42 | 6 | 290 |

TŌ; ATARU, TO HIT, TO STRIKE, TO SUCCEED,
TO WIN, (I.V.); ATERU, TO HIT, TO SUCCEED,
TO GUESS, (T.V.).

TO HIT, TO STRIKE, TO SUCCEED, TO WIN,
TO GUESS 当 IS A COMPOSITE OF THE GLEAMING
(AS IN LIGHT, BRILLIANCE, TO SHINE 光 JME 72)
TUSKS ON THE SNOUTED HEAD 彐 OF THE WILD
BOAR. THE WILD BOAR IS FAMOUS FOR THE
FEROCITY OF HIS CHARGE WHICH HITS, STRIKES,
SUCCEEDS, WINS 当. HIS VERY FEROCITY MAY
RESULT IN A MISS, THUS SUGGESTING TO GUESS 当. NOTE HOW
THE BOAR'S HEAD OR SNOUT 彐 IS LIKE A HAND 彐 (AS IN
TO HURRY 急 JME 186). THE SNOUT IS MARVELOUSLY ADAPTED
FOR USE AS A HAND (AS IN DIGGING TRUFFLES). THE SNOUT CAN
DIG, PUSH, PROBE, AND ACT AS A LEVER.

| BABYLONIAN SYMBOL FOR BOAR | TYPE OF AUSTRAL-ASIAN BOAR | SUPERIMPOSITION ON FUSION OF HAND WITH BOAR'S HEAD |
|---|---|---|

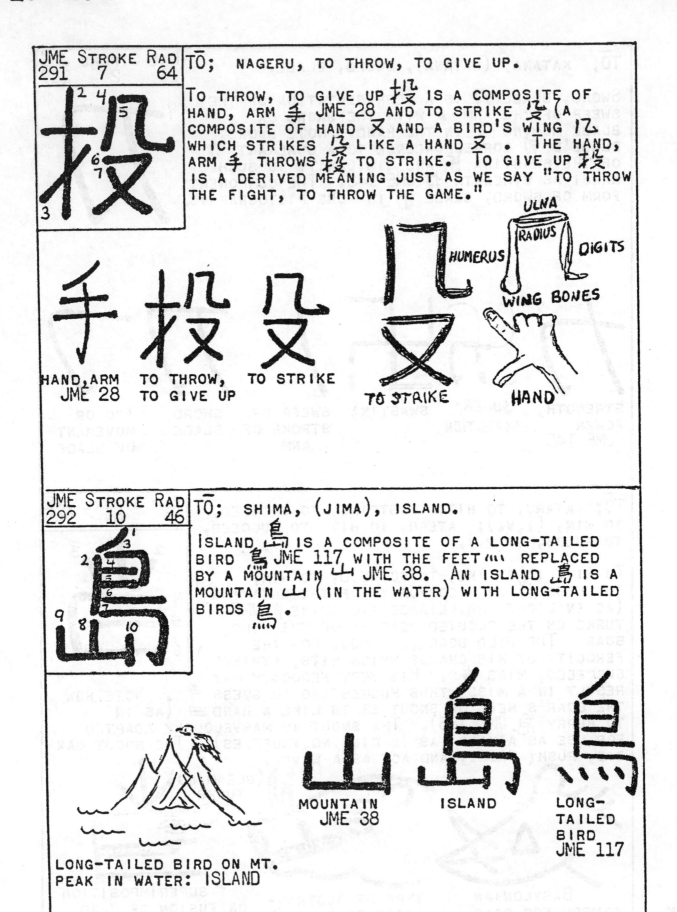

| JME 291 | Stroke 7 | Rad 64 |
|---|---|---|

TŌ; NAGERU, TO THROW, TO GIVE UP.

TO THROW, TO GIVE UP 投 IS A COMPOSITE OF HAND, ARM 手 JME 28 AND TO STRIKE 殳 (A COMPOSITE OF HAND 又 AND A BIRD'S WING 几 WHICH STRIKES 殳 LIKE A HAND 又. THE HAND, ARM 手 THROWS 投 TO STRIKE. TO GIVE UP 投 IS A DERIVED MEANING JUST AS WE SAY "TO THROW THE FIGHT, TO THROW THE GAME."

HAND, ARM
JME 28

TO THROW,
TO GIVE UP

TO STRIKE

HUMERUS
ULNA
RADIUS
DIGITS
WING BONES

TO STRIKE

HAND

| JME 292 | Stroke 10 | Rad 46 |
|---|---|---|

TŌ; SHIMA, (JIMA), ISLAND.

ISLAND 島 IS A COMPOSITE OF A LONG-TAILED BIRD 鳥 JME 117 WITH THE FEET 灬 REPLACED BY A MOUNTAIN 山 JME 38. AN ISLAND 島 IS A MOUNTAIN 山 (IN THE WATER) WITH LONG-TAILED BIRDS 鳥.

LONG-TAILED BIRD ON MT.
PEAK IN WATER: ISLAND

MOUNTAIN
JME 38

ISLAND

LONG-
TAILED
BIRD
JME 117

TŌ, (DŌ); KOTAE, ANSWER;
KOTAERU, TO ANSWER.

ANSWER, TO ANSWER 答 IS A COMPOSITE OF THE
BAMBOO 竹 (LEAVES RUSTLING FOR THE SOUND OF
THE ANSWER 答 ), THE LARGE ROOF 八 (FOR A
SCHOOL SETTING, ETC.), AND ONE 一 MOUTH 口
(FOR THE ANSWER'S 答 CONFORMITY OR AUTHORITY.

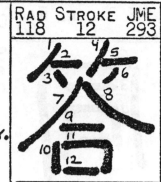

| RAD | STROKE | JME |
|-----|--------|-----|
| 118 | 12     | 293 |

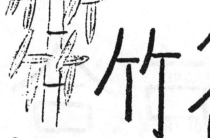

RUSTLE
OF
BAMBOO
LEAVES
ANSWERS

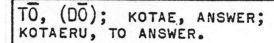

竹
BAMBOO
JME 113

答
ANSWER,
TO ANSWER

合
TO FIT,
TO SUIT,
TO AGREE,
TO BE TO-
GETHER
JME 77

ANSWER AS
FROM ONE
MOUTH UNDER
THE ROOF

---

TŌ, (DŌ), ZU; ATAMA, HEAD, BRAIN, TOP,
                                    LEADER.

HEAD, BRAIN, TOP, LEADER 頭 IS A COMPOSITE
OF 豆 PEA, BEAN, MINIATURE (DOLL, ETC.)
AND HEAD 頁 AS IN FACE 顔 JME 179. THE
IMPLICATION OF PEA, BEAN, MINIATURE 豆
SOMETHING IS DIMINUTIVE RESEMBLANCE TO THE
HEAD 頁 AS WE SAY "PEA-BRAINED." ORIGINALLY
PEA, BEAN, ETC. WAS A VASE 豆 ALSO HEAD-
SHAPED. HEAD 頁 SHOWS A COVERED EYE OR
HEAD 自 WALKING AS IT SUPERVISES.

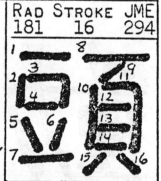

| RAD | STROKE | JME |
|-----|--------|-----|
| 181 | 16     | 294 |

CREST OR
COVERING

VASE
(RESEMBLES
AND/OR
HOLDS
PEAS, BEANS,
    ETC.)

豆
PEA,
BEAN,
MINIATURE
SOMETHING

HEAD,
BRAIN,
TOP,
LEADER

COMPO-
NENT
HEAD

FACE
JME 179

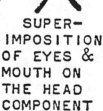
SUPER-
IMPOSITION
OF EYES &
MOUTH ON
THE HEAD
COMPONENT

| JME 295 | Stroke 6 | Rad 30 |
|---|---|---|

DŌ; ONAJI, SAME.

SAME 同 IS ONE — MOUTH 口 IN A SPACE 冂
FOR SAMENESS 同 OF OPINION, OF ECONOMIC BASE,
OF POLITICAL STRUCTURE, ETC.

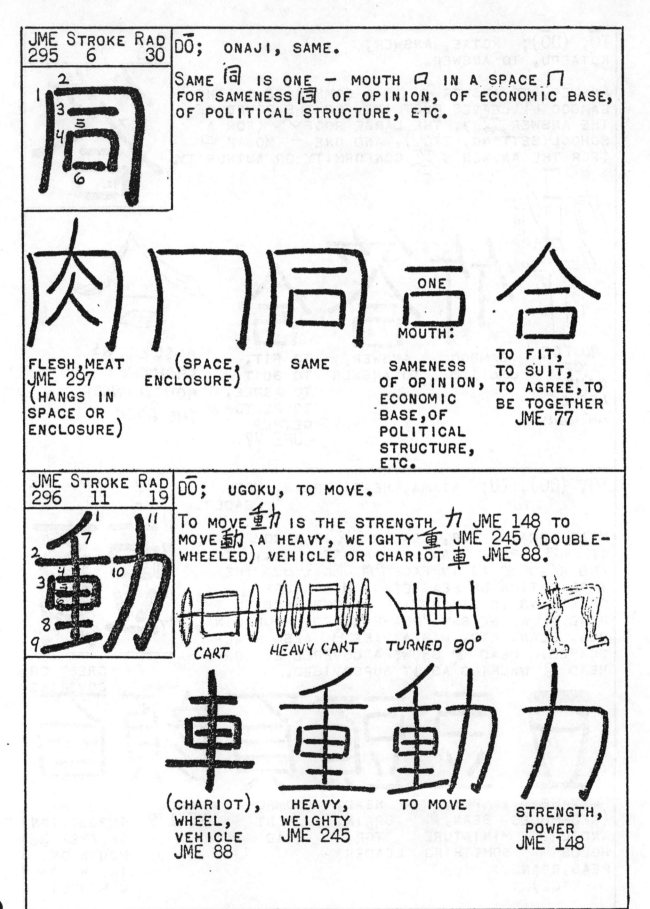

肉
FLESH, MEAT
JME 297
(HANGS IN
SPACE OR
ENCLOSURE)

冂
(SPACE,
ENCLOSURE)

同
SAME

口
ONE
MOUTH:
SAMENESS
OF OPINION,
ECONOMIC
BASE, OF
POLITICAL
STRUCTURE,
ETC.

合
TO FIT,
TO SUIT,
TO AGREE, TO
BE TOGETHER
JME 77

| JME 296 | Stroke 11 | Rad 19 |
|---|---|---|

DŌ; UGOKU, TO MOVE.

TO MOVE 動 IS THE STRENGTH 力 JME 148 TO
MOVE 動 A HEAVY, WEIGHTY 重 JME 245 (DOUBLE-
WHEELED) VEHICLE OR CHARIOT 車 JME 88.

CART   HEAVY CART   TURNED 90°

車
(CHARIOT),
WHEEL,
VEHICLE
JME 88

重
HEAVY,
WEIGHTY
JME 245

動
TO MOVE

力
STRENGTH,
POWER
JME 148

NIKU, FLESH, MEAT.

FLESH, MEAT 肉 IS A PICTOGRAPH OF FLESH,
MEAT 仌 (HANGING TO CURE OR DRY) IN A PARTLY
ENCLOSED SPACE 冂.

| RAD | STROKE | JME |
|-----|--------|-----|
| 130 | 6 | 297 |

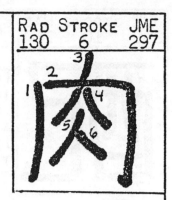

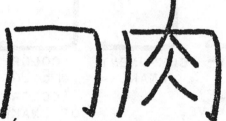 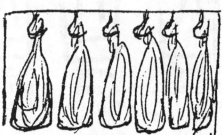

(SPACE OR         FLESH, MEAT      TWO FLITCHES        MEAT HANGING TO AGE
ENCLOSURE)                         OF MEAT ARE         OR CURE OR DRY
                                   HANGING TO
                                   DRY OR CURE

HA;  NAMI, WAVE.

WAVE 波 IS A COMPOSITE OF SKIN 皮 JME 307
AND WATER 氵 JME 14.  THE WAVE 波 IS THE
SKIN 皮 OF THE WATER 氵.
SKIN 皮 JME 307 SHOWS THE HAND 又 HOLDING
A KNIFE OR SHELL 丨 SCRAPING THE SKIN
OF THE BODY 厂 (AS IN SHOP 屋 JME 161).

| RAD | STROKE | JME |
|-----|--------|-----|
| 85 | 8 | 298 |

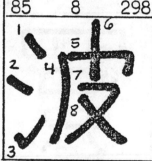

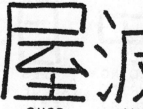  

SHOP          WAVE           SKIN          HAND &       PICTURE      BODY,
JME 161       (SKIN OF       JME 307       SCRAPER      OF HAND      CORPSE
              WATER OR                                  AND
              WATER HAND                                SCRAPER
              SCRAPES &
              STRIKES
              THE CLIFF)

MEASURE
OF LENGTH

| JME | STROKE | RAD |
|-----|--------|-----|
| 299 | 10 | 164 |

HAI, (PAI); KUBARU, TO DISTRIBUTE, TO DELIVER, TO ALLOCATE.

TO DISTRIBUTE, TO DELIVER, TO ALLOCATE 配 IS A COMPOSITE OF A WINE JUG 酉 AND WHAT IS PRIVATE 己 TURNING OR CIRCLING 己 LIKE A SNAKE 巴.
THE WINE JUG 酉 IS A PICTOGRAPH COMBINING THE STOPPER 丌 , JUG 口 , AND LIQUOR LEVEL 一.

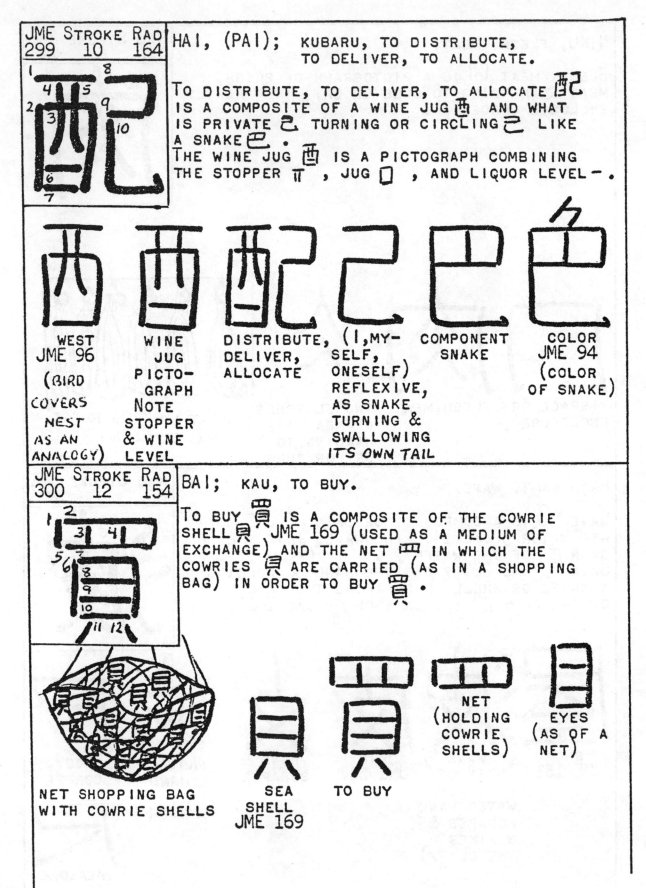

WEST
JME 96
(BIRD COVERS NEST AS AN ANALOGY)

WINE JUG PICTO-GRAPH NOTE STOPPER & WINE LEVEL

DISTRIBUTE, DELIVER, ALLOCATE

(I, MY-SELF, ONESELF) REFLEXIVE, AS SNAKE TURNING & SWALLOWING ITS OWN TAIL

COMPONENT SNAKE

COLOR
JME 94
(COLOR OF SNAKE)

| JME | STROKE | RAD |
|-----|--------|-----|
| 300 | 12 | 154 |

BAI; KAU, TO BUY.

TO BUY 買 IS A COMPOSITE OF THE COWRIE SHELL 貝 JME 169 (USED AS A MEDIUM OF EXCHANGE) AND THE NET 罒 IN WHICH THE COWRIES 貝 ARE CARRIED (AS IN A SHOPPING BAG) IN ORDER TO BUY 買 .

NET SHOPPING BAG WITH COWRIE SHELLS

SEA SHELL
JME 169

TO BUY

NET (HOLDING COWRIE SHELLS)

EYES (AS OF A NET)

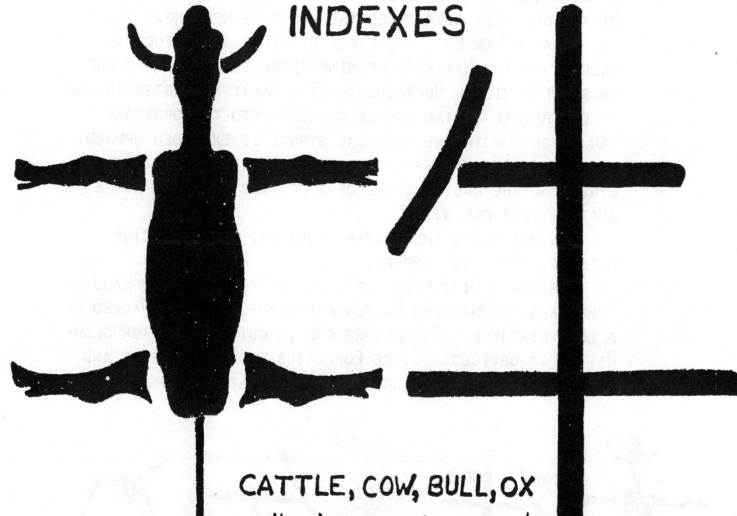

# VOLUME FOUR: KANJI 301-338; INDEXES

**CATTLE, COW, BULL, OX**
in the Japanese <u>kanji</u> and
in the Chinese characters

## THE KANJI HORSE AND THE KANJI COW    (THE KONJAKU)
### (TRANSLATION BY Y. DYKSTRA)

ON ANOTHER OCCASION, CONFUCIUS WAS WALKING AS HE LED A GROUP OF HIS DISCIPLES.  CONFUCIUS SAW A HORSE'S HEAD PROTRUDING FROM A ROADSIDE HEDGE.  CONFUCIUS SAID TO HIS DISCIPLES, "HERE IS A COW STICKING OUT ITS HEAD."

THE DISCIPLES WONDERED, "INDEED, THE MASTER SPOKE OF A COW RATHER THAN A HORSE.  HOW STRANGE! BUT AS THEY WALKED ON, THEY CONSIDERED THE MASTER'S MEANING.

FINALLY YEN HUI, THE FIRST DISCIPLE OF CONFUCIUS, UNDERSTOOD THE MASTER'S MEANING AFTER THEY HAD GONE ONE-THIRD OF A MILE.  HE THOUGHT, "THE KANJI FOR HORSE IN OUR TWELVE ANIMAL ZODIAC CAN BE CHANGED INTO THE ORDINARY KANJI FOR COW IF THE VERTICAL STROKE IS EXTENDED UPWARD, AS THOUGH THE HEAD PROJECTED OVER THE UPPER HORIZONTAL LINE.  SO THE MASTER SPOKE OF A COW INSTEAD OF A HORSE JUST TO TEST OUR WIT."

YEN HUI ASKED THE MASTER ABOUT IT, AND CONFUCIUS REPLIED, "THAT IS CORRECT."

THE OTHER DISCIPLES ALSO, ONE AFTER ANOTHER, GRADUALLY COMPREHENDED WHAT THE MASTER HAD MEANT, AS THEY WALKED ON A LONG DISTANCE.  SO WHETHER ONE IS QUICK-WITTED OR SLOW-WITTED IS OBVIOUS.  SINCE CONFUCIUS WAS INTELLIGENT AND WISE, THE PEOPLE ALL SHOWED THEIR RESPECT BY LOWERING THEIR HEADS.

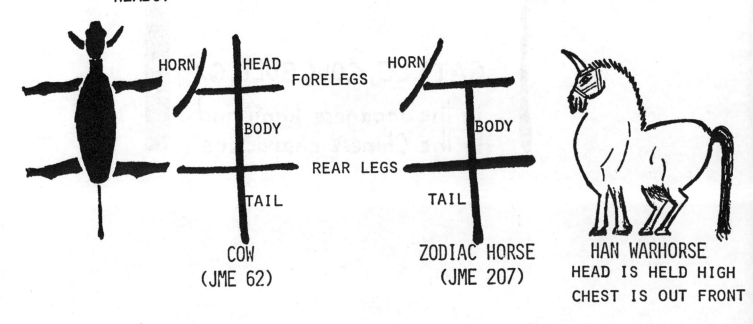

COW
(JME 62)

ZODIAC HORSE
(JME 207)

HAN WARHORSE
HEAD IS HELD HIGH
CHEST IS OUT FRONT

BAI; URI, SALE; URU, TO SELL.

SALE, TO SELL 売 IS A COMPOSITE OF A GENTLEMAN, FIGURE 士 JME 410 AT A DESK OR STAND 冗 (AS IN TO READ 読 JME 123) SELLING, TO SELL 売. 読

RAD 33 | STROKE 7 | JME 301

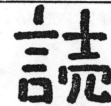

仕
WORK,
TO SERVE
JME 221

士
PERSON,
MAN,
FIGURE,
GENTLEMAN
JME 410

-l-
PICTURE
OF MAN'S
FEATURES

売
TO SELL

冗
DESK

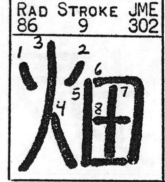
TO SELL,
SALE
(MAN IS
AT DESK
SELLING)

読
TO READ
JME 123

---

HATA, HATAKE, (BATAKE), FARM, FIELD,
CULTIVATED FIELD, PLANTATION.

FARM, FIELD, CULTIVATED FIELD, PLANTATION IS A COMPOSITE OF FIRE 火 JME 13 AND RICE FIELD 田 JME 40. A FARM, FIELD, CULTIVATED FIELD, PLANTATION 田 IS PREPARED FOR CULTIVATION BY FIRING 火 OR BURNING THE WILD GROWTH OR STUBBLE FROM THE PREVIOUS HARVEST.

RAD 86 | STROKE 9 | JME 302

火
FIRE
JME 13

畑
FARM, FIELD,
CULTIVATED
FIELD,
PLANTATION

田
PADDY,
RICE
FIELD

FIRE
(PICTURE)

| 10 acres | 10 acres |
| 10 acres | 10 acres |

FORTY ACRES
& NO MULE

MAYAN FIELDS WERE CULTIVATED BY THE "SLASH AND BURN" (MILPA) TECHNIQUE; SWIDDEN ARE CLEARINGS BY SHIFTING CULTIVATORS.

| JME 303 | Stroke 9 | Rad 105 |
|---|---|---|

HATSU, (PATSU), (DEPARTURE, TO LEAVE, TO SHOOT).

DEPARTURE, TO LEAVE, TO SHOOT 発 IS A COMPOSITE OF THE LEGS 癶 STRETCHED OUT WITH TWO SHORT LINES ` ` ON EACH SIDE FOR THE HIP AND KNEE JOINTS (LIKE THE KNEE JOINT IN FOOT, LEG 足 JME 29) AND 尤 A COMPOSITE OF THE FEET HOLDING A BOW, THE HANDS DRAWING THE ARROW, AND THE ARROW LASHING OUT ㄴ LIKE A BOLT OF LIGHTNING ㄴ (AS IN LIGHTNING 電 JME 286 WHERE THE BOLT ㄴ IS BELOW AND TO THE RIGHT).

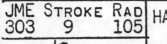

| MOVEMENT OF LEG JOINTS IN SHOOTING THE ARROW | LEGS SHOWING HIP & KNEE JOINTS | 発 DEPARTURE, TO LEAVE, TO SHOOT | 尤 HANDS ON THE BOWSTRING | BOW-STRING | 電 LIGHTNING JME 286 |
|---|---|---|---|---|---|

| JME 304 | Stroke 7 | Rad 32 |
|---|---|---|

HAN; SAKA, (ZAKA), A SLOPE, HILL.

A SLOPE, HILL 坂 IS THE ANTITHESIS, OPPOSITE 反 JME 492 OF EARTH, SOIL 土 JME 17 (WHICH IS LEVEL). ANTI-, ANTITHESIS, OPPOSITE 反 IS REPRESENTED BY THE HAND 又 FROM THE CLIFF 厂 (AS IN ROCK, CLIFF, CRAG 岩 JME 178) WHICH IS THAT OF THE MOUNTAINEER WHO IS AGAINST, ANTI-, OPPOSED 反 TO ANY INCURSION BY TRADITION AND INCLINATION.

| 土 EARTH, SOIL, JME 17 | 坂 A SLOPE, HILL | 反 ANTI-, ANTITHESIS, OPPOSITE JME 492 | THE SLOPE, HILL (BY THE HAND THAT THROWS FROM THE CLIFF) | 岩 ROCK, CLIFF, CRAG JME 178 |
|---|---|---|---|---|

HAN, (BAN); ITA, BOARD.

A BOARD 板 (OF FINISHED WOOD) IS THE ANTITHESIS, OPPOSITE 反 JME 492 OF A (LIVING GROWING) TREE 木 JME 15. ANTITHESIS, OPPOSITE 反 IS A COMPOSITE OF THE HAND 又 FROM THE CLIFF 厂 (AS IN ROCK, CLIFF, CRAG 岩 JME 178) OF THE MOUNTAINEER WHO IS OPPOSED BY TRADITION AND INCLINATION TO ANY ALIEN INCURSION.

| RAD | STROKE | JME |
|-----|--------|-----|
| 75  | 8      | 305 |

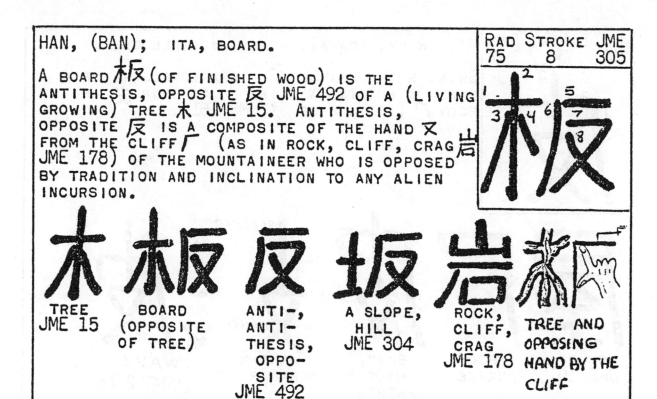

TREE
JME 15

BOARD
(OPPOSITE
OF TREE)

ANTI-,
ANTI-
THESIS,
OPPO-
SITE
JME 492

A SLOPE,
HILL
JME 304

ROCK,
CLIFF,
CRAG
JME 178

TREE AND
OPPOSING
HAND BY THE
CLIFF

BAN, WATCH, GUARD, NUMBER, ORDER, TURN.

WATCH, GUARD, NUMBER, ORDER, TURN 番 IS THE WATCHING, GUARDING 番 BY NUMBER, ORDER, TURN 番 OF THE RICE FIELD 田 JME 40 AGAINST ANIMALS (REPRESENTED BY THE HORN 丿 AND THE TRACK OR PAW PRINT 米.) THERE IS ALSO THE SUGGESTION THAT THE RICE 米 IS RIPE 米 AND MUST BE GUARDED 番.

| RAD | STROKE | JME |
|-----|--------|-----|
| 165 | 12     | 306 |

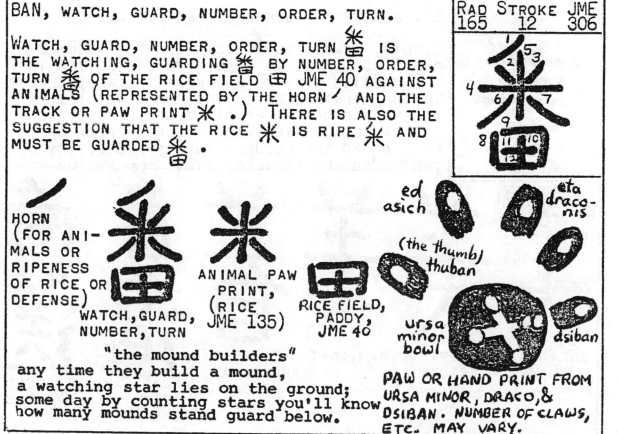

HORN
(FOR ANI-
MALS OR
RIPENESS
OF RICE OR
DEFENSE)

WATCH, GUARD,
NUMBER, TURN

ANIMAL PAW
PRINT,
(RICE
JME 135)

RICE FIELD,
PADDY,
JME 40

ed
asich

eta
draco-
nis

(the thumb)
thuban

ursa
minor
bowl

dsiban

PAW OR HAND PRINT FROM
URSA MINOR, DRACO, &
DSIBAN. NUMBER OF CLAWS,
ETC. MAY VARY.

"the mound builders"
any time they build a mound,
a watching star lies on the ground;
some day by counting stars you'll know
how many mounds stand guard below.

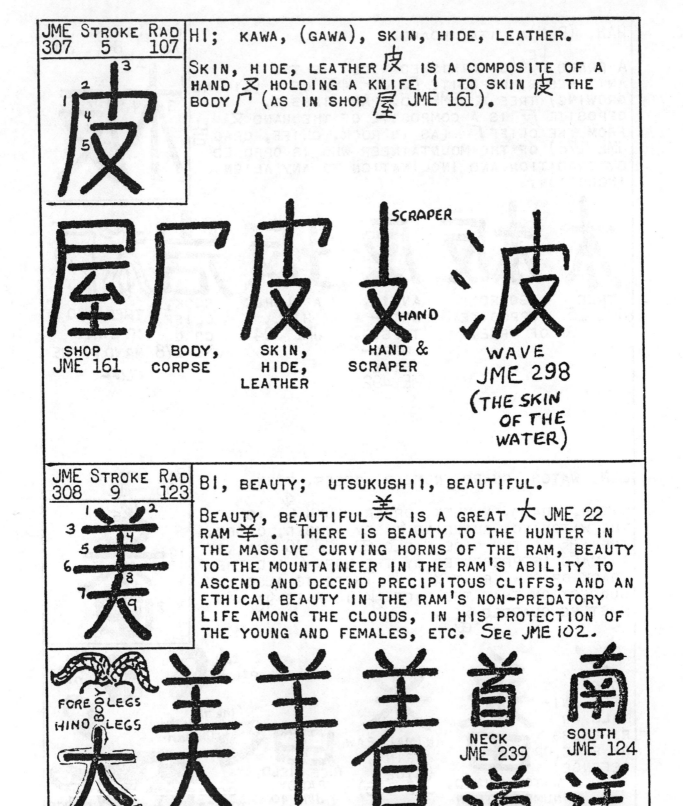

| JME 307 | Stroke 5 | Rad 107 |
|---|---|---|

HI; KAWA, (GAWA), SKIN, HIDE, LEATHER.

SKIN, HIDE, LEATHER 皮 IS A COMPOSITE OF A HAND 又 HOLDING A KNIFE | TO SKIN 皮 THE BODY 尸 (AS IN SHOP 屋 JME 161).

SHOP
JME 161

BODY, CORPSE

SKIN, HIDE, LEATHER

HAND & SCRAPER

SCRAPER

HAND

WAVE
JME 298
(THE SKIN OF THE WATER)

| JME 308 | Stroke 9 | Rad 123 |
|---|---|---|

BI, BEAUTY; UTSUKUSHII, BEAUTIFUL.

BEAUTY, BEAUTIFUL 美 IS A GREAT 大 JME 22 RAM 羊. THERE IS BEAUTY TO THE HUNTER IN THE MASSIVE CURVING HORNS OF THE RAM, BEAUTY TO THE MOUNTAINEER IN THE RAM'S ABILITY TO ASCEND AND DECEND PRECIPITOUS CLIFFS, AND AN ETHICAL BEAUTY IN THE RAM'S NON-PREDATORY LIFE AMONG THE CLOUDS, IN HIS PROTECTION OF THE YOUNG AND FEMALES, ETC. SEE JME 102.

FORE LEGS
HIND LEGS
BODY

GREAT, BIG
JME 22

BEAUTIFUL, BEAUTY

RAM, GOAT

TO WEAR, ARRIVE AT, REACH
JME 276

NECK
JME 239

ROAD, WAY, PATH
JME 122

SOUTH
JME 124

TO SEND
JME 268

HYŌ, (PYŌ), LIST, SCHEDULE, TABLE;
OMOTE, THE EXTERIOR, FRONT, SURFACE;
ARAWASU, TO SHOW, INDICATE, DISPLAY, EXPOSE,
EXPRESS.

| Rad | Stroke | JME |
|---|---|---|
| 145 | 8 | 309 |

THE EXTERIOR, FRONT, SURFACE 表 OF THE
LAYERS 主 OF CLOTHING, ROBES 衣 JME 341
IS SHOWN, DISPLAYED, EXPOSED 表. OTHER
MEANINGS SUCH AS LIST, SCHEDULE, TABLE 表
RESULT SINCE LISTS, SCHEDULES, TABLES 表 表
ARE NECESSARILY SHOWN, DISPLAYED, EXPOSED 表.
THE COMPONENT FOR LAYERS 主 WAS IN BLUE, GREEN, INEXPER-
IENCED 青 JME36 AND IN SPRING 春 JME 91. CLOTHING, ROBES
衣 WAS A COMPONENT IN GARDEN 園 JME 159 AND IN DISTANT,
FAR 遠 JME 160.

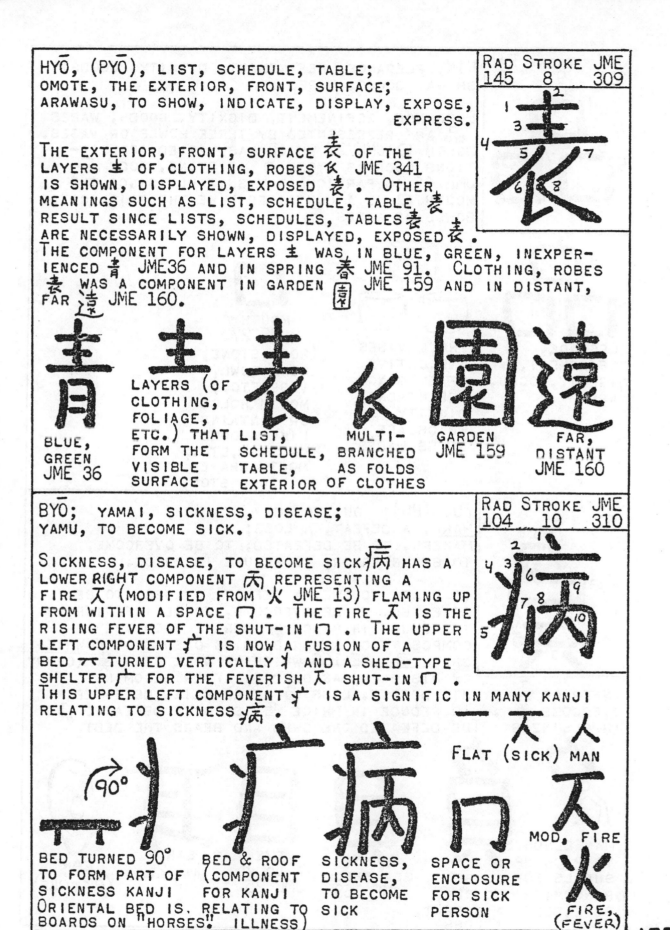

BLUE,
GREEN
JME 36

LAYERS (OF
CLOTHING,
FOLIAGE,
ETC.) THAT
FORM THE
VISIBLE
SURFACE

LIST,
SCHEDULE,
TABLE,
EXTERIOR OF CLOTHES

MULTI-
BRANCHED
AS FOLDS

GARDEN
JME 159

FAR,
DISTANT
JME 160

BYŌ; YAMAI, SICKNESS, DISEASE;
YAMU, TO BECOME SICK.

| Rad | Stroke | JME |
|---|---|---|
| 104 | 10 | 310 |

SICKNESS, DISEASE, TO BECOME SICK 病 HAS A
LOWER RIGHT COMPONENT 丙 REPRESENTING A
FIRE 大 (MODIFIED FROM 火 JME 13) FLAMING UP
FROM WITHIN A SPACE 冂. THE FIRE 大 IS THE
RISING FEVER OF THE SHUT-IN 冂. THE UPPER
LEFT COMPONENT 疒 IS NOW A FUSION OF A
BED 爿 TURNED VERTICALLY 爿 AND A SHED-TYPE
SHELTER 广 FOR THE FEVERISH 大 SHUT-IN 冂.
THIS UPPER LEFT COMPONENT 疒 IS A SIGNIFIC IN MANY KANJI
RELATING TO SICKNESS 病.

FLAT (SICK) MAN

MOD. FIRE

BED TURNED 90°
TO FORM PART OF
SICKNESS KANJI
ORIENTAL BED IS
BOARDS ON "HORSES"

BED & ROOF
(COMPONENT
FOR KANJI
RELATING TO
ILLNESS)

SICKNESS,
DISEASE,
TO BECOME
SICK

SPACE OR
ENCLOSURE
FOR SICK
PERSON

FIRE,
(FEVER)

| JME 311 | Stroke 9 | Rad 30 |
|---|---|---|

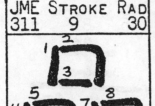

HIN, ELEGANCE, REFINEMENT, DIGNITY, GOODS; SHINA, GOODS, WARES.

ELEGANCE, REFINEMENT, DIGNITY, GOODS, WARES 品 ARE REPRESENTED BY THREE BOWLS OR VASES. MOUTH 口 JME 27 WHICH HAS VARIED APPLICATIONS SUCH AS STONE 口 IN STONE, ROCK 石 JME 44 IS PARTICULARLY SUITABLE SINCE THE MOUTH 口 IS A CONTAINER LIKE THE TRIPLICATED BOWLS OR VASES 品.

ELEGANCE, REFINEMENT, DIGNITY, GOODS, WARES

THREE VASES INDICATIVE OF ELEGANCE, REFINEMENT, DIGNITY, & WHICH ARE GOODS, WARES

MOUTH JME 27 (ROCK, STONE, SEAT, BOWL, VASE, ETC.) MOUTH HOLDS OR CONTAINS LIKE A BOWL OR VASE, ETC.; MOUTH SHAPED AS ROUND STONE

| JME 312 | Stroke 9 | Rad 154 |
|---|---|---|

FU, (BU); OU, TO BEAR, TO OWE; MAKE, A DEFEAT, A LOSS; MAKERU, TO BE DEFEATED, TO BE OVERCOME, TO BE INFERIOR, TO REDUCE IN PRICE.

TO BEAR, TO OWE, A DEFEAT, A LOSS, TO BE DEFEATED, TO BE OVERCOME, TO BE INFERIOR, TO REDUCE IN PRICE 負 DERIVE FROM THE COMPOSITE OF A MAN BENDING OVER ク A COWRIE SHELL 貝 JME 169 WHICH HE WILL BEAR 負 (CARRY ON HIS BACK) AS OWED 負 AFTER BECOMING INFERIOR 負 BY HIS DEFEAT, LOSS 負 AFTER BEING DEFEATED, OVERCOME 負. TO REDUCE IN PRICE 負 IS TO BE DEFEATED 負 IN BUSINESS. THE DEFEATED ONE OWES AND BEARS THE DEBT.

MAN BENDS TO PICK UP SHELLS FOR RANSOM, TRIBUTE, DEBT

TO BEAR, TO OWE, A DEFEAT, A LOSS

SEA SHELL JME 169

EYE, A LOOK JME 25

EAR JME 26

EAR (PICTURE)

BUTSU, MOTSU;  MONO, THING, ARTICLE, OBJECT, GOODS.

| RAD | STROKE | JME |
|-----|--------|-----|
| 93  | 8      | 313 |

THING, ARTICLE, OBJECT, GOODS 物 IS REPRE-
SENTED BY A COMPOSITE OF COW, OX, CATTLE,
BULL 牛 (THE LARGEST ANIMAL COMMON ON THE
FARM) AND THE LEGS AND TAIL 勿 OF THE LIZARD
OR CHAMELEON 易 (WHICH IS THE SMALLEST).
THUS THINGS, ARTICLES, OBJECTS, GOODS RANGE
AS FROM THE COW TO THE CHAMELEON.

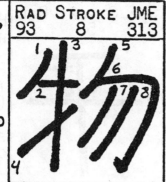

牛　牛　物　勿　易

COMPONENT / FOR COW,OX, CATTLE — COW,OX, CATTLE, BULL JME 62 — THING, ARTICLE, OBJECT, GOODS — LEGS & TAIL OF LIZARD OR CHAMELEON (SUGGESTS ALSO RAYS OF SUN IN WHICH HE BASKS) — (EASY), DIVINATION JME 545 CHAMELEON OR LIZARD PICTOGRAPH (SEE JME 252) — PICTURE OF CHAMELEON OR LIZARD (FOURTH LEG IS BEHIND BODY)

BUN;  KIKU, TO HEAR, TO LISTEN TO, TO ASK,
TO OBEY, TO HEAR OF;  KIKOERU, TO BE HEARD.

| RAD | STROKE | JME |
|-----|--------|-----|
| 128 | 14     | 314 |

TO HEAR, TO LISTEN TO, TO ASK, TO OBEY,
TO HEAR OF, TO BE HEARD 聞 IS A COMPOSITE OF
THE EAR 耳 JME 26 (OF THE PERSON) WITHIN THE
(OUTER, DOUBLE) GATES 門 JME 143 (AS OF THE
ESTATE) WHO HEARS, LISTENS TO, ASKS, HEARS
OF, AND BY WHOM THINGS ARE HEARD 聞.  THE
MEANING TO OBEY 聞 PROBABLY DERIVES FROM THE
PERSON OFTEN BEING THE WATCHMAN OR GATEMAN
WHO IS A SERVANT OBEYING 聞.

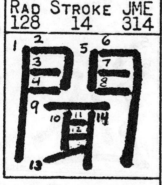

耳　聞　門　　開　間

EAR JME 26 — TO HEAR, TO LISTEN, TO ASK, TO OBEY, TO HEAR OF, TO BE HEARD — GATE JME 143 — (EAR IN THE GATE-WAY) HEARS, LISTENS — TO OPEN JME 171 — INTERVAL, SPACE, DISTANCE, ROOM, TIME JME 58

*To hear is to obey, my lord.*

| JME 315 | Stroke 5 | Rad 51 |
|---|---|---|

HEI, BYŌ; TAIRA, FLATNESS, EVENNESS; HIRATAI, EVEN, LEVEL, SIMPLE.

FLATNESS, EVENNESS, EVEN, LEVEL, SIMPLE 平 IS REPRESENTED BY THE SHINING, GLEAMING (SURFACE) OF A SHIELD 干 (AS IN NOON 午 JME 207). ALSO REVIEW GOLD, MONEY 金 JME 16 FOR THE SHIELD 干 AND SHINING NUGGETS ソ AS COMPONENTS. LIGHT, BRILLIANCE, TO SHINE 光 JME 72 ALSO HAS RAYS OF LIGHT ソ AS A COMPONENT.

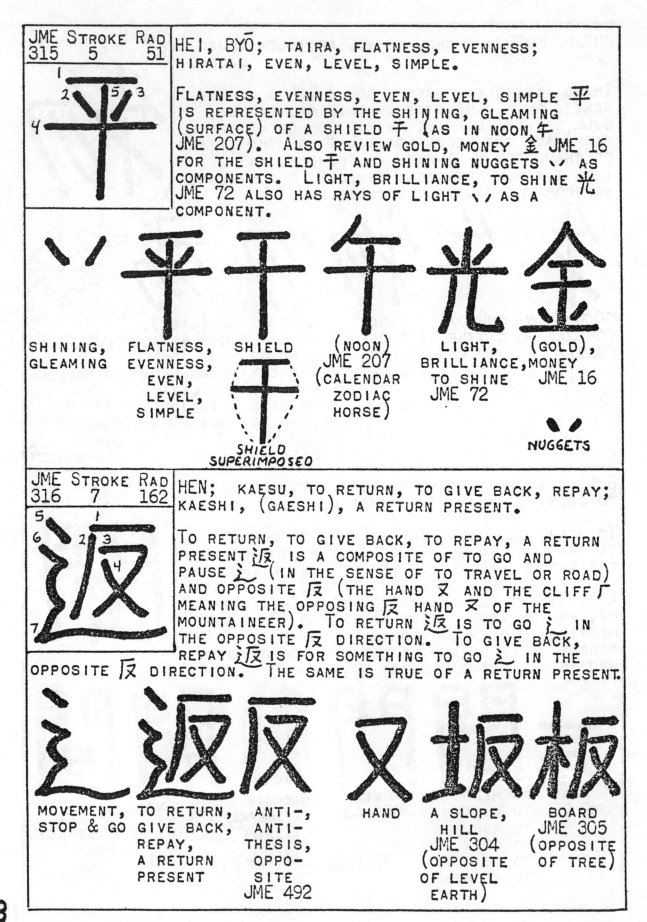

SHINING, GLEAMING — FLATNESS, EVENNESS, EVEN, LEVEL, SIMPLE — SHIELD — SHIELD SUPERIMPOSED — (NOON) JME 207 (CALENDAR ZODIAC HORSE) — LIGHT, BRILLIANCE, TO SHINE JME 72 — (GOLD), MONEY JME 16 — NUGGETS

| JME 316 | Stroke 7 | Rad 162 |
|---|---|---|

HEN; KAESU, TO RETURN, TO GIVE BACK, REPAY; KAESHI, (GAESHI), A RETURN PRESENT.

TO RETURN, TO GIVE BACK, TO REPAY, A RETURN PRESENT 返 IS A COMPOSITE OF TO GO AND PAUSE 辶 (IN THE SENSE OF TO TRAVEL OR ROAD) AND OPPOSITE 反 (THE HAND 又 AND THE CLIFF 厂 MEANING THE OPPOSING 反 HAND 又 OF THE MOUNTAINEER). TO RETURN 返 IS TO GO 辶 IN THE OPPOSITE 反 DIRECTION. TO GIVE BACK, REPAY 返 IS FOR SOMETHING TO GO 辶 IN THE OPPOSITE 反 DIRECTION. THE SAME IS TRUE OF A RETURN PRESENT.

MOVEMENT, STOP & GO — TO RETURN, GIVE BACK, REPAY, A RETURN PRESENT — ANTI-, ANTITHESIS, OPPOSITE JME 492 — HAND — A SLOPE, HILL JME 304 (OPPOSITE OF LEVEL EARTH) — BOARD JME 305 (OPPOSITE OF TREE)

BEN, (TO EXERT ONESELF, BE DILIGENT, BE INDUSTRIOUS).

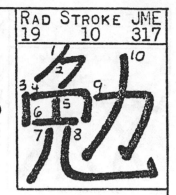

| RAD | STROKE | JME |
|-----|--------|-----|
| 19 | 10 | 317 |

TO EXERT ONESELF, BE DILIGENT, BE INDUSTRIOUS 勉 IS A COMPOSITE OF OGRE, FIEND, GHOST, DEMON 免 (AS A COMPONENT) AND STRENGTH 力 JME 148. OGRE, FIEND, GHOST, DEMON 免 IS A PICTOGRAPH. THERE IS A SUGGESTION HERE AS OF DEMONIAC STRENGTH, BUT IT IS MILDER AND INVOLVES STUDY, WORK, PHYSICAL EXERTION, ETC.

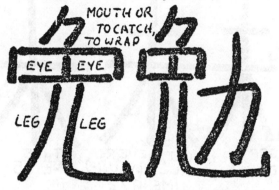
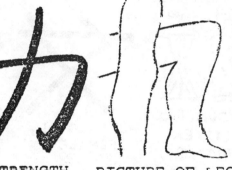

| OGRE, FIEND GHOST, DEMON | TO EXERT ONESELF, BE DILIGENT BE INDUSTRIOUS | STRENGTH JME 148 | PICTURE OF LEGS REPRESENTING STRENGTH OR POWER |

MAI, EVERY (USED AS A PREFIX).

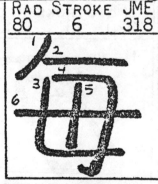

| RAD | STROKE | JME |
|-----|--------|-----|
| 80 | 6 | 318 |

EVERY 毎 IS A COMPOSITE OF MAN ㇒ JME 30 (AS A TOP COMPONENT) AND MOTHER 母 JME 137.
EVERY 毎 MAN ㇒ HAS A MOTHER 母.

MILK CAN BE POISON BECAUSE OF CONTAMINATION OR BECAUSE CATTLE OR SHEEP EAT POISONOUS AND SOMETIMES MILKY WEEDS. SO THE KANJI FOR POISON AND FOR MOTHER ARE RELATED.

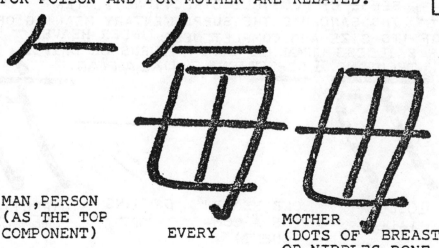

| MAN, PERSON (AS THE TOP COMPONENT) | EVERY | MOTHER (DOTS OF BREASTS OR NIPPLES DONE AS A LINE) | MOTHER JME 137 |
| | | | POISON JME 686 |

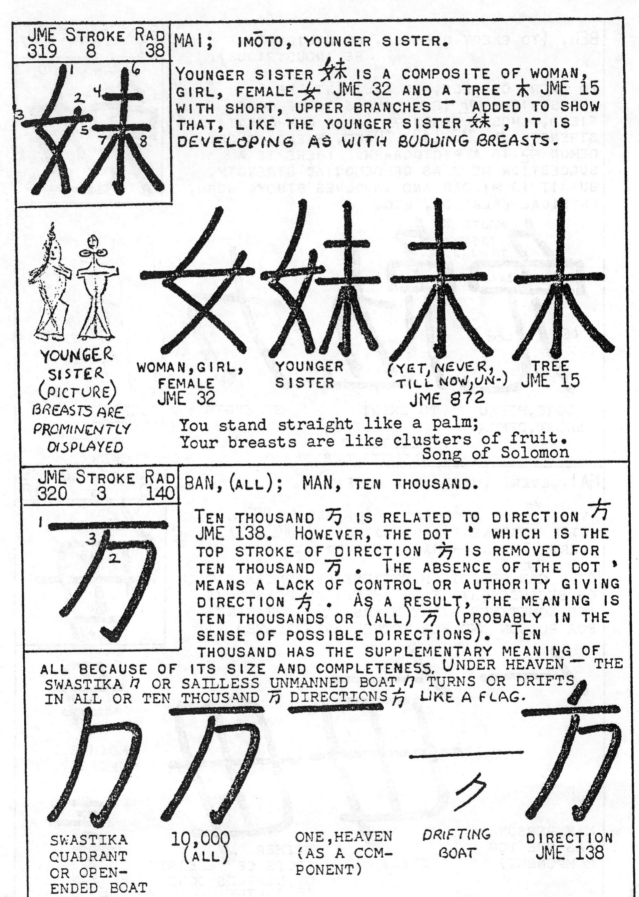

| JME 319 | Stroke 8 | Rad 38 |
|---|---|---|

MAI; IMŌTO, YOUNGER SISTER.

YOUNGER SISTER 妹 IS A COMPOSITE OF WOMAN, GIRL, FEMALE 女 JME 32 AND A TREE 木 JME 15 WITH SHORT, UPPER BRANCHES 一 ADDED TO SHOW THAT, LIKE THE YOUNGER SISTER 妹, IT IS DEVELOPING AS WITH BUDDING BREASTS.

YOUNGER SISTER (PICTURE) BREASTS ARE PROMINENTLY DISPLAYED

WOMAN, GIRL, FEMALE JME 32

YOUNGER SISTER

(YET, NEVER, TILL NOW, UN-) JME 872

TREE JME 15

You stand straight like a palm;
Your breasts are like clusters of fruit.
Song of Solomon

| JME 320 | Stroke 3 | Rad 140 |
|---|---|---|

BAN, (ALL); MAN, TEN THOUSAND.

TEN THOUSAND 万 IS RELATED TO DIRECTION 方 JME 138. HOWEVER, THE DOT ' WHICH IS THE TOP STROKE OF DIRECTION 方 IS REMOVED FOR TEN THOUSAND 万. THE ABSENCE OF THE DOT ' MEANS A LACK OF CONTROL OR AUTHORITY GIVING DIRECTION 方. AS A RESULT, THE MEANING IS TEN THOUSANDS OR (ALL) 万 (PROBABLY IN THE SENSE OF POSSIBLE DIRECTIONS). TEN THOUSAND HAS THE SUPPLEMENTARY MEANING OF ALL BECAUSE OF ITS SIZE AND COMPLETENESS. UNDER HEAVEN 一 THE SWASTIKA 万 OR SAILLESS UNMANNED BOAT 万 TURNS OR DRIFTS IN ALL OR TEN THOUSAND 万 DIRECTIONS 方 LIKE A FLAG.

SWASTIKA QUADRANT OR OPEN-ENDED BOAT

10,000 (ALL)

ONE, HEAVEN (AS A COMPONENT)

DRIFTING BOAT

DIRECTION JME 138

MEI; NAKU, TO SING, TWITTER (BIRDS),
TO HUM, BUZZ (INSECTS), TO GRUNT, GROWL,
ROAR (ANIMALS).

TO SING, TWITTER, HUM, BUZZ, GRUNT, GROWL,
ROAR 鳴 IS A COMPOSITE OF A MOUTH 口 JME 27
AND A LONG-TAILED BIRD 鳥 JME 117. THE
SINGING OR TWITTERING 鳴 FROM THE MOUTH 口
OF LONG-TAILED BIRDS 鳥 WAS EXTENDED TO
BIRD, INSECT, AND ANIMAL SOUNDS GENERALLY.

| Rad | Stroke | JME |
|-----|--------|-----|
| 30  | 14     | 321 |

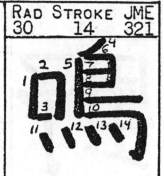

MOUTH
JME 27

TO SING,
TWITTER,
HUM, BUZZ,
GRUNT,
GROWL, ROAR

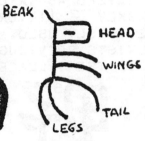

LONG-
TAILED
BIRD
JME 117

BEAK
HEAD
WINGS
TAIL
LEGS
ANCIENT
BIRD
SYMBOL

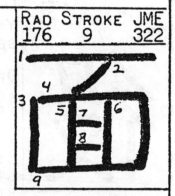

ISLAND
JME 292

MEN, FACE, FEATURES, MASK; OMO, SURFACE;
OMOTE, FACE, EXTERIOR, FRONT, SURFACE.

FACE, FEATURES, MASK, SURFACE, EXTERIOR,
FRONT 面 IS A PICTOGRAPH OF A MASK 面 AND
A FUSED CONGLOMERATE OF THE ARCHAIC KANJIS
FOR HEAD 百, FOR NOSE 自, FOR BEARD 而 ;
AND THE CURRENT KANJIS FOR EYE 目 JME 25,
AND FOR EAR 耳 JME 26 AS PART OF THE FUSED
CONGLOMERATE.

| Rad | Stroke | JME |
|-----|--------|-----|
| 176 | 9      | 322 |

EAR
JME 26

EYE
JME 25

ARCHAIC
NOSE
KANJI

HEAD
COMPONENT

ARCHAIC
BEARD
KANJI

FACE,
FEATURES,
MASK,
SURFACE,
EXTERIOR,
FRONT

MASK

MASK

MASK

| JME 323 | Stroke 11 | Rad 166 |
|---|---|---|

YA; <u>NO</u>, FIELD, PLAIN.

FIELD, PLAIN 野 IS A COMPOSITE OF VILLAGE, NATIVE PLACE, LINEAR UNIT 里 JME 332, AND PREVIOUS 予 JME 525. VILLAGE, NATIVE PLACE 里 IS A COMPOSITE OF RICE FIELD 田 JME 40 AND EARTH 土 JME 17 (SUGGESTING ONE'S RURAL OR COUNTRYSIDE ORIGIN). THE LINEAR UNIT <u>RI</u> (2.44 MI.) WAS USUALLY A MEASUREMENT USED TOWARDS A VILLAGE 里. PREVIOUS 予 MAY BE ANALYZED AS NAILS 丁 (AS IN TOWN 町 JME 115) TAKEN FROM THE BASKET マ (INVERTED AS IN TO PASS 通 JME 281) PREVIOUSLY OR PREVIOUSLY USED. THE CONCEPTION IS THAT A FIELD, PLAIN 野 EXISTS PREVIOUS 予 TO A VILLAGE 里 (BEFORE THE CONSTRUCTION OF THE VILLAGE).

| | | | | |
|---|---|---|---|---|
| PADDY 田 EARTH 土 | VILLAGE, NATIVE PLACE, <u>RI</u> (2.44 MI.) 里 | FIELD, PLAIN 野 | PREVIOUS JME 525 予 | NAILS, SPIKES ア | INVERTED BASKET OR CONTAINER WHOSE CONTENTS SPREAD OR EXPAND マ |

| JME 324 | Stroke 7 | Rad 60 |
|---|---|---|

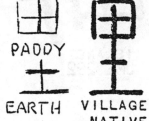

YAKU, OFFICE, POST, POSITION, DUTY, ROLE, SERVICE; EKI, WAR, CAMPAIGN.

OFFICE, POST, POSITION, DUTY, ROLE, SERVICE, WAR, CAMPAIGN 役 IS A COMPOSITE OF MEN 彳 (AS IN TO WAIT FOR 待 JME 271) AND TO STRIKE 殳 (AS IN TO THROW 投 JME 291). MEN 彳 IS A DOUBLING OF THE COMPONENT MAN 亻 JME 30. STRIKE 殳 IS A COMPOSITE OF HAND 又 (WHICH STRIKES 几 LIKE THE WING OF A BIRD) AND A STRIKING OR FLAPPING 几 WING. THE STRIKING MEN 役 DEALT OUT PUNISHMENT IN THE COURTS WITH BAMBOO RODS. THEIR OFFICE, POST, POSITION, DUTY, ROLE, SERVICE, ETC. WAS EXTENDED TO WAR OR CAMPAIGNS IN WHICH THEY COULD ACCOMPANY THE MAGISTRATE.

| | | | | |
|---|---|---|---|---|
| MEN: DOUBLED COMPONENT 彳 | OFFICE, POST 役 | HAND 又 | STRIKING WING 几 | WING BONES | TO THROW JME 291 投 |

YŪ, YU;  YOSHI, REASON, SIGNIFICANCE.

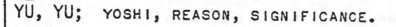

REASON, SIGNIFICANCE 由 IS A PICTOGRAPH OF A TORTOISE 甲 (WITH BODY 田 AND PROJECTING HEAD ｜ ) INVERTED 由 FOR HIS DEATH SO THAT THE TORTOISE SHELL CAN BE USED IN DIVINATION TO DIVINE REASONS, SIGNIFICANCE 由 .  THE TORTOISE SHELL WAS HEATED AND THE RESULTING CRACKS USED IN DIVINATION AS MENTIONED IN OUTSIDE, FOREIGN, OTHER 外 JME 56, STORE 店 JME 284, AND MARKS, POINT, SPOT 点 JME 285.

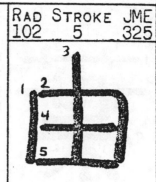

TORTOISE VIEWED FROM UNDERNEATH (PLASTRON)

TORTOISE SHELL: CARAPACE, GRADE A, BACK OF HAND

REASON, SIGNIFICANCE

(FOREIGN), OUTSIDE, OTHER JME 56

STORE JME 284

MARKS, POINT, SPOT JME 285

---

YŪ;  ASOBU, TO PLAY, TO AMUSE ONESELF, TO BE IDLE.

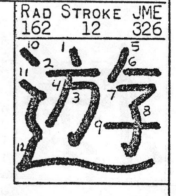

TO PLAY, TO AMUSE ONESELF, TO BE IDLE 遊 IS A MAN 𠂊 JME 30 (WHO IS) LIKE A CHILD 子 JME 31 GOING AND PAUSING 辶 (AS IN ROAD, WAY, PATH 道 JME 122) IN SOME DIRECTION 方 JME 138 AS HE PLAYS, AMUSES HIMSELF.

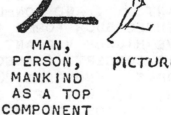

MOVEMENT, STOP & GO

TO PLAY, AMUSE ONE- SELF, TO BE IDLE

DIRECTION JME 138

CHILD JME 31

MAN, PERSON, MANKIND AS A TOP COMPONENT

PICTURE

| JME | STROKE | RAD |
|-----|--------|-----|
| 327 | 12 | 140 |

YŌ; HA, (BA), LEAF, FOLIAGE.

LEAF, FOLIAGE 葉 IS THE GRASS 艹 (GRASS 艹 COMPONENT AS IN GRASS, VEGETATION 草 JME 106) OF THE WORLD 世 JME 263 OF TREES 木 JME 15.

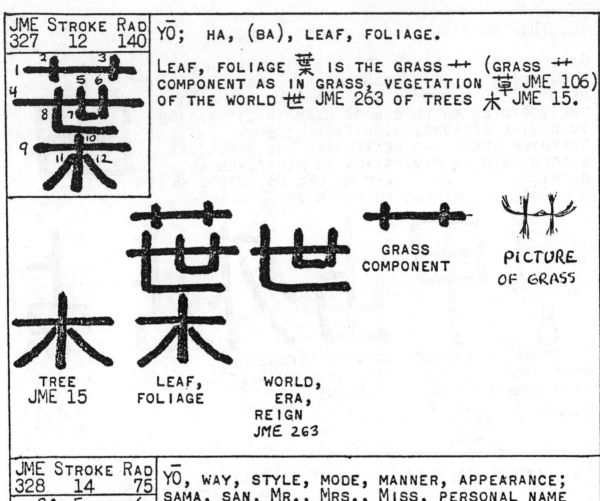

GRASS COMPONENT

PICTURE OF GRASS

TREE
JME 15

LEAF, FOLIAGE

WORLD, ERA, REIGN
JME 263

| JME | STROKE | RAD |
|-----|--------|-----|
| 328 | 14 | 75 |

YŌ, WAY, STYLE, MODE, MANNER, APPEARANCE; SAMA, SAN, MR., MRS., MISS, PERSONAL NAME SUFFIX (I.E. TERI-SAN), ETC.; SAMA, STATE, CONDITION.

WAY, STYLE, MODE, MANNER, APPEARANCE, STATE, CONDITION 様 IS A COMPOSITE AND FUSION OF TREE 木 JME 15, OF A GOAT COMPONENT 羊 (AS IN BEAUTY, BEAUTIFUL 美 JME 308), AND OF A WATER COMPONENT 水 (AS IN GLOBE, SPHERE 球 JME 188). THESE THREE COMPONENTS ARE OUTSTANDING IN THEIR DIFFERENCES REPRESENTING ANIMAL 羊, PLANT 木, AND NON-LIVING SUBJECT MATTER, WATER, WHICH 水 ASSUMES SUCH FORMS AS ICE, STEAM, AND WAVES. ALL THREE HAVE HIGHLY VARIANT WAYS, STYLES, MODES, CONDITIONS 様. THIS CONCEPT IS ALSO APPLIED TO APPEARANCES 様, ETC. OF PEOPLE. PROVERBS 30:19 SAYS, "THE WAY OF AN EAGLE IN THE AIR; THE WAY OF A SERPENT UPON A ROCK; THE WAY OF A SHIP IN THE MIDST OF THE SEA; AND THE WAY OF A MAN WITH A MAID."

GLOBE, SPHERE
JME 188

TREE

WAY, STYLE

WATER

WATER

GOAT, RAM

YŌ, (USED IN THE NAMES OF THE DAYS OF THE WEEK).

YŌ 日曜 IS A COMPOSITE OF SUN, DAY 日 JME 11, OF CLAWS ヨヨ, AND OF THE SHORT-TAILED BIRD 隹 (AS IN TO ADVANCE 進 JME 259). THE SHORT-TAILED BIRDS 隹 WINGING 羽 OR PERCHED ヨヨ (GREET) THE DAY, SUN 日 EACH DAY OF THE WEEK.

| Rad 72 | Stroke 18 | JME 329 |
|---|---|---|

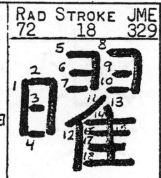

DAY, SUN JME 11

YŌ: USED IN DAYS OF THE WEEK

CLAWS (HANDS) OF BIRDS

WINGS (AT TIMES WINGS MAY BE PRINTED INSTEAD OF CLAWS (OR HANDS)

SHORT-TAILED BIRD

OLD SYMBOL FOR SHORT-TAILED BIRD

RAKU; OCHIRU, TO FALL, TO DROP, (I.V.); TO BE INFERIOR TO, TO BE OMITTED; OTOSU, TO DROP, TO LET FALL, TO LOSE, (T.V.); TO DEBASE, TO MAKE WORSE.

TO FALL, TO DROP, TO BE INFERIOR TO, TO BE OMITTED, TO LET FALL, TO LOSE, TO DEBASE, TO MAKE WORSE 落 IS A COMPOSITE OF GRASS 艹, OF WATER シ, AND OF THE SEATED GUEST 各 (AS IN GUEST 客 JME 184, BUT LACKING THE ROOF 宀). OBJECTS OFTEN FALL, DROP, OR ARE DROPPED 落 INTO GRASS 艹 OR WATER シ AND ARE LOST 落. FOR A GUEST 客 TO LET SOMETHING FALL 落 OR DROP 落 IS A BREACH OF ETIQUETTE INVOLVING INFERIORITY 落, OMISSION 落, DEBASEMENT 落, OR MAKING MATTERS WORSE 落. THE SAME IS TRUE IF SUCH A THING HAPPENS IN THE PRESENCE OF A GUEST ON THE PART OF THE HOST.

| Rad 140 | Stroke 12 | JME 330 |
|---|---|---|

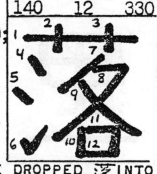

WATER COMPONENT

落 TO FALL, TO DROP, TO LOSE

GRASS COMPONENT

EACH, EVERY JME 568

PICTURE OF GUEST DROPPING 'CUP

GUEST JME 184

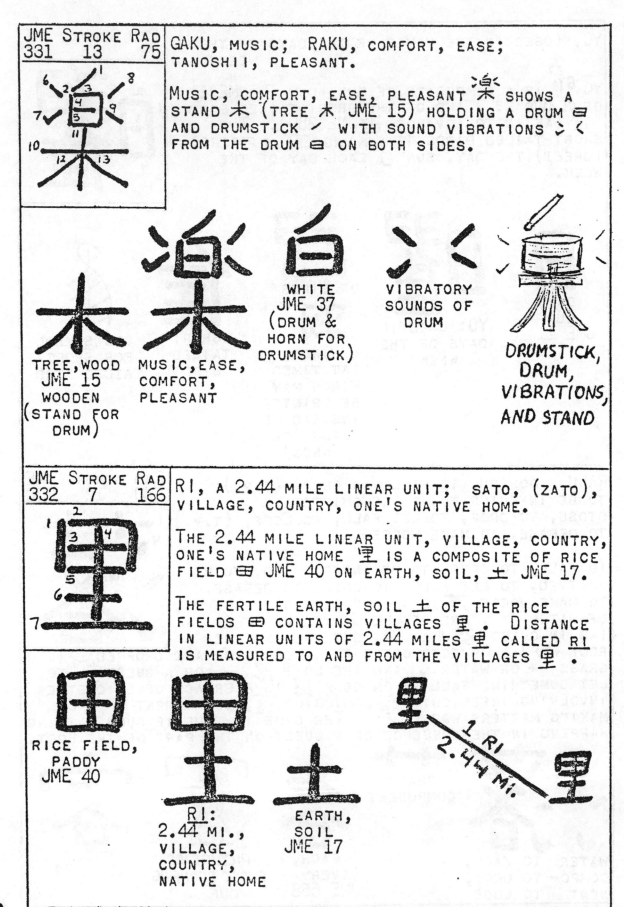

| JME | Stroke | Rad |
|-----|--------|-----|
| 331 | 13 | 75 |

GAKU, MUSIC; RAKU, COMFORT, EASE; TANOSHII, PLEASANT.

MUSIC, COMFORT, EASE, PLEASANT 楽 SHOWS A STAND 木 (TREE 木 JME 15) HOLDING A DRUM 日 AND DRUMSTICK ′ WITH SOUND VIBRATIONS ⸯ⟨ FROM THE DRUM 日 ON BOTH SIDES.

TREE, WOOD
JME 15
WOODEN
(STAND FOR DRUM)

MUSIC, EASE, COMFORT, PLEASANT

WHITE
JME 37
(DRUM & HORN FOR DRUMSTICK)

VIBRATORY SOUNDS OF DRUM

DRUMSTICK, DRUM, VIBRATIONS, AND STAND

| JME | Stroke | Rad |
|-----|--------|-----|
| 332 | 7 | 166 |

RI, A 2.44 MILE LINEAR UNIT; SATO, (ZATO), VILLAGE, COUNTRY, ONE'S NATIVE HOME.

THE 2.44 MILE LINEAR UNIT, VILLAGE, COUNTRY, ONE'S NATIVE HOME 里 IS A COMPOSITE OF RICE FIELD 田 JME 40 ON EARTH, SOIL, 土 JME 17.

THE FERTILE EARTH, SOIL 土 OF THE RICE FIELDS 田 CONTAINS VILLAGES 里. DISTANCE IN LINEAR UNITS OF 2.44 MILES 里 CALLED RI IS MEASURED TO AND FROM THE VILLAGES 里.

RICE FIELD, PADDY
JME 40

RI:
2.44 MI.,
VILLAGE,
COUNTRY,
NATIVE HOME

EARTH,
SOIL
JME 17

1 RI
2.44 MI.

RI, REASON, LOGIC.

REASON, LOGIC 理 IS FOR THE VILLAGES, COUNTRYSIDE, NATIVE HOMES 里 TO HAVE A KING 王 JME 49 (SYMBOLIC OF GOVERNMENT). REASON, LOGIC 理 IS TO HAVE A KING'S 王 JME 49 (STANDARD) UNIT OF LINEAR MEASURE 里, THE RI OF 2.44 MILES. (IT IS ANALOGOUS TO THE KING'S FOOT, ETC. AS STANDARD MEASURE).

| RAD | STROKE | JME |
|-----|--------|-----|
| 96  | 11     | 333 |

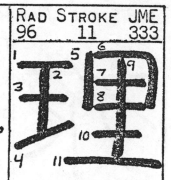

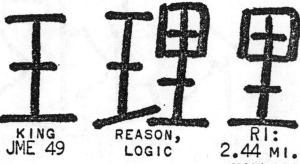

王
KING
JME 49

理
REASON,
LOGIC

里
RI:
2.44 MI.,
VILLAGE,
COUNTRY-
SIDE,
NATIVE
HOME

田
RICE FIELD,
PADDY
JME 40

土
EARTH,
SOIL
JME 17

RYŪ, RU; NAGARE, STREAM, CURRENT; NAGARERU, TO FLOW, TO RUN, TO STREAM, (I.V.); NAGASU, TO POUR, TO SET ADRIFT, TO WASH AWAY, (T.V.).

STREAM, CURRENT, TO FLOW, TO RUN, TO STREAM, TO POUR, TO SET ADRIFT, TO WASH AWAY 流 IS A COMPOSITE OF WATER 氵, DIRECTIONAL 亠 (AS IN THE CAP OF AUTHORITY OR THE TERMS HEADSTREAM, HEAD WATERS, FOUNTAINHEAD), A SECRET, CLOUDY, SELFISH, BASKET-LIKE 厶 (PLACE ABOVE, WHICH TEMPORARILY HOLDS THE WATERS), AND THE STREAM 川 (AS OF THREE CHANNELS LIKE RIVER 川 JME 39 AND WATER 水 JME 14).

| RAD | STROKE | JME |
|-----|--------|-----|
| 85  | 10     | 334 |

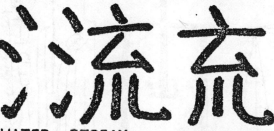

氵
WATER
COM-
PONENT

流
STREAM,
CURRENT,
TO FLOW,
TO RUN,
TO STREAM

亠厶川
DIRECTIONAL
HEADWATERS
RELEASE A
3-CHANNELED
STREAM

WATER FROM
ABOVE FLOWS
AWAY

川
RIVER,
JME 39

水
WATER
JME 14

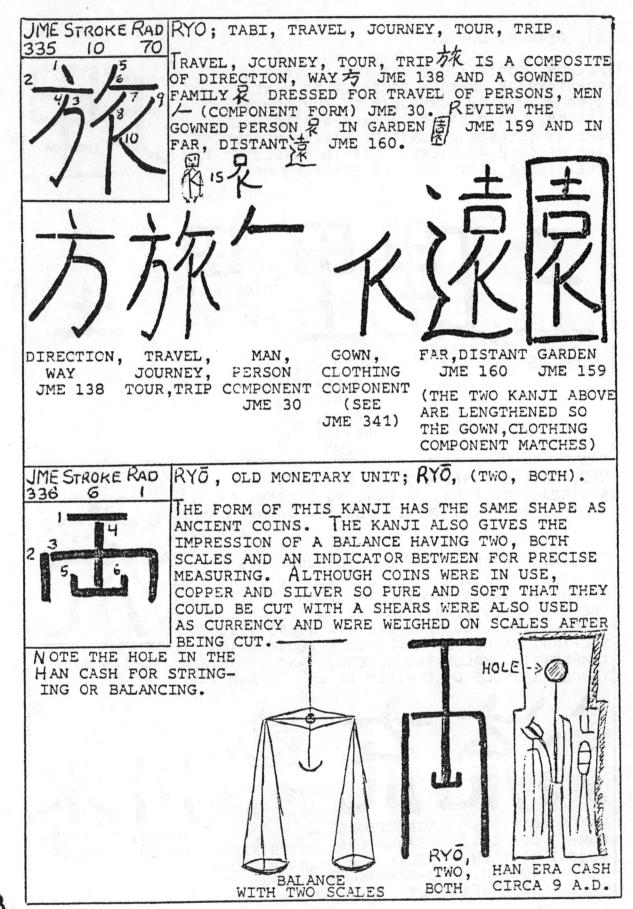

| JME | STROKE | RAD |
|-----|--------|-----|
| 335 | 10 | 70 |

RYO; TABI, TRAVEL, JOURNEY, TOUR, TRIP.

TRAVEL, JOURNEY, TOUR, TRIP 旅 IS A COMPOSITE OF DIRECTION, WAY 方 JME 138 AND A GOWNED FAMILY 氏 DRESSED FOR TRAVEL OF PERSONS, MEN 亻 (COMPONENT FORM) JME 30. REVIEW THE GOWNED PERSON 衣 IN GARDEN 園 JME 159 AND IN FAR, DISTANT 遠 JME 160.

| DIRECTION, WAY JME 138 | TRAVEL, JOURNEY, TOUR, TRIP | MAN, PERSON COMPONENT JME 30 | GOWN, CLOTHING COMPONENT (SEE JME 341) | FAR, DISTANT JME 160 | GARDEN JME 159 |

(THE TWO KANJI ABOVE ARE LENGTHENED SO THE GOWN, CLOTHING COMPONENT MATCHES)

| JME | STROKE | RAD |
|-----|--------|-----|
| 336 | 6 | 1 |

RYŌ, OLD MONETARY UNIT; RYŌ, (TWO, BOTH).

THE FORM OF THIS KANJI HAS THE SAME SHAPE AS ANCIENT COINS. THE KANJI ALSO GIVES THE IMPRESSION OF A BALANCE HAVING TWO, BOTH SCALES AND AN INDICATOR BETWEEN FOR PRECISE MEASURING. ALTHOUGH COINS WERE IN USE, COPPER AND SILVER SO PURE AND SOFT THAT THEY COULD BE CUT WITH A SHEARS WERE ALSO USED AS CURRENCY AND WERE WEIGHED ON SCALES AFTER BEING CUT.

NOTE THE HOLE IN THE HAN CASH FOR STRINGING OR BALANCING.

HOLE ->

BALANCE WITH TWO SCALES

RYŌ, TWO, BOTH

HAN ERA CASH CIRCA 9 A.D.

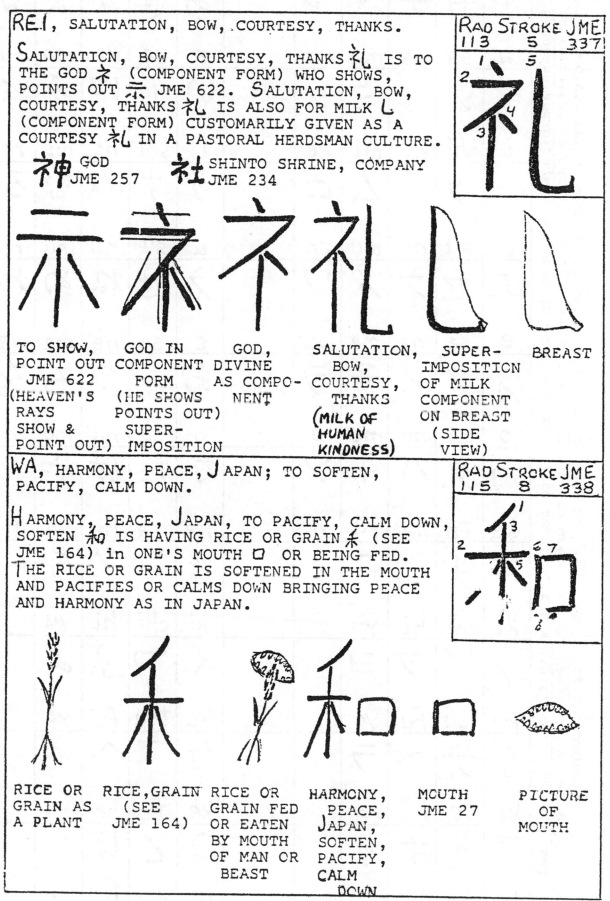

REI, SALUTATION, BOW, COURTESY, THANKS.

SALUTATION, BOW, COURTESY, THANKS 礼 IS TO THE GOD ネ (COMPONENT FORM) WHO SHOWS, POINTS OUT 示 JME 622. SALUTATION, BOW, COURTESY, THANKS 礼 IS ALSO FOR MILK し (COMPONENT FORM) CUSTOMARILY GIVEN AS A COURTESY 礼 IN A PASTORAL HERDSMAN CULTURE.

神 GOD JME 257      社 SHINTO SHRINE, COMPANY JME 234

| RAD | STROKE | JME |
|-----|--------|-----|
| 113 | 5 | 337 |

TO SHOW, POINT OUT JME 622 (HEAVEN'S RAYS SHOW & POINT OUT)

GOD IN COMPONENT FORM (HE SHOWS POINTS OUT) SUPER-IMPOSITION

GOD, DIVINE AS COMPO-NENT

SALUTATION, BOW, COURTESY, THANKS (MILK OF HUMAN KINDNESS)

SUPER-IMPOSITION OF MILK COMPONENT ON BREAST (SIDE VIEW)

BREAST

WA, HARMONY, PEACE, JAPAN; TO SOFTEN, PACIFY, CALM DOWN.

HARMONY, PEACE, JAPAN, TO PACIFY, CALM DOWN, SOFTEN 和 IS HAVING RICE OR GRAIN 禾 (SEE JME 164) in ONE'S MOUTH 口 OR BEING FED. THE RICE OR GRAIN IS SOFTENED IN THE MOUTH AND PACIFIES OR CALMS DOWN BRINGING PEACE AND HARMONY AS IN JAPAN.

| RAD | STROKE | JME |
|-----|--------|-----|
| 115 | 8 | 338 |

RICE OR GRAIN AS A PLANT

RICE, GRAIN (SEE JME 164)

RICE OR GRAIN FED OR EATEN BY MOUTH OF MAN OR BEAST

HARMONY, PEACE, JAPAN, SOFTEN, PACIFY, CALM DOWN

MOUTH JME 27

PICTURE OF MOUTH

### KATAKANA

| | | | | |
|---|---|---|---|---|
| ア a | サ sa | ナ na | マ ma | ル ru |
| イ i | シ shi | ニ ni | ミ mi | レ re |
| ウ u | ス su | ヌ nu | ム mu | ロ ro |
| エ e | セ se | ネ ne | メ me | ワ wa |
| オ o | ソ so | ノ no | モ mo | ヲ o |
| カ ka | タ ta | ハ ha | ヤ ya | ン n |
| キ ki | チ chi | ヒ hi | ユ yu | |
| ク ku | ツ tsu | フ fu | ヨ yo | |
| ケ ke | テ te | ヘ he | ラ ra | |
| コ ko | ト to | ホ ho | リ ri | |

### HIRAGANA

| | | | | |
|---|---|---|---|---|
| あ a | さ sa | な na | ま ma | る ru |
| い i | し shi | に ni | み mi | れ re |
| う u | す su | ぬ nu | む mu | ろ ro |
| え e | せ se | ね ne | め me | わ wa |
| お o | そ so | の no | も mo | を o |
| か ka | た ta | は ha | や ya | ん n |
| き ki | ち chi | ひ hi | ゆ yu | |
| く ku | つ tsu | ふ fu | よ yo | |
| け ke | て te | へ he | ら ra | |
| こ ko | と to | ほ ho | り ri | |

Katakana and hiragana are used in Japanese writing to supplement the kanji. Katakana are used to represent sounds in foreign languages. Hiragana are used with the kanji for easier writing to conclude verbs, when the meaning is clear, or when no kanji exists for the purpose.

170

# THE 214 RADICALS

|  | 0 | 10 | 20 | 30 | 40 | 50 |
|---|---|---|---|---|---|---|
| 0 | THE 214 RADICALS | 10 儿 man, legs. | 20 勹 wrap. | 3 STROKES / 30 口 mouth. | 40 宀 roof. | 50 巾 cloth, kerchief. |
| 1 | 1 STROKE / 1 一 one, unity. | 11 入 to enter. | 21 匕 spoon, pointer, corpse. | 31 囗 enclosure, boundaries. | 41 寸 "inch," unit of length. | 51 干 shield, weapon. |
| 2 | 2 丨 (up or down movement). | 12 八 eight, to divide. | 22 匚 basket, chest, vessel, enclosure. | 32 土 earth, soil, ground. | 42 小 small, little. | 52 幺 small. |
| 3 | 3 丶 point, dot. (extended power). | 13 冂 borders, empty space. | 23 匸 cover, conceal, squareness, capacity. | 33 士 samurai, scholar. | 43 尢 feeble, weak, lame. | 53 广 lean-to, shed, shelter. |
| 4 | 4 丿 support, horn, scyth. | 14 冖 cover. | 24 十 ten, perfect, complete. | 34 夂 follow, march, end. | 44 尸 corpse. | 54 辶 walk. |
| 5 | 5 乙 (tail of snake or dragon). | 15 冫 ice. | 25 卜 to divine (scapula & plastron cracks). | 35 夊 walk. | 45 屮 sprout, sprouting plant. | 55 廾 joined hands raised or folded. |
| 6 | 6 亅 (barbed hook, nail body). | 16 几 table, stool. | 26 卩 seal. | 36 夕 evening, end, moon. | 46 山 mountain. | 56 弋 a dart. |
| 7 | 2 STROKES / 7 二 two, duality, (heaven & earth). | 17 凵 open vessel. | 27 厂 cliff. | 37 大 big, great. | 47 川 river, stream. | 57 弓 a bow. |
| 8 | 8 亠 head, cover, authority of heaven. | 18 刀 sword, knife. | 28 厶 private, selfish, basket, cocoon. | 38 女 woman, girl, female. | 48 工 work(man), square or plumb line. | 58 彐 boar's or pig's head. |
| 9 | 9 人 man, human, person. | 19 力 strength, power, energy. | 29 又 rt. hand, again, also. | 39 子 child, son. | 49 己 personal, self. | 59 彡 hair, shape. |

| | 60 | 70 | 80 | 90 | 100 | 110 | |
|---|---|---|---|---|---|---|---|
| 0 | 60 彳 step, walk. | 70 方 square, direction, way. | 80 毋 do not. | 90 爿 slice, bed. wood, tree's left half | 100 生 birth, life, grow. | 110 矛 spear, lance. | 0 |
| 1 | 4 STROKES 61 小 忄 心 heart, mind. | 71 旡 无 not, no, have not. | 81 比 比 compare, sort, kind. | 91 片 side, strip, tree's rt. half. | 101 用 use, business. | 111 矢 arrow. | 1 |
| 2 | 62 戈 spear. | 72 日 sun, day. | 82 毛 hair, wool, fur, feathers. | 92 牙 tooth, tusk. | 102 田 field, paddy. | 112 石 stone. | 2 |
| 3 | 63 戶 door, house. | 73 曰 say, speak. | 83 氏 clan, family. | 93 牛 cow, ox, bull. | 103 正 足 cloth, foot in motion. | 113 衤 示 to show, inform. | 3 |
| 4 | 64 扌 手 hand, arm. | 74 月 moon, month. | 84 气 air. | 94 犭 犬 dog. | 104 疒 disease, sickness. | 114 禸 禸 pawprint, track. | 4 |
| 5 | 65 支 branch, obstinate. | 75 木 tree, wood. | 85 氵 水 water. | 5 STROKES 95 玄 dark, black, mysterious | 105 癶 leg joints | 115 禾 grain or rice (as plants). | 5 |
| 6 | 66 攴 to rap. | 76 欠 exhale, owe, yawn. | 86 灬 火 fire. | 96 王 玉 gem, jade. | 106 白 white, clear. | 116 穴 hole, cave, pit. | 6 |
| 7 | 67 文 literary, pattern. | 77 止 stop. | 87 爫 爪 claw, hoof. | 97 瓜 melon, cucumber. | 107 皮 skin, leather, fur, bark. | 117 立 to stand. | 7 |
| 8 | 68 斗 unit of capacity, Great Dipper. | 78 歹 歺 bad, evil. | 88 父 father. | 98 瓦 瓦 tile, pottery. | 108 皿 dish, saucer, vessel. | 6 STROKES 118 竹 竹 bamboo. | 8 |
| 9 | 69 斤 unit of weight, axe. | 79 殳 lance, to kill, to strike. | 89 爻 mix, interwind. | 99 甘 sweet. | 109 罒 目 eye. | 119 米 rice (polished but uncooked) | 9 |

| | 120 | 130 | 140 | 150 | 160 | 170 |
|---|---|---|---|---|---|---|
| 0 | 120 糸 silk, thread, string. | 130 朋月肉月 flesh, meat. | 140 艹卅 grass, plants. | 150 谷 valley, ravine. | 160 bitter, painful, metallic taste. 辛 | 170 阝阜 mound, hill. |
| 1 | 121 缶 clay pot, vessel. | 131 臣 minister. | 141 虍 tiger. | 151 豆 bean, pea, vessel. | 161 辰 dragon, hour. | 171 隶 reach. |
| 2 | 122 罓罒网 ⺲罦 net, trap. | 132 自 self. | 142 虫 insect, bug, worm. | 152 豕 pig, hog. | 162 辶辶辵 go fast and stop suddenly. | 172 隹 short-tailed bird. |
| 3 | 123 羊 sheep. | 133 至 reach, arrive. | 143 血 blood. | 153 豸 beast, reptile, worm. | 163 阝邑 village, city. | 173 雨 rain. |
| 4 | 124 羽羽 wings, feathers. | 134 臼 mortar. | 144 行 go, walk, conduct, a row. | 154 貝 shell, cowrie. | 164 酉 bird, wine vessel. | 174 blue, green, unripe, inexperi- enced. 青 |
| 5 | 125 耂老 old. | 135 舌 tongue. | 145 衤衣 clothes, garment. | 155 赤 red. | 165 釆 distin- guish, divide. | 175 非 not, is not. |
| 6 | 126 而 and, but. | 136 舛 confuse, oppose. | 146 西 a cover. | 156 走 run, walk fast. | 166 里 village, unit of distance. | 9 STROKES 176 face, front, surface, mask. 面 |
| 7 | 127 耒 plow handle, till, cultivate | 137 舟 boat, ship. | 7 STROKES 147 見 see, show. | 157 𧾷足 foot, leg. | 8 STROKES 167 金 gold, money, metal. | 177 革 leather, hide, skin. |
| 8 | 128 耳 ear. | 138 艮 hard, perverse, obstinate. | 148 角 horn, corner. | 158 身 body. | 168 镸長 chief, senior, grow, long | 178 韋 leather, to rebel. |
| 9 | 129 聿 pen, pencil. | 139 色 color. | 149 言 word, expression. | 159 車 vehicle, chariot, carriage, cart. | 169 門 gate, door. | 179 韭 leeks, onions. |

173                                                                                          173

# THE 214 RADICALS

The 214 radicals are used to construct kanji or characters much as words are formed from letters of the alphabet. Some of the radicals are complicated; some are seldom used; some have more than one form. Learn their meanings as separate "building blocks" and try to understand how and why they belong in the character or kanji. The radicals are the keys to the meaning of the kanji. They may have different meanings just as words in English may have different meanings. Often you can guess at the meaning of a strange or new character by examining the radical. Sometimes a radical such as "tree" is used as part of the kanji(s) for many different kinds of trees. The same thing is true of the radical for "gold" and different metals.

| | 180 | 190 | 200 | 210 |
|---|---|---|---|---|
| 0 | 180 音 sound, noise, voice, tone. | 190 髟 hair. 髟 | 200 麻 hemp. 麻 | 210 齊 even, level. |
| 1 | 181 頁 head, page. | 191 鬥 fight. | 12 STROKES 201 黃 yellow. 黄 | 15 STROKES 211 齒 tooth. |
| 2 | 182 風 wind, style, fashion, custom. | 192 鬯 wine. | 202 黍 millet. | 16 STROKES 212 龍 dragon. |
| 3 | 183 飛 fly, jump, leap. | 193 鬲 caldron. | 203 黑 black. 黒 | 213 龜 tortoise. |
| 4 | 184 食 eat. | 194 鬼 devil, ogre, demon. | 204 黹 embroidery, needlework. | 17 STROKES 214 龠 flute, fife. |
| 5 | 185 首 head, neck. | 11 STROKES 195 魚 fish. | 13 STROKES 205 黽 toad, frog. | |
| 6 | 186 香 odor, fragrance, incense. | 196 鳥 bird. | 206 鼎 tripod. | |
| 7 | 10 STROKES 187 馬 horse. | 197 鹵 brine, barren, plunder. | 207 鼓 drum. | |
| 8 | 188 骨 bone. | 198 鹿 deer. | 208 鼠 rat, mouse. | |
| 9 | 189 高 high, tall. | 199 麥 wheat, barley. | 14 STROKES 209 鼻 nose. | |

KANJI LOCATOR I, STROKE INDEX FOR JME NUMBERS IN THE KANJI ABC
Look up kanji of your text by stroke number
to get their JME numbers in The Kanji ABC.

| | | | | | | | | | | | |
|---|---|---|---|---|---|---|---|---|---|---|---|
| **1** | 下 21 | 中 23 | 引 156 | 犬 66 | 外 5G | 皮 307 | 同 295 | 気 59 | **7** | 村 107 | 走 105 |
| 一 1 | 千 101 | 五 5 | 心 95 | 王 49 | 左 18 | 目 25 | 名 140 | 池 110 | 住 244 | 決 202 | 足 29 |
| **2** | 口 27 | 今 81 | 戸 69 | **5** | 市 222 | 石 44 | 向 213 | 当 290 | 何 51 | 汽 60 | 身 255 |
| 七 7 | 土 17 | 元 68 | 手 28 | 世 263 | 平 315 | 礼 337 | 回 169 | 百 130 | 作 82 | 男 109 | 車 88 |
| 九 9 | 夕 98 | 公 210 | 文 134 | 主 237 | 広 211 | 立 149 | 地 111 | 竹 113 | 体 270 | 町 115 | 近 195 |
| 二 2 | 大 22 | 六 6 | 方 138 | 仕 221 | 本 45 | 台 272 | 多 108 | 米 135 | 来 147 | 社 234 | 返 316 |
| 人 30 | 女 32 | 分 133 | 日 11 | 兄 199 | 正 46 | 号 215 | 字 86 | 糸 83 | 助 248 | 究 185 | 里 332 |
| 入 125 | 子 31 | 切 99 | 月 12 | 冬 120 | 母 137 | **6** | 安 53 | 考 74 | 君 198 | 声 97 | 麦 128 |
| 八 8 | 小 24 | 化 163 | 木 15 | 出 90 | 玉 64 | 交 212 | 寺 228 | 耳 26 | 図 261 | 花 43 | **8** |
| 刀 289 | 山 38 | 午 207 | 止 220 | 北 139 | 生 34 | 休 61 | 年 126 | 肉 297 | 坂 304 | 見 67 | 事 230 |
| 力 148 | 川 39 | 友 145 | 毛 142 | 半 129 | 用 146 | 先 33 | 早 104 | 自 229 | 局 194 | 角 173 | 京 63 |
| 十 10 | 工 71 | 円 48 | 水 14 | 去 189 | 田 40 | 光 72 | 会 54 | 色 94 | 弟 282 | 谷 78 | 使 224 |
| **3** | 才 217 | 天 119 | 火 13 | 古 70 | 由 325 | 全 267 | 次 227 | 虫 114 | 形 200 | 貝 169 | 取 238 |
| 三 3 | 万 320 | 太 269 | 父 131 | 右 19 | 申 254 | 両 336 | 死 223 | 行 73 | 役 324 | 売 301 | 愛 240 |
| 上 20 | **4** | 少 93 | 牛 62 | 四 4 | 白 37 | 合 77 | 毎 318 | 西 96 | 投 291 | 赤 35 | 和 338 |

KANJI LOCATOR I, STROKE INDEX FOR JME NUMBERS IN THE KANJI ABC
Look up kanji of your text by stroke number
to get their JME numbers in The Kanji ABC.

| | | | | | | | | | | | |
|---|---|---|---|---|---|---|---|---|---|---|---|
| 国 79 | 波 298 | 乗 251 | 春 91 | 級 187 | **10** | 病 310 | 球 188 | 黒 80 | 落 330 | 新 256 | 駅 158 |
| 夜 144 | 注 277 | 前 102 | 昭 249 | 美 308 | 勉 317 | 紙 85 | 理 333 | **12** | 葉 327 | 暗 154 | 鳴 321 |
| 妹 319 | 物 313 | 南 124 | 昼 279 | 茶 275 | 原 205 | 荷 165 | 第 273 | 勝 250 | 買 300 | 楽 320 | **15** |
| 始 225 | 画 167 | 品 311 | 柱 278 | 草 106 | 夏 52 | 記 180 | 細 218 | 場 252 | 遊 326 | 話 151 | **16** |
| 学 57 | 知 112 | 客 184 | 活 174 | 計 201 | 家 53 | 起 181 | 終 241 | 寒 175 | 運 157 | 遠 160 | 橋 193 |
| 実 233 | 空 65 | 室 232 | 海 55 | 自 312 | 島 292 | 通 281 | 組 103 | 晴 265 | 道 122 | 鉄 283 | 親 260 |
| 岩 178 | 者 235 | 屋 161 | 炭 274 | 追 280 | 庫 206 | 配 299 | 船 266 | 暑 247 | 開 171 | 電 286 | 頭 294 |
| 岸 177 | 苦 197 | 度 288 | 界 170 | 送 268 | 弱 236 | 馬 127 | 週 242 | 朝 118 | 間 58 | **14** | **17** |
| 店 284 | 表 309 | 待 277 | 畑 302 | 重 245 | 旅 335 | 高 76 | 進 259 | 期 183 | 集 243 | 様 328 | **18** |
| 所 246 | 金 16 | 後 208 | 発 303 | 面 322 | 時 87 | **11** | 都 287 | 森 41 | 雲 47 | 歌 166 | 曜 329 |
| 明 141 | 長 116 | 思 84 | 県 203 | 音 50 | 書 92 | 動 296 | 野 323 | 温 162 | **13** | 算 219 | 顔 179 |
| 東 121 | 門 143 | 急 186 | 研 204 | 風 132 | 校 75 | 強 192 | 雪 100 | 番 306 | 園 159 | 聞 314 | |
| 板 305 | 雨 42 | 持 231 | 神 257 | 食 253 | 根 216 | 悪 152 | 魚 190 | 答 293 | 意 155 | 語 209 | |
| 林 150 | 青 36 | 指 226 | 秋 89 | 首 239 | 帰 182 | 教 191 | 鳥 117 | 絵 172 | 感 176 | 読 123 | |
| 歩 136 | **9** | 星 264 | 科 164 | 点 285 | 流 334 | 深 258 | 黄 214 | 着 276 | 数 262 | 銀 196 | |

176

# ALPHABETICAL JAPANESE WORD INDEX FOR JME NUMBERS

(On readings are in capitals; kun readings in small letters).

## A

agaru 上 20
ageru 上 20
aida 間 58
aka 赤 35
akai 赤 35
akarui 明 141
akeru 明 141
aki 秋 89
akiraka 明 141
AKU 悪 152
ame 雨 42
ame 天 119
AN 行 73
AN 安 153
AN 暗 154
ani 兄 199
ao 青 136
aoi 青 136
aratani 新 256
arawasu 表 309
aruku 歩 136
asa 朝 118
ashi 足 29
asobu 遊 326
atama 頭 294
atarashii 新 256
ataru 当 290
ateru 当 290
atsui 暑 247
atsumaru 集 243
atsumeru 集 243
au 会 54
au 合 77
ayumu 歩 136
aza 字 86

## B

BA 馬 127
ba 場 252
BAI 買 300
bakasu 化 163
bakeru 化 163
BAKU 麦 128
BAN 番 306
BAN 万 320
BEI 米 135
BEN 勉 317
BI 美 308
BO 母 137
BOKU 木 15
BU 分 133
BU 歩 136
BUN 分 133
BUN 文 134
BUN 聞 314
BUTSU 物 313
BYAKU 白 37
BYŌ 病 310
BYŌ 平 315

## C

CHA 茶 275
CHAKU 着 276
CHI 池 110
CHI 地 111
CHI 知 112
chi 千 101
chichi 父 131
chiisai 小 24
chikai 近 195
chikara 力 148
CHIKU 竹 113
CHŌ 町 115

CHŌ 長 116
CHŌ 鳥 117
CHŌ 朝 118
CHŌ 重 245
CHŪ 中 23
CHŪ 虫 114
CHŪ 注 277
CHŪ 柱 278
CHŪ 昼 279

## D

DAI 大 22
DAI 台 272
DAI 第 273
DAI 弟 282
DAN 男 109
dasu 出 90
DEN 田 40
DEN 電 286
deru 出 90
DO 土 17
DO 度 288
DŌ 道 122
DŌ 同 295
DŌ 動 296
DOKU 読 123

## E

E 会 54
E 絵 172
EI 泳 352
EI 英 353
EKI 駅 158
EKI 役 324
EN 円 48
EN 園 159
EN 遠 160

## F

FU 父 131
FU 負 312
FŪ 風 132
fukai 深 258
fukasa 深 258
FUN 分 133
funa 船 266
fune 船 266
furui 古 70
futa 二 2
futatsu 二 2
futoi 太 269
futoru 太 269
fuyu 冬 120

## G

GA 画 167
GAI 外 56
GAKU 学 57
GAKU 楽 331
GAN 元 68
GAN 岸 177
GAN 岩 178
GAN 顔 179
-gata 形 200
GATSU 月 12
GE 下 21
GE 外 56
GEN 元 68
GEN 原 205
GETSU 月 12
GIN 銀 196
GO 五 5
GO 期 183
GO 午 207
GO 後 208

mi-SE

tori 鳥 117
toru 取 238
tōru 通 281
toshi 年 126
TSU 都 287
TSŪ 通 281
tsuchi 土 17
tsugi 次 227
tsugu 次 227
TSUI 追 280
tsukaeru 仕 221
tsukau 使 224
tsuki 月 12
tsuku 着 276
tsukuru 作 82
tsuno 角 173
tsuyoi 強 192

**U**

U 右 19
U 雨 42
ue 上 20
ugoku 動 296
uke 受 240
ukeru 受 240
uma 馬 127
umareru 生 34
umi 海 55
umu 生 34
UN 雲 47
UN 運 157
uo 魚 190
uri 賣 301
uru 賣 301
ushi 牛 62
ushiro 後 208
uta 歌 166
utau 歌 166
utsukushii 美 308

**W**

WA 話 151
WA 和 338
wakareru 分 133
wakeru 分 133
warui 悪 152

**Y**

YA 夜 144
YA 野 323
ya 家 53
ya 屋 161
YAKU 役 324
yama 山 38
yamai 病 310
yamu 病 310
yashiro 社 234
yasui 安 153
yasumi 休 61
yasumu 休 61
yattsu 八 8
yawaragu 和 338
yo 四 4
yo 夜 144
yo 世 263
YŌ 用 146
YŌ 葉 327
YŌ 様 328
YŌ 曜 329
yoko 横 355
yomu 読 123
yon 四 4
yoru 夜 144
yoshi 由 325
yottsu 四 4
yowai 弱 236
yowaru 弱 236
YU 由 325
yū 夕 98

**Z**

yubi 指 226
yuki 雪 100
yuku 行 73

**Z**

ZEN 前 102
ZEN 全 267

| | | | |
|---|---|---|---|
| 1 i², yi² 一 | 31 tzŭ³ 子 | 61 hsiu¹ 休 | 91 ch'un¹ 春 |
| 2 êrh⁴ 二 | 32 nü³ 女 | 62 niu² 牛 | 92 shu¹ 書 |
| 3 san¹ 三 | 33 hsien¹ 先 | 63 ching¹ 京 | 93 shao³ 少 |
| 4 szŭ⁴ 四 | 34 sheng¹ 生 | 64 yü⁴ 玉 | 94 se⁴ 色 |
| 5 wu³ 五 | 35 ch'ih⁴ 赤 | 65 k'ung¹ 空 | 95 hsin¹ 心 |
| 6 liu⁴ 六 | 36 ch'ing¹ 青 | 66 ch'üan³ 犬 | 96 hsi¹ 西 |
| 7 ch'i 七 | 37 pai² 白 | 67 chien⁴ 見 | 97 shêng¹ 聲 声 * |
| 8 pa¹ 八 | 38 shan¹ 山 | 68 yüan² 元 | 98 hsi⁴,¹ 夕 |
| 9 chiu³ 九 | 39 ch'uan¹ 川 | 69 hu⁴ 戶 | 99 ch'ieh⁴ 切 |
| 10 shih² 十 | 40 t'ien² 田 | 70 ku³ 古 | 100 hsüeh³ 雪 * |
| 11 jih⁴ 日 | 41 sên¹, shên¹ 森 | 71 kung¹ 工 | 101 ch'ien¹ 千 |
| 12 yüeh⁴ 月 | 42 yü³ 雨 | 72 kuang¹ 光 | 102 ch'ien² 前 |
| 13 huo³ 火 | 43 hua¹ 花 | 73 hsing² 行 | 103 tsu³ 組 |
| 14 shui³ 水 | 44 shih² 石 | 74 k'ao³ 考 | 104 tsao³ 早 |
| 15 mu⁴ 木 | 45 pen³ 本 | 75 hsiao⁴ 校 | 105 tsou³ 走 |
| 16 chin¹ 金 | 46 chêng⁴ 正 | 76 kao¹ 高 | 106 ts'ao³ 草 |
| 17 t'u³ 土 | 47 yün² 雲 | 77 ho² 合 | 107 ts'un¹ 村 |
| 18 tso³ 左 | 48 yüan² 圓 * | 78 ku³ 谷 | 108 to¹ 多 |
| 19 yu⁴ 右 | 49 wang² 王 | 79 kuo² 國 * 国 * | 109 nan² 男 |
| 20 shang⁴ 上 | 50 yin¹ 音 | 80 hei¹ 黑 * | 110 ch'ih² 池 |
| 21 hsia⁴ 下 | 51 ho² 何 | 81 chin¹ 今 | 111 ti⁴ 地 |
| 22 ta⁴ 大 | 52 hsia⁴ 夏 | 82 tso⁴ 作 | 112 chih¹ 知 |
| 23 chung¹ 中 | 53 chia¹ 家 | 83 mi⁴ 糸 | 113 chu² 竹 |
| 24 hsiao³ 小 | 54 hui⁴ 會 会 * | 84 szŭ¹ 思 | 114 ch'ung² 虫 |
| 25 mu⁴ 目 | 55 hai³ 海 * | 85 chih³ 紙 | 115 t'ing³ 町 |
| 26 êrh³ 耳 | 56 wai⁴ 外 | 86 tzŭ⁴ 字 | 116 chang² 長 |
| 27 k'ou³ 口 | 57 hsüeh² 學 * 学 * | 87 shih² 時 | 117 niao³ 鳥 |
| 28 shou³ 手 | 58 chien¹ 間 | 88 ch'e¹ 車 | 118 chao¹ 朝 |
| 29 tsu² 足 | 59 ch'i⁴ 氣 * | 89 ch'iu¹ 秋 | 119 t'ien¹ 天 |
| 30 jen² 人 | 60 ch'i⁴ 汽 | 90 ch'u¹ 出 | 120 tung¹ 冬 |

121 tung¹ 東
122 tao⁴ 道 *
123 tu² 讀 *
124 nan² 南
125 ju⁴ 入
126 nien² 年
127 ma³ 馬
128 mai⁴ 麥 *
129 pan⁴ 半
130 pai³ 百
131 fu⁴ 父
132 feng¹ 風 凨 *
133 fên¹ 分
134 wên² 文
135 mi³ 米
136 pu⁴ 步
137 mu³ 母
138 fang¹ 方
139 pei³ 北
140 ming² 名
141 ming² 明
142 mao² 毛
143 mên² 門
144 yeh⁴ 夜
145 yu³ 友
146 yung⁴ 用
147 lai² 來 来
148 li⁴ 力
149 li⁴ 立
150 lin² 林

151 hua⁴ 話
152 o⁴ 惡 *
153 an¹ 安
154 an⁴ 暗
155 i⁴ 意
156 yin³ 引
157 yün⁴ 運
158 i⁴,yi⁴ 驛 *
159 yüan² 園
160 yüan³ 遠
161 wu¹ 屋
162 wen¹ 溫
163 hua⁴ 化
164 k'o¹,k'e¹ 科
165 ho² 荷
166 ko¹,ke¹ 歌
167 hua⁴ 畫 * 画 *
168 hui² 回
169 pei⁴ 貝
170 chieh⁴ 界
171 k'ai¹ 開
172 hui⁴ 繪 *
173 chüeh² 角
174 huo² 活
175 han² 寒
176 kan³ 感
177 an⁴ 岸
178 yen² 岩
179 yen² 顏
180 chi⁴ 記

181 ch'i³ 起
182 kuei¹ 歸 * 归
183 ch'i¹'² 期
184 k'o⁴,k'e⁴ 客
185 chiu¹'⁴ 究
186 chi² 急 *
187 chi² 級
188 ch'iu² 球 *
189 ch'ü⁴ 去
190 yü² 魚
191 chiao⁴ 教 *
192 ch'iang³ 強
193 ch'iao² 橋
194 chü² 局
195 chin⁴ 近 *
196 yin² 銀
197 k'u³ 苦
198 chun¹ 君
199 hsiung¹ 兄
200 hsing² 形
201 chi⁴ 計
202 chüeh² 決
203 hsien⁴ 縣 *
204 yen² 研
205 yüan² 原
206 k'u⁴ 庫
207 wu³ 午
208 hou⁴ 後
209 yü³ 語
210 kung¹ 公

211 kuang³ 廣 *
212 chiao¹ 交
213 hsiang⁴ 向
214 huang² 黃 *
215 hao² 號 *
216 ken¹ 根
217 ts'ai² 才
218 hsi⁴ 細
219 suan⁴ 算
220 chih³ 止
221 shih⁴ 仕
222 shih⁴ 市
223 szu³ 死
224 shih³ 使
225 shih³ 始
226 chih³ 指
227 tz'u⁴ 次
228 szu⁴ 寺
229 tzu⁴ 自
230 shih⁴ 事
231 ch'ih² 持
232 shih⁴ 室
233 shih² 實
234 she⁴ 社
235 che³ 者
236 jo⁴,je⁴ 弱
237 chu³ 主
238 ch'ü³ 取
239 shou³ 首
240 shou⁴ 受

| 241 | chung¹ 終 | 271 | tai⁴ 待 | 301 | mai⁴ 賣 | 331 | le⁴ 樂* |
| 242 | chou¹ 週* | 272 | t'ai² 台 | 302 | 一 | 332 | li³ 里 |
| 243 | chi² 集 | 273 | ti⁴ 第 | 303 | fa¹ 發 | 333 | li³ 理 |
| 244 | chu⁴ 住 | 274 | t'an⁴ 炭 | 304 | fan³ 坂 | 334 | liu² 流 |
| 245 | chung⁴ 重 | 275 | ch'a² 茶 | 305 | pan³ 板 | 335 | lü³ 旅 |
| 246 | so³ 所 | 276 | cho²,⁵ 着 | 306 | fan¹ 番 | 336 | liang¹ 両雨* |
| 247 | shu³ 暑* | 277 | chu⁴ 注 | 307 | p'i² 皮 | 337 | li³ 礼 |
| 248 | chu⁴ 助 | 278 | chu⁴ 柱 | 308 | mei³ 美 | 338 | ho² 和 |
| 249 | chao¹ 昭 | 279 | chou⁴ 晝* | 309 | piao³ 表 | | |
| 250 | sheng⁴ 勝 | 280 | chui¹ 追* | 310 | ping⁴ 病 | | |
| 251 | ch'eng² 乘* | 281 | t'ung¹ 通* | 311 | p'in³ 品 | | |
| 252 | ch'ang² 場 | 282 | ti⁴ 弟 | 312 | fu⁴ 負 | | |
| 253 | shih² 食 | 283 | t'ieh³ 鉄 | 313 | wu⁴ 物 | | |
| 254 | shen¹ 申 | 284 | tien⁴ 店 | 314 | wen² 聞 | | |
| 255 | shen¹ 身 | 285 | tien³ 點* | 315 | p'ing² 平 | | |
| 256 | hsin¹ 新 | 286 | tien⁴ 電 | 316 | fan³ 返 | | |
| 257 | shen² 神 | 287 | tou¹ 都 | 317 | mien³ 勉* | | |
| 258 | shen¹ 深 | 288 | tu⁴ 度 | 318 | mei³ 每 | | |
| 259 | chin⁴ 進* | 289 | tao¹ 刀 | 319 | mei⁴ 妹 | | |
| 260 | ch'in¹ 親 | 290 | tang¹ 當当* | 320 | wan⁴ 万 | | |
| 261 | t'u² 圖* | 291 | t'ou² 投 | 321 | ming² 鳴 | | |
| 262 | shu⁴ 數* | 292 | tao³ 島 | 322 | mien⁴ 面 | | |
| 263 | shih⁴ 世 | 293 | ta² 答 | 323 | yeh³ 野 | | |
| 264 | hsing¹ 星 | 294 | t'ou² 頭 | 324 | i⁴,yi⁴ 役 | | |
| 265 | ch'ing² 晴 | 295 | t'ung² 同 | 325 | yu² 由 | | |
| 266 | ch'uan² 船* | 296 | tung⁴ 動 | 326 | yu² 遊* | | |
| 267 | ch'üan² 全 | 297 | jou⁴ 肉 | 327 | yeh⁴ 葉 | | |
| 268 | sung⁴ 送* | 298 | po¹ 波 | 328 | yang⁴ 樣* | | |
| 269 | t'ai⁴ 太 | 299 | p'ei⁴ 配 | 329 | yao⁴ 曜 | | |
| 270 | t'i³ 体骨體* | 300 | mai³ 買 | 330 | lao⁴ 落 | | |

*Chinese characters which may be variants are marked with an asterisk. The much-abbreviated recent characters are not given since explanations often do not apply. You need to learn the alternate forms because printed and written forms may differ and you may read older books as well as contemporary material. The numbers are for the tones. The meanings can be found in a Chinese-English dictionary such as Fenn's, but are usually much the same in Chinese and Japanese.

DR. ANDREW DYKSTRA has always been most
fascinated by the Japanese KANJI or the
Chinese characters used in reading and
writing and even thinking by nearly one
billion of the earth's peoples.  These
volumes of THE KANJI ABC are his first
publications on that subject.

The KANJI have usually been the difficult
part of an Oriental language course.  Dr.
Dykstra hopes to make the KANJI a subject
of intense interest to everyone.

As pictographs, the KANJI are an international language intelligible to all of
us human beings.  Many scientists and
humanists have assumed that ancient minds
are primitive, lacking the ability to
associate and reason logically.  But Dr.
Dykstra believes that the ancient minds are in no way
inferior to our own, and that we have not had the acumen
to understand what they are telling us.

Dr. Dykstra was born in the historic Lushan (mountains)
of Kiangsi Province and spent his youth in China where
he graduated from the Shanghai American School.  During
World War II, he received his commission from Columbia
Midshipman School, and his diploma from the Navy Oriental
Languages PostGraduate School at Colorado University and
Oklahoma State University.  He was later promoted with a
speciality in Psychology in the Medical Service Corps.

After the war, Dr. Dykstra was employed by the State of
California and also taught courses for Lassen College in
Psychology, Humanities, History, Political Science, and
German.  He was awarded fellowships in Law at Boalt Hall,
in Interpersonal Relations at Immaculate Heart College in
Los Angeles, in Chinese at Claremont Graduate School and
San Francisco State University, and in Japanese at UCLA.

Another of Dr. Dykstra's interests, Oriental humor, has
produced SEXY LAUGHING STORIES OF OLD JAPAN, printed by
Japan Publications, Inc., 1255 Howard Street, S.F. CA 94103.
"Laughing stories" are literally what the Japanese call
the sexy and humorous tales that for centuries have been
retold by travelling story tellers who accompanied words
with vivid facial expressions, gestures, and sounds.

Dr. Dykstra hopes to transmit his pleasure in the KANJI
by his writings.  His purpose is to promote understanding
between American and Oriental peoples through enjoyment
of the KANJI.  Strangely enough, even the Japanese and
Chinese often have done little more than to memorize the
meanings of the KANJI, practice their writing, and enjoy
their beauty.  The KANJI deserve far more than this.